The Cappadocian Mothers

The Cappadocian Mothers

*Deification Exemplified in the Writings
of Basil, Gregory, and Gregory*

Carla D. Sunberg

foreword by
T. A. Noble

James Clarke & Co

James Clarke & Co
P.O. Box 60
Cambridge
CB1 2NT
United Kingdom

www.jamesclarke.co
publishing@jamesclarke.co

ISBN: 978 0 227 17690 0

British Library Cataloguing in Publication Data
A record is available from the British Library

First published by James Clarke & Co, 2018

Copyright © Carla D. Sunberg, 2018

Published by arrangement
with Pickwick Publications

"Carla Sunberg presents powerful examples of women—mothers and sisters—who embodied and taught theosis, sometimes translated from the Greek as 'deification,' or growth in holiness, Christ-likeness, and love. We've only recently become aware of these ancient church women, and Sunberg unveils how their lives and teachings embody spiritually formative practices relevant today. *The Cappadocian Mothers* will inspire all who seek to live holy, Christ-like lives, full of love."

—**Don Thorsen,** Professor of Theology,
Azusa Pacific University Seminary

"Well-versed in feminist hermeneutical methodology, Carla Sunberg has crafted a significant piece of historical retrieval. She has mined the writings of fourth-century Cappadocian Fathers to learn of the significant witness and influence of the women who helped shape their understanding of how one becomes a participant in the divine nature. Her meticulous research demonstrates that without these mothers in faith, the fathers would lack living witnesses for their formulation of early Christian understandings of Christology, mystical theology, and Trinitarian construction. Besides, these remarkable women challenged regnant notions of the inferiority of women. Sandberg has bridged a major gap in scholarship, and the whole church will profit."

—**Molly T. Marshall,** President, Professor of Theology and
Spiritual Formation, Central Seminary

"History has provided stories of the men who became heroes of the Christian faith in Cappadocia. Stories of the women were simply pushed aside, partly because of the culture of the fourth-century Roman Empire. Dr. Carla Sunberg brings to the forefront seven women who had significant impact on those men church history has hailed as heroes. But it isn't just that these women influenced the patristic church; rather, they're lives were used as illustrations of *theosis*, 'Christ in me the hope of glory': our human process of becoming like Christ as we seek to follow Christ closely. This informative, well-researched, and accessible volume is important for women and men, pastors and teachers, historians and storytellers."

—**MaryAnn Hawkins,** Dean, Anderson University School of
Theology and Christian Ministry

"In this volume on *The Cappadocian Mothers*, Carla Sunberg has provided a great gift to the modern church, and its release cannot be more timely. At the dawn of the twenty-first century, the ancient Cappadocian witness of the possibility of living a life characterized by ever-greater participation in God speaks to a growing hunger among Christians for living and vibrant faith. In addition to this hunger for knowing and living in God, there are many of us who hunger to hear the voices of our mothers in the faith as well as the voices of our fathers. While the first part of *The Cappadocian Mothers* is a treasure trove of ancient wisdom, the latter part 'brings it home' to the life of contemporary Christians. Sunberg addresses issues such as gender and class equality, women in ministry leadership, as well as how the life of *theosis* is grounded in the Christian household."

—Cheryl Bridges Johns, Robert E. Fisher Chair of Spiritual
Renewal & Christian Formation,
Pentecostal Theological Seminary

To the great men in my life:

My husband, Chuck Sunberg, without whom
this never would have come about,

My father, Jerald D. Johnson, who has been
my champion.

To the women in my life who lived in the
model of the great Cappadocian Mothers:

My grandmother, L. Marie Johnson, a Godly woman
who had more skills and abilities than the world
could handle at her time;

My mother, Alice Johnson, who was the equal partner
of her husband, the priest;

My mother-in-law, Thelma Sunberg, a modern-day Nonna
who dedicated her life in prayer for her children, all five
of whom have given their lives in service to the Lord.

Contents

Foreword

Every student of Christian theology, even if only a dilettante, has heard of the Cappadocian Fathers. But who were the Cappadocian Mothers?

The "Fathers" of the church were those bishops and teachers of the first six centuries who formulated the doctrines of the faith summarized in the creeds. And the Cappadocian Fathers were those three great bishops of the province of Cappadocia in the fourth century, two brothers and their friend, who played a key role in shaping the final form of the "Nicene" Creed. Basil was archbishop of Caesarea, the capital of the province of Cappadocia in the Greek-speaking Eastern Roman Empire (found today in central Turkey). As a student in Athens, he had become a close friend of Gregory from Nazianzus, who eventually was to become the archbishop of Constantinople, the eastern imperial capital. Nazianzen was the great poet and orator who went to the city to win it over to the orthodox Christian faith in the full deity of Christ. He is famous for his great Theological Orations on the Holy Trinity and was given the title of "The Divine" or "The Theologian" along with the Apostle John. The other Gregory was the younger brother of Basil, educated at home on the family estate, appointed bishop of Nyssa by his older brother as part of an ecclesiastical power struggle. He outshone both his elders as the great Christian philosophical theologian of his day.

But who were the Cappadocian Mothers?

Dr. Carla Sunberg, in this book, rich in theology, spirituality, and patristic scholarship, provides an introduction to these influential women. In brief, they were the mothers and sisters of these three great doctors of the church. And what the book demonstrates is that, although the "Fathers" have had all the fame, it was these "Mothers" who shaped their character. Basil's grandmother, Macrina, his mother, Emelia, and his older sister, Macrina, were the strong influences on his life and that of his younger brother, Gregory. They called the younger Macrina their teacher. It was Gregory Nazianzen's mother, Nonna, who won his father to the Christian faith and gave her son a Christian upbringing, and it was his sister, Gorgonia, who exemplified for him in her suffering the holy life. In addition there were Basil's two younger sisters, Theosebia and one whose name we do not know who went back on her vows of virginity to be married.

Patristics has become a passionate interest among many Western evangelicals over the past few decades. Many self-styled "conservatives" have come to see that learning from our Christian past cannot stop at the Reformation. And many who would never think of themselves as "conservative" have discovered the rich seam of spirituality in the ancient church. To inform our Christian living in this post-Christian age, many have come to see that it is of inestimable benefit to learn from the great preachers and thinkers who wrestled with the questions of Christian doctrine and ethics in ancient multicultural society. While Augustine has influenced us all in the West, the great doctors of the Eastern Church have often been ignored. But living and working in Russia for thirteen years, Dr. Sunberg came to love the Orthodox Church, whose life, liturgy and spirituality are shaped by the Eastern Fathers and Mothers. This book is therefore a feast of patristic scholarship.

But feminism is also a lively area of fresh thinking in our generation, challenging the church to rethink many of its cultural assumptions about the role of women. Dr. Sunberg is an ordained elder in the Wesleyan "holiness" tradition, which has recognized the call of women to preach and minister since the pioneering ministry of the Methodist Phoebe Palmer in the mid-nineteenth century, foreshadowed by John Wesley himself. Another of the contributions of this book therefore is to help us learn from these strong Christian women of a distant age and culture who, while they did not preach or publish, shaped and formed the character and outlook of their close male relatives who did. They were the exemplars of holy living—powerfully compassionate, faith-full, disciplined living.

That points to a third area of interest and concern. This is a book about Christian holiness. Far from being an abstract treatise of doctrinal ideas, it helps us to understand that, as Stanley Hauerwas and others have emphasized, Christian holiness is a matter of *character*. It is of course rooted in the spiritual life with its deep emotional undercurrent, its passionate love for God and for others, but it not mere emotionalism. It shows itself in disciplined living, in careful stewardship of resources, in generous giving, in compassionate caring, in the living fellowship of Christian community. In all of these it is "deification," reflecting the image of God. That word is, of course, easily misunderstood by Western Christians. But Dr. Sunberg helps us to see from the study of the lives of these women what it does, and what it does not, mean.

This is a book which will bring alive the practical daily circumstances in which these women lived and truly loved. It was in a culture and a time far distant from our own. But here we can find a fresh vision not only of the powerful influence of the Christian family and home, but of the way in which Christian women—even with all the restrictions they faced in a patriarchal society—influenced and shaped the world of their day. It will help us to see what Christian holiness looks like, lived out in real life.

Thomas A. Noble

Research Professor of Theology
Nazarene Theological Seminary, Kansas City

Senior Research Fellow in Theology
Nazarene Theological College, Manchester

Preface

Within the last century there has been a renewed interest in the writings of the Cappadocian Fathers and particularly their understanding of deification or theosis. The Cappadocian Fathers, building upon the work of Origen, took a pagan Greek concept and Christianized it so that by the fourth century, the goal of Christians was to be transformed into the image of God by living a life of virtue in imitation of Christ. This was their concept of theosis.

Basil, Gregory and Gregory did not write about their theological concepts in a vacuum, but rather, they were influenced by their social contexts. Quite specifically this included the women in their lives. Much has been written about Macrina, the elder sister of Basil and Nyssen. She is the perfect unsullied virgin who is transformed into the bride of Christ. While Macrina's story has received considerable attention, little has been written regarding the remaining women who are found within their texts. These include Basil and Nyssen's grandmother, Macrina the Elder and their mother Emmelia. Both of these women had deification or theosis as the telos for their lives and they became living models of Basil and Gregory's theology. Not only were they models, but also the home they created was an incubator for the development of future saints. Within Basil and Gregory's texts we find other women as well, including their sister Theosebia and another unnamed "Fallen Virgin." Each one of these lives exemplifies what it means to be living a life with the goal of theosis.

Basil's friend, Gregory of Nazianzus, was also greatly affected by the women in his life. He wrote the panegyric on his sister, Gorgonia, in which he shares in great detail about her life and that of their mother. His mother Nonna and his sister Gorgonia are both presented as the new Eve as they become models for the restoration of female flesh. Throughout Nazianzen's writings we see these women as models for deification. This study explores the way in which the women exemplify and bring greater understanding to their theology of deification.

When combined these seven females, six of whom we know are canonized as saints, present a picture of deification which takes one beyond the purely theological language of the Cappadocian Fathers. Instead, a complex sociological and theological picture develops and ultimately it becomes impossible to separate the women from their theology or their theology from the women. The Cappadocian Mothers bring new life to the Cappadocians' theology which places it within a realistic milieu and provides differing perspectives on theosis.

Acknowledgments

THIS WORK COMES AT the end of a very long journey which began many years ago in Russia. Spending hours in Russian Orthodox churches, watching and learning from the liturgy and then observing the women involved in the life of the church, my interest was sparked. After suffering under seventy years of communism and atheism the Russian Orthodox Church was just again coming to life. Could the church survive and what would be her future? What would be the role of women in the life of the church? If I could go back far enough in time, before there was any East or West in the church, could I find truths that would be relevant for all of Christianity, and reveal the impact that women had made in the life of the church?

A journey began to search back in time and seek out truths from the past. Special thanks must be given to those who inspired me during my graduate studies at Nazarene Theological Seminary (NTS) including Dr. Alex Deasley who worked tirelessly to teach us about holiness in the early years of Christianity and Dr. Paul Bassett who taught himself Old-School Slavonic so that he could better teach us about Russian Orthodoxy. Thanks to Dr. Ed Robinson, Dean of NTS who encouraged the development of a Russian-language faculty for the training of Protestant pastors in the former Soviet Union. Thanks to all my Russian language students who helped me fall in love with the country, the language, the church and with all of them! They have forever changed my life.

The faculty and staff at Nazarene Theological College (NTC), Manchester have been more than supportive throughout this journey. Without their help and support this work would never have been completed. Dr. Kent Brower has been the proverbial "thumb in my back" and Dr. Tom Noble has been the patient and wise advisor. There are not enough words to thank them. Grace Point Church of the Nazarene in Fort Wayne, Indiana has been more than gracious in giving me time and space to complete my studies. Their kingdom perspective is greatly appreciated.

Finally, I must thank my husband who spent days, weeks and even months alone as he provided me with the privilege of studying. He is my partner and fellow image-bearer as we walk this journey of life together.

I am not sure whether this is the end of the journey, or whether, just as the Cappadocians may have discovered, it is simply the beginning of more than we can ever comprehend.

Abbreviations

ACW	Ancient Christian Writers
ANF	Ante-Nicene Fathers
CC	In Cantica Cantic. (Commentary on the Canticle)
CH	Church History
CCSG	Corpus Christianorum: Series graeca. Turnhout, 1977–
CCSL	Corpus Christianorum: Series Latina. Turnhout, 1953–
CSEL	Corpus scriptorum ecclesiasticorum latinorum
Cont. Eun.	Contra Eunomius
CWS	Classics of Western Spirituality
DAR	De Anima et Resurrectione (On the Soul and the Resurrection)
DHO	De Hominis Opificio (On the Making of Man)
DOP	Dumbarton Oaks Papers
DP	De Perfectione (On Perfection)
DV	De Virginitate (On Virginity)
DVM	De Vita Macrinae (The Life of Macrina)
DVMo	De Vita Moysis
Ep.	Epistula
Epigr.	Epigrammata
FC	Fathers of the Church. Washington, D.C., 1947–
GCS	Die griechischen christlichen Schriftsteller der ersten Jahrhunderte, Akademie-Verlage: Berlin.
GNO	Gregorii Nyseni Opera
HTR	Harvard Theological Review

J	Jaeger
JECS	Journal of Early Christian Studies
JFSR	Journal of Feminist Studies in Religion
JTS	Journal of Theological Studies, Oxford
LCL	Loeb Classical Library
LR	Long Rule
LXX	Septuagint
NPNF1	Nicene and Post-Nicene Christian Fathers, Series 1
NPNF2	Nicene and Post-Nicene Christian Fathers, Series 2
Or.	Orator, oratoria, oratio
OC	Oratio Catechatica (The Great Catechism)
PG	J.-P. Migne (ed.), Patrologia Graeca, Paris, 1857–66
PL	J.-P. Migne (ed.), Patrologia Latina, Paris, 1844–64
SBL	Society of Biblical Literature
SC	Sources chrétiennes. Paris, 1943–
SJT	Scottish Journal of Theology, Edinburgh
SR	Short Rule
StPat	Studia Patristica, Louvain
VigChr	Vigiliae Christianae, Amsterdam
WUNT	Wissenchaftliche Untersuchungen zum Neuen Testament

CHAPTER 1

Introduction

THE CAPPADOCIAN FATHERS OF the fourth century, Basil of Caesarea, his brother, Gregory of Nyssa, and his friend Gregory of Nazianzus, are best remembered as theologians of the Trinity. However, theologians of their day not only wrote theology, they embodied theology. Wilken reminds us, "The intellectual effort of the early church was at the service of a much loftier goal than giving conceptual form to Christian belief. Its mission was to win the hearts and minds of men and women to change their lives."[1] For the Cappadocians, it was their life, but it was also a lifestyle. This included a lifelong quest to grow in a relationship with, and seek the face of God, intent on becoming more like God. Within the writings of the Cappadocians we discover a unique pathway to their understanding of *theosis*, one which broadens our understanding for it includes the women in their lives. These women, the *Cappadocian Mothers*, both married and virgins, exemplified deification for the Fathers and provided a model for a female restored in the image of God. The result is an optimistic message that provides a road map for pathways to deification for women but even more, a fuller understanding of the Cappadocians' theology when all of humanity is taken into account.

This early Christian theology "is the work of an unparalleled company of gifted thinkers whose lives are interwoven with their thought."[2] These theologians were not necessarily trying to establish something as they were trying to understand and explain what they were personally experiencing. "The desire to understand is as much part of believing as is the drive to act on what one believes."[3] According to Sheldrake, "*Being a theologian* is as much a quality of *being* in relation to the reality we reflect upon as a concern for the technology of a specific discipline."[4] Sheldrake's conclusion is that

1. Wilken, *Spirit of Early Christian Thought*, xiv.
2. Ibid., xviii.
3. Ibid., 3.
4. Sheldrake, *Spirituality & History*, 6.

1

"some kind of transformation is implied by the search for knowledge."[5] The result is that doctrine traditionally develops because of an embodiment of spiritual traditions within the lives of people and is not simply the result of abstract ideas.[6] The Cappadocians' relationships, involvement in the life of the church, social origins and education all helped to form their theology, which in turn was fundamentally pastoral.[7]

The synthesis of Cappadocian theology "encapsulates an idea of Christian knowledge in which biblical exegesis, speculative reasoning and mystical contemplation are fused."[8] This synthesis included the relationships and sociological world of their families. Basil and Gregory of Nyssa grew up in a Christian family consisting of five boys and five girls. Their Christian roots can be traced back to their grandparents who had been disciples of Gregory Thaumaturgus, missionary to Pontus. The turn of the fourth century had been greeted with the persecution of Christians. Basil and Gregory's grandparents were survivors of this persecution. Their grandmother, Macrina the Elder, taught them sayings she had learned from Gregory Thaumaturgus.[9] Basil, in the midst of the great Trinitarian debates, comments, "Nay, the conception of God which I received in childhood from my blessed mother and my grandmother Macrina, this, developed, have I held within me; for I did not change from one opinion to another with the maturity of reason, but I perfected the principles handed down to me by them. . . . The teaching about God which I had received as a boy from my blessed mother and my grandmother Macrina, I have ever held with increased conviction."[10]

Basil's friend, Gregory of Nazianzus, was also raised in a Christian home. Basil and Nazianzen, both of whom were raised in Cappadocia, studied classical literature but did not meet until their paths led them to Athens. Here while continuing their studies they met and became lifelong friends.[11] While they studied at Athens these two young Cappadocians became known for their "diligence and success in work, their stainless and devout life, and their close mutual affection."[12] Gregory described their behavior while in Athens: "The sole object of us both was virtue and living for

---

5. Ibid.

6. Ibid., 41.

7. Ibid., 46–48.

8. Ibid., 46.

9. Wilken, *Spirit of Early Christian Thought*, 138–39. See also Rousseau, *Basil of Caesarea*, 3.

10. Basil of Caesarea, *Ep.* 223.3 (PG 32) (Deferrari, LCL).

11. Van Dam, *Kingdom of Snow*, 5.

12. *NPNF2* 8:xv.

future hopes, having detached ourselves from this world before departing from it . . . our great concern, our great name, was to be Christians and be called Christians."[13] These young men who had been raised in Christian homes, furthered their education and made a mark on their world. Wilken believes this "continuity within Christian families over several generations helped spark the flowering of Christian intellectual life in the late fourth century."[14] In this case, this flowering left us with the writings of the Cappadocian Fathers.

Within the families and writings of the Cappadocians we find seven women: Macrina the Elder, grandmother of Basil and Nyssen; Emmelia, mother of Basil and Nyssen; Macrina, older sister of Basil and Nyssen; Theosebia and an unnamed virgin, both younger sisters of Basil and Nyssen; Nonna, mother of Nazianzen; and Gorgonia, Nazianzen's sister. These women, according to McGuckin, "seemed almost like a new breed—powerful as matriarchs, yet adding a decidedly new twist to that power base, for in their radical espousing of the principle that 'there is no longer male nor female in Christ,' they passed over psychological and social barriers that still contained their pagan sisters within the social mores of an immensely strong patriarchy."[15] The result was that these women, just as the men, were an embodiment of theology.

Structural framework

The Cappadocian Mothers remained lost within the pages of ancient manuscripts for generations and not until the last century did scholars begin to uncover them. Feminism and Christian feminist writings in the past half-century have helped us to rediscover these women at the same time feminist writings have been brought to the forefront of scholarship. Christian feminism believes that the arc of biblical teachings trends toward equality between men and women; church history increasingly bears out this egalitarian affirmation. Medievalist Allen Frantzen reminds us, "If writing about women was once an innovation, it is now an imperative."[16]

Faced with this imperative, we struggle with the manner or methodology in which we are to confront these women of history. Averil Cameron reminds us, "For early Christianity itself women seem to have been an object of attention in a way which calls for explanation, while clearly any feminist

13. Gregory Nazianzen, *Or.* 43.20–21 (PG 36:493) (SC 384) (FC, 39–41).

14. Wilken, *Spirit of Early Christian Thought*, 138–39.

15. McGuckin, *St. Gregory of Nazianzus*, 5. See also Gal 3:28.

16. Frantzen, "When Women Aren't Enough," 445–71.

in our day, or indeed anyone interested in the history of women, is going to find that understanding their role in Christianity presents a particularly acute methodological problem."[17] This methodological problem must be confronted.

Any methodological approach involving women necessitates a consideration of feminist hermeneutical principles. These must include their application in the midst of a shifting historical context where radical women's studies have given way to a more inclusive gender studies model. In an effort to tackle this methodological problem, Elizabeth Schüssler Fiorenza developed a series of four interdependent hermeneutical principles providing us with a remarkable model for feminist biblical and historical studies.[18] These include the *Hermeneutic of Suspicion*, the *Hermeneutic of Proclamation*, the *Hermeneutic of Remembrance* and, finally, the *Hermeneutic of Creative Actualization*.[19] According to Schüssler Fiorenza, these principles assist us in a "critical feminist theology of liberation."[20]

The *Hermeneutic of Suspicion* allows us to recognize where the text is androcentric and patriarchal. Therefore, one approaches the text with caution, asking what or whose purposes are being served.[21] Schüssler Fiorenza reinforces the importance of this feminist hermeneutic and its relationship to contemporary society.

> This critical insight of feminist hermeneutics has ramifications not only for historical scholarship but also for our contemporary-political situation because the Bible still functions today as a religious justification and ideological legitimization of patriarchy.
>
> To speak of power is to speak of political realities and struggles although we might not be conscious of this when we speak of the power of the Word. The Bible is not simply a religious but also a profoundly political book as it continues to inform the self-understandings of American and European "secularized" societies and cultures. Feminist biblical interpretations therefore

17. Cameron, "Virginity as Metaphor," 181.

18. O'Donovan, "Doing It Differently," 161. While Schüssler Fiorenza describes her principles in relation to biblical studies, Sheldrake and Coon utilize her principles in relation to Christian historical study through the centuries therefore not confining her concepts to biblical studies.

19. Schüssler Fiorenza, *Bread Not Stone*, 1–22.

20. Ibid., 15.

21. Kassian, "History of Feminism."

have a critical political significance not only for women in biblical religion but for all women in Western societies.[22]

The *Hermeneutic of Suspicion* highlights as fact the historical texts have been written by men and generally for men, permitting us to move beyond what may have traditionally been a singular interpretation.

Schüssler Fiorenza's *Hermeneutic of Proclamation* allows us to recover texts which permit us to proclaim freedom and liberation for the oppressed women of our day.[23] In other words, the ancient texts are interpreted so they inform the present day. Within more extreme feminism, the texts which "promote sexism or patriarchy [are] no longer to be proclaimed in the worship assembly."[24] However, it is within the *Hermeneutic of Remembrance* we are able to "search the texts for traces of women's history."[25] Not only have these women of history been found, but their struggles, too, are identified. Determined by the written text or by their obvious absence within the text,[26] the end result is the proclamation of good news for today's women.

Finally, there is the *Hermeneutic of Creative Actualization* whereby we reactualize the challenge given by the text, the personalities and communities encompassed therein.[27] Here feminist theologians may "read into, embellish or augment" the text.[28] According to Kassian, this final hermeneutic has enabled feminist theologians "to open up the door for a usable feminist *future*."[29]

While Schüssler Fiorenza has developed this hermeneutic model, at the same time, there have been major concurrent changes occurring within academia and different fields of study affecting our methodology and these must be included. Elizabeth Clark, church historian, provides us with a framework of understanding the three phases of development within the historical study of women. The first phase came to be known as *Women's Studies*. This was the "more innocuous task of merely describing women's

22. Schüssler Fiorenza, *Bread Not Stone*, xi.

23. Kassian, "History of Feminism."

24. Barbara Reid, *Choosing the Better Part?*, 10. This would raise serious questions as to whether feminist theologians accept the canon. Elizabeth Cady Stanton's *Women's Bible* is an example of this revisionist writing for suffragettes, and her version of the Bible was met with limited success.

25. Kassian, "History of Feminism."

26. Reid, *Choosing the Better Part?*, 10.

27. Doohan, "Scripture and Contemporary Spirituality."

28. Kassian, "History of Feminism."

29. Ibid.

activities."[30] This recovery of women became political as it became celebratory in lauding our foremothers.[31]

As the focus of recovery became more political, it developed into the next phase, *Feminist Studies*. Because of its politically charged nature, at its most extreme, *Feminist Studies* developed the goal of the "final eradication of women's oppression."[32] This phase is waning as the focus on *Gender Studies* emerges. "At the most simple level, gender studies *lets men in*—both as subjects for discussion and as authors."[33] Of course, historians focused on a feminist agenda have been critical of this shift toward gender, contending it undercuts the power of women. "For them, privileging gender and language seemed to signal a retreat in the wider historical discipline in which the battle had not yet been won for *women's* history."[34] At the same time, Frantzen is very positive about the shift to gender. In his opinion, gender has become a "tool for reconceptualizing male as well as female roles, reconfiguring the power struggles between the sexes, and merging sexual distinctions founded on reproductive difference. Gender studies, where those reconceptualizations are carried out, examine how males and females choose to think and act in reference to the conventions expected of the men and women of their ages."[35] It also leaves room for the relationship between males and females and, subsequently, the influences of each on historical writings.

Recent works have been influenced by post-structural interpretation. This type of interpretation is open to "social and cultural construction of gender, sexuality, and the body."[36] Coon explains: "Historians focusing on these constructions examine the fluidity of gender models and means by which various cultures recreate the categories of 'masculine' and 'feminine' in order to accommodate changing social, political, economic, and spiritual precepts. This methodology also considers more fully the relationship between author and text and between sacred image and didactic purpose."[37] It is then within this context of *Gender Studies* we can examine the writings of the Cappadocian Fathers, male writers, and attempt to understand the role their feminist writings play in their theology. We will attempt to meld

---

30. Clark, "Women, Gender, and the Study of Christian History," 396. See Liz James's introduction to *Women, Men and Eunuchs*, xii–xiv.

31. Clark, "Lady Vanishes," 30–31.

32. Clark, "Women, Gender, and the Study of Christian History," 396.

33. Ibid., 419–20. See Frantzen, "When Women Aren't Enough," 451.

34. Clark, "Women, Gender, and the Study of Christian History," 417.

35. Frantzen, "When Women Aren't Enough," 445.

36. Coon, *Sacred Fictions*, xx.

37. Ibid.

the hermeneutic model of Schüssler Fiorenza within the world of *Gender Studies*.

Throughout the phase of *Women's Studies*, we find the greatest use of the *Hermeneutic of Remembrance*. This began with a search through history to find the women who had been lost for so long. Sheldrake reminds us, "Who is permitted to have a history and who is not is a vital issue because those who have no memories or story have no life."[38] In the nineteenth century, we hear the prophetic voice of Rev. Dr. Thomas Upham, "One of the results of God's great work which is now going on in the world will be to raise and perfect woman's position and character. The darkest page in human history is that of the treatment of woman."[39] According to Clark, in the past thirty years, the feminist movement has endeavored to recover the history of those who have not had a voice, and hence no memory.[40] Sheldrake contends, "Some historians object to contemporary attempts to retrieve the forgotten women in history by arguing that *significant* women find a place in history as readily as men. Presumably there just happen to have been fewer significant women in history than men!"[41] However, the bias of traditional history has been toward the viewpoint of the powerful, and as a result, elite groups in history have had the greatest exposure.[42]

Traditional historical theory, according to Hayden White, has told us a story about the past but did not provide us with any explanation pertaining to those events.[43] According to Sheldrake, this traditional historical theory has been *teleological*, until recently. "That is, it approached the past in order to explain the results that we supposed that it produced."[44] The danger is, when anticipating a result, certain elements of a story may have been overemphasized, resulting in a misunderstanding of the outcome.[45] Feminism has attempted to correct this traditional approach, yet caution is in order. "Historical revision may conclude that previous accounts reached conclusions for unsound reasons, and yet we cannot simply *assume*, from the start, that the conclusion was undoubtedly false. All that can be said initially is that there are new questions which must be asked."[46] For example,

---

38. Sheldrake, *Spirituality & History*, 65.

39. Upham, as quoted in Palmer, *Promise of the Father*, 52.

40. Clark, "Women, Gender, and the Study of Christian History," 423–24.

41. Sheldrake, *Spirituality & History*, 77–78.

42. Ibid., 65.

43. White, "Question of Narrative," 3.

44. Sheldrake, *Spirituality & History*, 19.

45. Ibid.

46. Ibid.

by revisiting the history of the Cappadocians with an intentional inclusion of the women about whom they have written, is there anything new to be asked?

The initial period of the *Hermeneutic of Remembrance* involved a rediscovery of patristic hagiography. The Cappadocian fathers, according to Coon,

> combined the simple beauty of Christian parable with the highly stylized rhetoric of late antiquity in *vitae* that immortalized the sanctity of their most intimate friends and family. Patristic hagiography served a variety of purposes, which included evoking the experience of desert asceticism, reinforcing theological orthodoxy, promoting virginity, and sanctifying members of patrician families who would then serve as models for worldly renunciation.[47]

While the Cappadocian hagiographical documents of women could be found in Migne,[48] written in Greek and Latin, they seemed to have been lost until they were republished in English and occasionally French.

In 1916 W. K. Lowther Clarke published Nyssen's *Life of Macrina* in English.[49] The rediscovery and availability of material in English opened the door for further study. A generation later, building on the work of Jaeger, in 1967, Virginia Callahan published a new English translation of that work.[50] Maraval published the critical French version in *Sources Chrétiennes* in 1971.[51] Nazianzen's funeral oration for his sister Gorgonia had been printed in English in Schaff's *Nicene and Post-Nicene Fathers of the Christian Church* in 1894.[52] This piece of hagiography provided information on the life of his sister Gorgonia as well as the life of his mother, Nonna. As these works began to appear, they became the objects of further study.

Feminist authors have examined these hagiographic documents in a more critical manner and have tried to determine what, in fact, they are trying to tell us. Elizabeth Clark, beginning in the 1980s, has become one

47. Coon, *Sacred Fictions*, 7.

48. Patrologia Graeca, edited by J. P. Migne, 162 vols. (Paris, 1857–1886).

49. Nyssen, *DVM* (PG 46:960–1000), in Clarke, *Life of Saint Macrina*, 965–66.

50. Nyssen, *Ascetical Works*, trans. Virginia Woods Callahan (FC, 58), 159–91.

51. Grégoire de Nysse, *Vie de Sainte Macrine*, ed. and Fr. trans. by Maraval.

52. Nazianzen, *Or.* 8 (PG 35:789) (NPNF2 7). Also to be found in Schaff is Basil of Caesarea's *Ep.* 223 (PG 32) (NPNF2 7:599–601), in which we find biographical information regarding Basil's mother, Emmelia, and his grandmother Macrina the Elder. This information is more biographical than hagiographical. Today newer sources exist in English, including McCauley's translations in the Father's of the Church series, and Daley, in *Gregory of Nazianzus: The Early Church Fathers*.

of the more prolific feminist authors in the field of patristics,[53] helping us to examine the documents in a critical manner. Hagiography, however, presents us with a problem because it is a representation of an idealized world and "presents only what the writer wants the reader to believe and to value and what, at the time of writing, is in need of reform."[54] According to Harvey, "Hagiography often showed acute tension in its presentation of women. It portrayed holy women as conforming to established social norms even when their actions contradicted these norms."[55] As a result, Gregory of Nyssa espoused virginity as the path to God.[56] At the same time, his friend Gregory of Nazianzus praised his mother and sister for being godly wives and mothers.[57] Ultimately, the problem with hagiography is it is impossible to separate the factual from the fictional. Sheldrake reminds us hagiographies may "offer some factual insights, but this does not demand that we accept as 'fact' every last, extraordinary detail."[58] We recognize the people of the past understood reality within their context. In studying the past, we attempt to contextualize our understanding, recognizing we will always fall short.

Interestingly, Coon sees the hagiography of female saints as replicating the process of redemption. "By transforming profane female flesh into a vehicle of grace, women's conversion extends the hope of universal salvation to sinful humanity."[59] She sees holy women as both masculine and feminine, representing the spirit and the flesh. The sum of these considerations lead us to conclude "their sacred biographies both empower and restrain their spiritual activities."[60] Coon argues that the biographies "compelled the faithful to worship the omnipotence of God which manifested itself through the miraculous deeds of the saints."[61] These arguments take us beyond the

---

53. Clark's works include: *Ascetic Piety and Women's Faith*; "Authority and Humility"; "Ideology, History and the Construction of 'Woman'"; "Early Christian Women"; *Women in the Early Church* (this includes a copy of Gregory of Nyssa, *DV* [PG 45:317–416] [SC 119, 1966]); "Holy Women, Holy Words"; "Lady Vanishes" (this article provides an excellent history of feminist studies and provides an excellent road map bringing us current); "Theory and Practice"; "Women, Gender, and the Study of Christian History."

54. Sheldrake, *Spirituality & History*, 105–6.

55. Harvey, "Sacred Bonding," 27–57, 31.

56. Nyssen, *DV* (PG 45:317–416) (SC 119) (GNO VIII.I) (FC, 3–75).

57. Nazianzen, *Or. 8*.

58. Sheldrake, *Spirituality & History*, 23.

59. Coon, *Sacred Fictions*, xvii–xviii.

60. Ibid., xviii–xix.

61. Ibid., 9–10.

documents creating a problem for the historian. According to White, the narrative historian's method "consists in the investigation of the documents in order to determine what is the true or most plausible story that can be told about the events of which they are evidence."[62] Unfortunately, it was soon discovered that the women themselves were not uncovered in these hagiographical works. Rather, a number of literary pieces written by male authors were encountered. According to Clark, the *literariness* of the texts presented a theoretical problem.[63]

Nyssen's *On the Soul and the Resurrection* (newly translated in 1993 into English by Roth)[64] is an example of a text posing this theoretical problem. This document is not hagiographic, but rather is a dialogue modeled after Socrates' muse Diotima, with words modeled after Plato's *Phaedo*.[65] This style creates a literary challenge, raising the question as to whether the ideas presented are those of Macrina or simply Nyssen's. Wilken believes the thoughts are truly hers and that Gregory admires her for her "theological acumen as well as her piety. In the treatise it is Macrina who instructs Gregory about the resurrection, not the bishop Gregory who teaches Macrina."[66] On the other hand, Schaff believes Macrina is simply the mouthpiece of her brother Gregory. "Into her mouth he put his theological instructions on the soul, death, resurrection, and final restoration."[67] We are left with a good theological and philosophical piece of work, but we are unsure whether Macrina herself can be found there.

The questions posed by these varying opinions create a problem for feminist historical scholarship in light of post-structuralist critique. Clark argues many feminist historians view the post-structuralist critique of *objectivity* versus *subjectivity* as an encouragement to abandon any evidence which may create a "connection between people of the past and the description of them in historians' records."[68] In other words, categories have become so blurred, according to Clark, "we are forbidden to speak of *women* anymore."[69] In the process, the male subject has become decentered "leaving no space for the female subject, either. Why, many feminists query, are we told to abandon *subjectivity* just at the historical moment when women

62. White, *Question of Narrative*, 2.

63. Clark, "Holy Women, Holy Words," 416.

64. Nyssen, *DAR* (PG 46:11–160), trans. Roth.

65. Plato, "Phaedo," in *Dialogues*, trans. Jowett.

66. Wilken, *Spirit of Early Christian Thought*, 139.

67. Schaff, *History of the Christian Church*, 905.

68. Clark, "Holy Women, Holy Words," 416.

69 Ibid.

have begun to claim it?"[70] It appears that precisely when women have been found, the fruit of literary criticism and post-structuralism's labor, there is the possibility that they may disappear. Clark asks, "Why . . . was the 'end of woman' authorized without consulting her?"[71]

Averil Cameron poses this very poignant question, "How then to get beyond the texts?"[72] Her response is that "feminist writers wishing to recapture a positive role for early Christian women must proceed by reinterpreting the texts which provide their main evidence."[73] Clark, speaking for feminist historians, asks how "might they profitably combine literary theorists' emphasis on the role of language in shaping *reality* with more traditional historical concerns for the extra textual world? What, for example, might we be able to claim about *holy women* and *holy words* in late ancient Christianity?"[74] Feminist historians fear "that post-structuralists are apolitical (or worse), that they vastly overrate the place of language in the constitution of the world, are insensitive to issues of gender, and by decentring subjectivity, authorship, and agency, leave no ground on which a feminist politic can be built."[75] The issues that theoretically-informed feminist historians raise are helpful to church historians.[76] Specifically, historians must be able to examine not only the question of *how*, but also *why*, *what meaning*, and *who*?[77] Spiegel tells us, "It is perhaps to be expected that the current movement away from structuralist and post-structuralist readings of history and historiography is similarly governed by the needs and goals of social history, albeit of a kind quite different from that which preceded the advent of the *linguistic turn*."[78] We are currently in a state of accommodation and revision and looking for a solution.[79] Václev Havel posits it in this manner: "We are looking for an objective way out of the crisis of objectivism."[80]

Clark provides a solution and methodology for this problem. Specifically in the area of ancient Christianity and patristics, Clark notes the

70 Ibid. Influential theorists of structuralism and poststructuralism include Luce Irigaray, Julia Kristeva, and Jacques Derrida.

71. Clark, "Holy Women, Holy Words," 416. Miller, "Text's Heroine," 118, discussing Foucault's essay, "What Is an Author?"

72. Cameron, "Virginity as Metaphor," 187.

73. Ibid.

74. Clark, "Holy Women, Holy Words," 417.

75. Clark, "Lady Vanishes," 2.

76. Ibid.

77. Ibid., 10.

78. Spiegel, introduction to *Practicing History*, 4.

79. Ibid., 24.

80. Havel, "End of the Modern Era."

numerous historians who have played the role of anthropologist and yet have not paid attention "to the ways in which *woman* or *the female* becomes a rhetorical code for other concerns."[81] Her criticism in the area of patristics stems from those historians who wish to reject theoretical incursions into the field. Clark argues, "Now we should register more fully that the written materials surviving from late ancient Christianity are almost exclusively *texts*, not *documents*."[82] Averil Cameron reminds us, "Language is one of the first and most fundamental elements in the construction of sexual identity."[83] As a result, according to Clark, patristic historians must pay greater attention to the manner in which they construct the concept of *woman*.[84] While we cannot recover woman in a pure and simple way, we can find traces of her in our exploration because, according to Clark, women are "imbedded in a larger social-linguistic framework."[85] As we explore this framework, we will find them and their influence. *Women's studies* in religion have appropriated the social model for study, while *gender studies* have, according to Clark, "begun to adopt the hermeneutical paradigm of historical studies."[86] Her suggestion for methodology is to utilize both models, with the final result being a more enriched study.[87]

Clark is not alone. Sheldrake, as well, believes the time has come for analysis and historical enquiry to become more analytical with a greater emphasis placed on the interrelationship of events.[88] This interrelationship of events allows us to explore the theological concepts anticipated within the texts. The feminist theorist Irigaray encourages us to take up the theological question. Her work allows space for the Divine, and as a result, has freed us from having to accept the antireligious bias, which is often found in modern feminist theory.[89] Ursula King declares feminist scholars have become frustrated because historical study has become so text-oriented it has become over-intellectualist and "thus often excluded women from serving

---

81. Clark, "Women, Gender, and the Study of Christian History," 423–24.

82. Ibid. This is in the sense that we have tried to prove the role of a particular document, such as a letter, an epitaph, or a panegyric, rather than examining the very words, or texts for the meanings to be found in the writings themselves.

83. Cameron, "Sacred and Profane Love," 17.

84. Clark, "Women, Gender, and the Study of Christian History," 423–24.

85. Clark, "Lady Vanishes," 31.

86. Clark, "Women, Gender, and the Study of Christian History," 397.

87. Ibid.

88. Sheldrake, *Spirituality & History*, 27.

89. Jones, "Divining Women," 42–67, 44.

as subjects of study."[90] It is time to give attention to religious experience and its interrelatedness.[91]

This brings us to a new way in which to examine the text. Gabrielle Spiegel devises the phrase *social logic* "to register both social and formal concerns"[92] within a text. The *social logic* of a text begins to emerge when we view it from the *theological perspective*.[93] The *social logic* of the text, according to Clark, "has less to do with *real women* than with an elaboration of theological points that troubled their authors."[94] Clark, playing on Spiegel's words, encourages us to expand the concept of *social logic* to include the *theological logic* within a text as well.[95] She provides us with an example from *De Vita Macrinae*, noting "even though we retreat from the project of locating the *real Macrina* in this and other treatises by Gregory of Nyssa, a reading that attends to the social and theological context of these works reveals that the character of Macrina here plays a role in the contemporary controversy that tried to secure the place of a modified Origenism for *orthodoxy*."[96] In this regard, Macrina becomes "a tool with which Gregory can think through various troubling intellectual and theological problems that confronted male theologians of his day; in a special way, she exemplifies the claim that Christian males, as well as other ancient men, used women to *think with*."[97] Therefore, one function of Macrina in this text is to "serve as a spokesperson for Gregory's revised Origenist theology."[98]

Certain concerns must be mentioned in regard to subjectivity because criticism has developed against feminist writing in regard to experience. Several factors are at play, including the fact that much of the writing seems to present a picture of white middle-class women, which has been "represented as if it were the experience of *all* women."[99] Historians who are responsibly aware of the potential cross contamination during research readily admit they bring their subjectivity with them to the text. Goldstein speaks of this quite openly:

90. Clark, "Women, Gender, and the Study of Christian History," 407.

91. Ibid.

92. Clark, "Lady Vanishes," 13.

93. Ibid., 23.

94. Ibid., 24.

95. Ibid., 31.

96. Ibid.

97. Ibid., 27. See Brown, *Body and Society*, 153.

98. Clark, "Lady Vanishes," 27.

99. Clark, "Women, Gender, and the Study of Christian History," 407.

I am a student of theology; I am also a woman. Perhaps it strikes you as curious that I put these two assertions beside each other, as if to imply that one's [gender] has some bearing on his theological views. I myself would have rejected such an idea when I first began my theological studies. But now . . . I am no longer as certain as I once was that, when theologians speak of *man*, they are using the word in its generic sense. It is, after all, a well-known fact that theology has been written almost exclusively by men.[100]

The feminist must be aware of her own subjectivity, because without this awareness there will be the potential for abuse in interpretation.[101] Leclerc warns us: "When the feminist agenda becomes so *apologetic* as to force patristic rhetoric in certain, perhaps even contrived directions, the integrity of the interpretation can be legitimately questioned."[102] One direction, which may potentially be forced, is the search for early Christian feminism within certain texts, which Cameron asserts are "in the main highly misogynistic."[103] Christian feminist theologians stress that the gospel brought the good news to all people, including the poor and uneducated, and presumably, this included most women. Therefore, no matter what the text itself may imply, the assertion remains that "there was once a golden age of early Christianity in which women played a role they were scarcely to enjoy again until the rise of the feminist movement."[104] This argument will affect the manner in which a feminist historian or theologian approaches the text.

We must accept that historical knowledge can never be completely objective and will always be subjective in relation to our interest and use of the material.[105] "What remains after events have been explained is both *historical* and *meaningful* insofar as it can be understood. And this remainder is understandable insofar as it can be *grasped* in a symbolization, that is, shown to have the kind of meaning with which plots endow stories."[106] The historian tells a story in order that he or she eventually reveals a plot symbolic of the meaning of the text.[107] In the wake of the contemporary focus

---

100. Goldstein, "Human Situation," 25–42. Leclerc, *Singleness of Heart*, 5.

101. Leclerc, *Singleness of Heart*, 6.

102. Ibid.

103. Cameron, "Virginity as Metaphor," 184.

104. Ibid. See also, e.g., Schüssler Fiorenza, *In Memory of Her*, and Ruether, "Mothers of the Church," 30–70.

105. Sheldrake, *Spirituality & History*, 29–30.

106. White, *Question of Narrative*, 29.

107. Ibid., 28–29.

on *gender studies* and utilizing Schüssler Fiorenza's *Hermeneutic of Creative Actualization*, we can take the time to find the theological rhetoric existent within the text. It is within this last period of time that we have shifted our approach in theology "towards a greater reflection on human experience as an authentic source of divine revelation."[108]

Therefore, we adopt concepts from the area of gender studies allowing both the male and the female figures to be represented, asking questions regarding their interaction. The *Hermeneutic of Remembrance* allows us to reveal the Cappadocian Mothers, both through biography and hagiography. Using the *social logic* of this melding we then begin to ask theological questions related to the presence of the Cappadocian Mothers within the writings of Basil, Gregory and Gregory. Specifically, then we look to the question of *theosis*, or *deification*, in the writings of the Cappadocians and how the presence of these women informs their theology.

Theological framework

This study will include an examination of the Cappadocian Fathers' texts in which we gain understanding of their doctrine of theosis. In Cappadocian thought, the goal of the Christian life was theosis: to become like God or union with God.[109] This concept of theosis signaled a return to the *telos* of humanity, a humanity that was made in the image and likeness of God. People are saved through their participation in theosis, culminating in their growth in holiness, love, and Christ-likeness. Throughout their lives, the Cappadocians worked toward this salvific goal. They believed that theosis involved a synergistic activity, one between God and people. For the Cappadocians, life and doctrine were always one and the same.[110] Scholars identify Gregory of Nazianzus as the first Christian theologian to utilize the term theosis frequently and consistently.[111] Origen utilized the term in a Christian sense, but according to Winslow, "Difficulties inherent in Origen's

---

108. Sheldrake, *Spirituality & History*, 41.

109. Finlan and Kharlamov, *Theosis*, 1.

110. Wilken, *Spirit of Early Christian Thought*, xviii.

111. Winslow, *Dynamics of Salvation*, 180. According to Winslow, "Theophilus of Antioch was the first to use the vocabulary of *theosis* but restricted its meaning to that of immortality. Irenaeus was the first to relate the incarnation of the Word to the deification of man, postulating a 'double metathesis' whereby God became man that man might become God" (*Adv. Haer.*, 3.19.1). "Clement of Alexandria was the first to use the word Θεοποιέω to indicate this 'deifying' action brought about by the incarnation, relating it to the contemporary Hellenic concept of 'assimilation to God'" (*Paed.* 1.12).

system tended to detract from the ultimate validity of the term."[112] Gregory of Nazianzus makes constant use of *theosis* or the doctrine of deification within the Christian context. While the term was not yet normalized within the Christian community, his use carved out a permanent place for the doctrine.[113]

The theological framework of the Cappadocians included the influences of Origen and Neoplatonism. However, this was not the only basis for their thought. While the Cappadocians and those before them utilized classical philosophies in an effort to explain their beliefs, the foundation of their beliefs was not found in those philosophies, but in the Bible, or Holy Scriptures. "Gregory [Nyssen] begins not with Plato nor Plotinus nor their followers, but the Hebrew Bible, or the Septuagint, and the collection of first-century writings that would come to be called the New Testament."[114] Winslow believes that this approach is also the case concerning Nazianzen's writings. "We see here in Gregory's language a recognizable conflation of two views, the biblical and the Platonic. . . . Gregory in no way indicates that these two views are incompatible, but blends them together in such a way as to draw, as he sees it, upon the best from each of the two traditions."[115] Gregory of Nyssa was considered the deeper thinker over his brother, Basil. He "gave greater attention to philosophical difficulties posed by the biblical narrative."[116]

At the same time, Basil made it clear that he based his faith and life in the Scriptures. In his *Preface on the Judgement of God*, he tells us, "I was reared from the very beginning by Christian parents. From them I learned even in babyhood the Holy Scriptures which led me to a knowledge of the truth."[117] The theological framework of the Cappadocians shaped daily life. A follower of Christ was expected to live life in a holy manner. Basil defines this holy life in his *Ascetical Works*.

> Knowledge of holy living is knowledge of meekness and humility. Humility is the imitation of Christ; highmindedness and boldness and shamelessness, the imitation of the Devil. Become an imitator of Christ, not of Anti-Christ; of God and not the

---

112. Winslow, *Dynamics of Salvation*, 180.

113. Ibid.

114. Bassett, *Holiness Teaching*, 1:127.

115. Winslow, *Dynamics of Salvation*, 173. "To this extent, at least, Gregory's description of the heavenly life parallels his 'theoretical' definition of Paradise in *Oration on Theophany 38.12*" (PG 36:324B–D) (SC 358).

116. Wilken, *Spirit of Early Christian Thought*, 144.

117. Basil, *Preface on the Judgment of God* (PG 31) (FC, 37).

adversary of God; of the Master, not the fugitive slave; of the merciful One, not the merciless; of the lover, not the enemy, of mankind; of the inmates of the bridal chamber, not the inhabitants of darkness.[118]

Basil's words summarize his teaching, "Let us carefully endeavour, then, in every work only to do the will of God, and so by remembering this we shall attain to union with God."[119]

Nyssen believed that this imitation of Christ in our daily lives was part of a salvific process, which helped us become transformed into the image of God. In his writing *On Perfection* he states "that we may become the Image by true imitation of the beauty of the Archetype, as Paul did, who by his virtuous life became an imitator of Christ."[120] This leads us to an important question within the study. Is the image of God present in woman? Is *theosis* possible for women?

Image of God

Both Basil and Nyssen provide us with thoughts on the topic of the image of God. Basil's *Homily on Psalm 1* provides us with insight into his thinking.[121] Horowitz interpreted Basil as having a "clear-cut declaration that the *image of God* is a spiritual gift shared equally by men and women."[122] Nyssen highlights his thoughts in *On the Making of Man*,[123] revealing he was "hesitant to give an opening to the heretical viewpoint which had seen propagation as a characteristic of the Trinitarian Godhead; thus he did not like the notion that the image was male and female, which to him implied the prototype was male and female."[124] Interestingly, Clark believes that Nyssen's *De Vita Macrinae* paints Macrina as a living example of a human being in the image of God.[125] This would beg the question as to whether he saw Macrina as being asexual, because of her life of virginity. Their thoughts on

118. Basil, *Ascetical Discourse* (PG 46) (FC, 30–31).

119. Morison, *St. Basil and His Rule* (LR 5.3), 27.

120. Keenan, "De Professione Christiana and De Perfectione," 196. Nyssen, *DP* (PG 46:272A–B). English trans., Nyssen, *DP* (PG 46:249), in Bassett, *Holiness Teaching*, 127–36.

121. Basil, *Homily on Psalm 1* (PG 29:216D–217A).

122. Horowitz, "Image of God in Man," 196.

123. Nyssen, *DHO* 16 (PG 44:185b–c). Cf. *DHO* 22 (PG 44:204–9) (*NPNF2* 5:747–830).

124. Horowitz, "Image of God in Man," 197.

125. Clark, "Holy Women, Holy Words," 428. See also Nyssen, *DHO* 22 (PG 44:204).

this subject appear, at first glance, to be contradictory and will need further consideration.

For the Cappadocians, asceticism plays a special role in *theosis*, which included specific biblical practices. Many young people in the fourth century chose the life of asceticism. Specifically, young women left the world for a life of virginity as the *bride of Christ*. Nyssen expresses his view in *De Virginitate*.[126] Notably, his sister Macrina dominates the work *De Vita Macrinae* to "represent the ideal of ascetic piety."[127] In his discourse *De Virginitate*, Nyssen paints virginity as "the central virtue through which man perfects himself and reaches his goal which is participation in the purity and incorruptibility of God."[128] Much modern scholarship has focused on the lives of these virgins, and feminist writing is divided over whether asceticism was beneficial for the women or not.[129] Sheldrake's conclusion is that women suffered more than men as a result of this emphasis on ascetic spirituality.[130] Van Dam is concerned that issues such as money and power have so dominated the discussion of female asceticism that we have lost the focus on "true religious piety."[131] "Once these modern analyses of virginity and continence begin to highlight issues of empowerment or suppression, they also become discussions of the cultural construction of gender and sex in antiquity. It is not surprising that modern scholarship has often transformed ancient virginity into an aspect of women's studies."[132] However, when the theological attitude of the Cappadocian Fathers is explored, their attitude is "much more positive than is often imagined."[133]

Macrina becomes the model of virginity in Nyssen's hagiographical document, *De Vita Macrinae*. The biography is written in the form of a letter to his friend Olympius. Here we learn much detail about the life of this distinguished family, as well as the character of Gregory. Nyssen ascribes to Macrina "the secret name of Thecla," thus depicting "his sister's life as following in the tradition of the great virgin saint."[134] While Nyssen has provided us with his philosophical thoughts on virginity in *De Virginitate*,

126. Nyssen, *DV* (PG 45:317–416) (SC 119) (GNO VIII.I).

127. Smith, "Just and Reasonable Grief."

128. Nyssen, *DV* (FC, 4).

129. Leclerc, *Singleness of Heart*, 26.

130. Sheldrake, *Spirituality & History*, 74.

131. Van Dam, *Families and Friends*, 84.

132. Ibid.

133. Beagon, "Cappadocian Fathers, Women and Ecclesiastical Politics."

134. Smith, "Just and Reasonable Grief," 65. For more on Thecla, see Barrier *Acts of Paul and Thecla*; and *Acts of Paul and Thecla*, trans. Jones.

it is in *De Vita Macrinae* that we find practical application. He equates her life of virginity, separation from social obligations and the desires of the flesh, "with the eschatological life of incorruptibility through participation in God's incorruptible nature."[135] Her day-to-day life is a "proleptic participation in the angelic life of the saints at the resurrection."[136]

Derek Kruger examines Nyssen's *De Vita Macrinae*, believing that the text itself becomes a holy relic, "a witness to her saintly life, held in the author's hands. Materializing her memory, text substitutes for body."[137] Through the text itself, we see the relationship to deification, and through the narrative, Gregory brings us to a point of transformation and unification. Macrina has been transformed during her life, and is now united to Christ. As she reaches the point of death, she says her evening prayers. Macrina quotes Psalm 141: "Let my prayer be counted as an incense offering before your face, and the lifting up of my hands as an evening sacrifice."[138] So her life, that of a virgin, has been and is a sacrifice to God.

Interestingly, in the Cappadocians' writings about their female relatives, Macrina and Theosebia are the only two who live lives of virginity.[139] Concern exists that the focus on these virgins, or *Brides of Christ*, has taken attention away from the real center of holiness or *theosis*. While there was a growing emphasis on asceticism, according to Brown, "The Christian household and the local church remained the *loci* of the female quest for holiness, as they had been, for men and women alike, in the earlier centuries of the church."[140] According to Sheldrake, we have, for too long, allowed holiness to be defined in the *clerical-monastic* role, or that of virginity, rather than in "the Christian life as a whole."[141] Within the life of the church, a priority was placed on the *spiritual* over *material*, resulting in a suspicion of human sexuality.[142] According to Sheldrake, "The flesh and involvement in material things were associated with original sin. It was difficult to conceive of the possibility of saintliness *through* marriage or labour in the fields!"[143]

---

135. Smith, "Just and Reasonable Grief," 67.

136. Ibid., 66.

137. Kruger, "Writing and the Liturgy," 504.

138. Nyssen, *DVM* (SC 178) (GNO VIII.I) (FC, 181); (Ps 141:2 NIV).

139. It could be argued that her mother, Emmelia, could be included here, since after becoming widowed, chose to live a life of celibacy and asceticism with Macrina.

140. Brown, *Body and Society*, 262.

141. Sheldrake, *Spirituality & History*, 68.

142. Ibid.

143. Ibid., 70.

Therefore, the position of these married women within the texts of the Cappadocians thickens the plot.

Gregory and Basil's grandmother, Macrina the Elder, as well as their mother, Emmelia, are referenced in their writings. In *Epistle* 204 and 233, Basil refers to the teaching which he received from his grandmother, Macrina.[144] In *De Vita Macrinae* Nyssen tells us of the life of Macrina, and his mother, Emmelia. Gregory of Nazianzus also tells us of the married women within his family, specifically his mother, Nonna, and his sister Gorgonia. In his *Oration 8, On His Sister Gorgonia*,[145] we learn much about his sister. As we are introduced to Nonna, we discover exactly how deep an imprint her life made on the family. His father, Gregory, became a Christian specifically from her persuasive and long-reaching influence. As these women have come to the attention of feminist historians, new questions have been raised. Cameron notes that Gorgonia was a wife and a mother and yet says, "She, too, is praised for leading a life of such chastity and restraint that she virtually overcame the taint of the married state."[146] While that may be true, eventually Nazianzen goes on to compare Gorgonia with Solomon's woman of Proverbs 31. In the panegyric, Gregory describes "his sister as the personification of many of the virtues conventionally associated with reputable women."[147]

It becomes obvious that the women were very present in the lives of the Cappadocian Fathers. This brought about challenges for them because, according to Cameron, "There was no simple way in which the Fathers of the fourth century could write about women, and there is no simple way in which the real women can be recaptured."[148] At the same time she also suggests that there is no way for the Fathers' writing not to have been affected by their relationships with real women.[149] These real women become living examples of the theological concepts of the day with which the Cappadocians were wrestling. One of these concepts was theosis, and Winslow reminds us that all of Nazianzen's writing is infused with theosis: "There is no part in Gregory's writings, whether theological, Christological or soteriological, whether contemplative, pastoral or ascetical, in which this constant concern for theosis is not a major motif, a motif by which we today are the more

---

144. Basil, *Ep.* 204, *To the Neocaesarcans* (PG 32:745) (Deferrari, LCL); Basil, *Ep.* 223 (PG 32:820) (Deferrari, LCL).

145. Nazianzen, *Or.* 8 (PG 35:789).

146. Cameron, "Virginity as Metaphor, 197. See Nazianzen, *Or.* 8.

147. Van Dam, *Families and Friends*, 93. Nazianzen, *Or.* 8.19.

148. Cameron, "Virginity as Metaphor," 200.

149. Ibid.

able faithfully to interpret his thought."[150] This motif of theosis, presumably, would include his relationship with his mother and sister. Finally, Winslow leaves us with this thought:

> Yet we must conclude that the constant reference to *theosis* made by Gregory throughout his writings, be they on whatever subject or in whatever context, indicates that it is more properly understood as a *theological* term. That is, it helps us the better to know (1) who God is, (2) what God has done for us, and therefore (3) who we are and can be.[151]

The three Cappadocian Fathers' theological thought and development was greatly intertwined and therefore one must also conceive that if theosis infused Nazianzen's writing, it infused the writing of Basil and Nyssen as well. The presence of the women within their writings as examples of deification help us better know who God is, what God has done for us, and the hope of what we can become. The women become examples, not just for the Cappadocians, but all of humanity. We are able to agree with Derek Kruger: "Like the bread [of the Eucharist], the *Life of Macrina*, is distributable; and like its consecration, repeatable."[152] It is not only the *Life of Macrina* which is distributable and repeatable, but the lives of all seven of the Cappadocian Mothers found within the writings of Basil, Gregory and Gregory.

150. Winslow, *Dynamics of Salvation*, 178.
151. Ibid., 199.
152. Kruger, "Writing and the Liturgy," 510.

CHAPTER 2

The Christianization
of Deification

WITHIN THE LAST CENTURY, we have experienced a reawakening and interest in the Eastern Orthodox theology of *theosis* or *deification*. Orthodox
theologians such as Lossky[1] and Meyendorff[2] brought this mystical
doctrine of theosis into the twentieth century. The result was a desire by
Orthodox, Catholic and Protestant theologians to peer into the past and
into the history of the Eastern Church to gain a greater understanding of
this belief. The concept of deification, or becoming like God, has often
seemed unpalatable to the West, and yet, interest has been piqued and a
desire exists to learn more about this doctrine. The American theologian
F. W. Norris has encouraged Protestants not to look on deification "as an
oddity of Orthodox theology but as an ecumenical consensus, a catholic
teaching of the Church, best preserved and developed by the Orthodox."[3]
Therefore, this theology is not for the Eastern Church alone, rather, theosis
exists for all of Christianity.

Long before the split between East and West, the church grappled with
the ideas inherent within deification. It was Irenaeus who first spoke of this
concept in a christological manner. In the preface of *Against Heresies* 5, he
stated, "The Word of God, our Lord Jesus Christ, who did, through His
transcendent love, become what we are, that He might bring us to be even

---

1. Lossky, *Mystical Theology*. Especially note ch. 10, "The Way of Union." A
lengthy discussion of *free will* is found here and is of importance because it is only as a
result of free will that humans may choose to be in a relationship, to be in union with
God.

2. Meyendorff, "Theosis in the Eastern Christian Tradition." Here Meyendorff
gives a very nice overview of the Eastern understanding of Christian spirituality. He
touches on deification/theosis with the subheadings: "God Became Man so that Man
Might Become God"; "The Spirit of Truth"; and "The One and the Three."

3. Norris, "Deification," 422.

22

what He is Himself."[4] More than a century later, Athanasius developed this writing in the *The Incarnation of the Word of God*: "For He was made man that we might be made God (θεοποιηθῶμεν)."[5] Both of these statements are based on the Petrine comments in 2 Pet 1:4, "Thus he has given us, through these things, his precious and very great promises, so that through them you may escape from the corruption that is in the world because of lust, *and may become participants of the divine nature*"[6] (γένεσθε Θείας κοινωνοί φύσεως).[7] This scripture becomes the crux of "the Orthodox understanding of salvation, namely release from the corruption and mortality caused by the evil desires of the world."[8] God's goal for humanity is to free humanity from corruption which is the consequence of sin. This freedom is found in the transformation of humanity through deification.

The Cappadocians were not enlightened by modern Orthodox theology. They were working out their theology within a particular historical context. The Council of Nicaea in 325 and the resulting discussions greatly defined the life and work of the Cappadocian Fathers. Arduously, they studied the writings of the earlier Fathers who had moved the controversies to the forefront during this period and remained in dialogue with many of their contemporaries. Brooks Otis defines Cappadocian thought as "an attempt to unite the doctrine of God with the doctrine of angels and the doctrine of man in a way which would equal the logical consistency of the system of Origen without involving its heretical consequences."[9] Beyond the theological tensions, new civic challenges were rising. The Arian controversies of their time produced political alliances created from these power struggles, scarring the landscape of the church. The Cappadocians experienced that one's theology could become the basis for ecclesial assignments. Both Nyssen and Nazianzen in later years resented Basil, then archbishop, when he assigned them to less than desirable sees, playing into the game of political stratagem.

The Cappadocians, while theologians, were at the same time passionate about their faith. Their intellectual pursuits were an attempt to explain, biblically and theologically, what they were experiencing personally. The

---

4. Irenaeus, preface to *Against Heresies* 5 (PG 7a:1120) (*ANF* 1). "Verbum Dei, Jesum Christum Dominum nostrum: qui propter immensam suam dilectionem factus est quod sumus nos, uti nos perficeret esse quod est ipse." This quote appears only in Latin and not in Greek.

5. Athanasius, *Incarnation of the Word* (PG 25:192)(SC 199)(*NPNF2* 4:54).

6. NRSV—emphasis mine.

7. Greek New Testament (Textus Receptus) with Strong's Numbers.

8. Karkkainen, *One with God*, 18.

9. Otis, "Cappadocian Thought," 101.

result is that the three Fathers, all prolific writers, have left us with numerous documents and records which give us a glimpse into their lives and their theology. Each of them plays a role in the development of the doctrine of theosis of their day, and yet together they give us a broader picture of their understanding.

Basil of Caesarea

Basil, the eldest of the three Cappadocians, was born in Caesarea in 329/330.[10] He was the first son and one of ten children born to his father, Basil the Elder, a teacher of rhetoric and a lawyer, and his wife, Emmelia. Basil the Elder had been raised in a Christian home by his mother, Macrina the Elder.[11] Macrina and her husband, disciples of Gregory Thaumaturgus, had suffered under the persecutions. Much of the family fortune was lost during the persecutions but was rebuilt to a substantial basis by the time Basil and Emmelia began their family. Emmelia, Basil's mother, was raised an orphan. Nyssen tells us:

> But as she was orphaned of both father and mother and was blooming in her physical prime, the fame of her beauty attracted men as suitors. There was a risk that if she were not voluntarily joined to a man, she might suffer some unwanted abuse, since those driven mad by her beauty were preparing to seize her. For this reason she chose a man known and attested for the seemliness of his life; thus she acquired a guardian for her own life.[12]

Six of Emmelia's ten children are remembered as saints: Basil; his older sister, Macrina the younger; younger sister Theosebia; and his brothers, Gregory of Nyssa, Naucratius and Peter of Sebaste.[13] This is an impressive Christian family "which gave to the church a mother superior, three bishops, a director of a home for the elderly, Naucratius, and the means for financing philanthropic work on a large scale."[14]

---

10. Nazianzen, *Ep.* 2 (PG 37:21) (GCS 53) (*NPNF2* 7:849).

11. We are told that the grandfather was also a Christian, but his name is not known.

12. Nyssen, *Life of Macrina*, trans. Clark, in *Women in the Early Church*, 235.

13. Meredith, *Gregory of Nyssa*, 20–21. Meredith says, "The materials for the life of Basil are copious. Aside from his own writings, among which are to be found some 350 letters, we also possess panegyrics from his brother and his friend, scattered notices in the letters and writings of the two Gregories and the notices on his life in Socrates' *Ecclesiastical History* (4.26)." Meredith does not include Theosebia in this list of sibling saints. The argument for this will be seen later, in ch. 8.

14. Osborn, "I'm Looking Over," 26.

Basil, as the eldest son, was encouraged to further his education. He became a great student, studying in Caesarea, Constantinople and eventually in Athens, "not unlike a modern progression from Pomona to Stanford to Harvard."[15] However, while still in Athens, Basil came under the influence of Eustathius of Sebaste, a relationship which would have lasting effects on his theology and church politic. It is in Basil's *Epistle* 1, *To Eustathius* that we learn why he leaves Athens rather abruptly. Eustathius had turned to a life of asceticism, which Basil found very appealing. He writes, "Owing to the repute of your philosophy, I left Athens, scorning everything there."[16] He returned home to Caesarea, where he stayed for some time teaching rhetoric, eventually taking time to travel to Syria, Palestine and Egypt to learn more about the monastic way of life, which his mentor Eustathius was developing. Following this journey, he encouraged his friend Nazianzen to join him near Annesi so that he could put into practice the things he had learned about philosophy and asceticism.

Basil was ordained while in his mid-thirties and became a very celebrated preacher, and was considered a great rhetorician throughout his life.[17] His most popular sermons were those on the Six Days of Creation, or the *Hexaemeron*. These sermons were copied and preached by many others of his day.[18] His sermons often spoke to current issues. In 369, Cappadocia suffered a failure of the wheat crop, and the result was a devastating famine. Having given up much of his family's wealth to serve the poor, Basil could speak with authority to the wealthy of his flock in regard to their response to the famine.[19] His sermon "I Will Pull Down My Barns" includes a rather scathing indictment against those with sufficient resources.

> He gave no heed to the words that commanded: *Do not withhold from doing good who is able;*[20] and again: *Let not mercy and truth leave thee;*[21] and also: *Deal thy bread to the hungry.*[22] . . . His barns were near to bursting with the great quantities of corn he had stored there; but his greedy heart was not yet filled. For he was ever adding new crops to the earlier ones; and the mass swelling upwards through yearly increase he found himself in

15. Ibid., 17.

16. Basil, *Ep. 1* (PG 32:61) (Deferrari, LCL).

17. Osborn, "I'm Looking Over," 17.

18. Ibid., 19. See also Basil, *On the Haxaemeron*, trans. Way.

19. Osborn, "I'm Looking Over," 19.

20. Prov 3:27.

21. Prov 3:3.

22. Isa 58:7.

this predicament of avarice, that he could not let go of the first yield, nor find room to store the last.[23]

Basil believed that all followers of Christ should be engaged in helping their brothers and sisters in Christ.

> *What shall I do?* Offhand I would say: "I shall fill the souls of the hungry. I shall open my barns, and I shall send for all who are in want. I shall be like Joseph[24] in proclaiming the love of my fellow man. I shall cry out with a mighty voice: 'Come to me all of you who have need of bread; for of the abundance that divine love has given to me, let each of you take according to his need.'"[25]

An impassioned preacher, he also embraced the life about which he preached.

The Council of Nicaea, held in 325 shortly before Basil's birth, became a defining factor for his life, much of which was spent defending Nicene orthodoxy. As an adult, Basil attended the council which Constantius convened at Constantinople in 360.[26] Around 365, the opposition party of the pro-Arians had the ear of the emperor, and Basil found himself on the defence. While "not himself a great pioneer of Christian thought, he nevertheless discerned the issues in the discussion regarding the Trinity and himself proposed particular terminology—*ousia*, essence, for the universal being of God and *hypostasis*, subsistence, for particular expressions as Father, Son, or Spirit, which contributed precision and clarity to the debates."[27] Basil laid the foundation for the Trinitarian line which would be upheld by the ecumenical councils of Constantinople in 381 and then finally of Chalcedon in 451. He was the dominant member of the Cappadocians and at age forty became archbishop of Caesarea.[28] Sadly, he died by age forty-nine, his health having been greatly affected by his austere lifestyle.

Gregory of Nazianzus

Basil's best friend was Gregory of Nazianzus. While Basil may be viewed as the more dominant member of the Cappadocians, the two were very similar

23. Basil, *Homilia(e)*, "I Will Pull Down My Barns," trans. Toal, 326.

24. Gen 47:2.

25. Basil, "I Will Pull Down My Barns," 327.

26. Van Dam, *Kingdom of Snow*, 2–3.

27. Osborn, "I'm Looking Over," 18.

28. Ibid., 17.

in education, experience and commitment to the Christian life. Socrates Scholasticus tells us, "If any one should compare Basil and Gregory with one another, and consider the life, morals, and virtues of each, he would find it difficult to decide to which of them he ought to assign the pre-eminence: so equally did they both appear to excel, whether you regard the rectitude of their conduct, or their deep acquaintance with Greek literature and the sacred Scriptures."[29] Gregory was born around 330 "on a country estate called *Karbala*, near Arianzus, a village in the hilly center of the Roman province of Cappadocia."[30] His parents both came from comfortably wealthy families, but early on their marriage was somewhat of a clash. Gregory's mother and her family were Christians, while his father belonged to an obscure sect called the Hypsistarians.[31] They were not Christian but observed "a monist theology of One supreme God," while at the same time using the Jewish Scriptures and following "certain Jewish practices in worship."[32] Nonna, Gregory's mother, fervently prayed for her husband, with the result that he eventually converted to Christianity.[33] Gregory held his parents in high esteem, "I will add still one more word more about them: they have been fairly and justly apportioned to the two sexes. He is the ornament of men, she of women, and not only the ornament but also a pattern of virtue."[34]

Nazianzen attended school in Athens along with Basil and the future emperor Julian. These relationships, whether good or bad, affected much of Nazianzen's life, for all three of these bright young men had differing views regarding the future of Greek culture. "Basil thought it [Greek culture] could serve as a preliminary step for biblical studies. Julian tried to prevent Christians from using it at all. Gregory of Nazianzus was so indignant at Julian's restrictions that he argued that it was possible to indulge a passion for classical culture while retaining a devotion to Christianity."[35] When Julian became emperor, Gregory and his father defied Julian in his restrictions.[36]

Gregory and Basil were both renown for their intelligence. Socrates Scholasticus reminds us, "Indeed, although Eunomius . . . and many others on the side of the Arians were considered men of great eloquence, yet whenever they attempted to enter into controversy with Gregory and Basil, they

29. Socrates Scholasticus, *Ecclesiastical Letter* 4.26 (*NPNF2* 2:111).

30. Daley, *Gregory of Nazianzus*, 3.

31. Nazianzen *Or.* 18 (PG 35:985).

32. McGuckin, *St. Gregory of Nazianzus*, 3.

33. Nazianzen, *Or.* 18.11 (PG 35:985).

34. Ibid., 8 (PG 35:789–814) (FC, 104).

35. Van Dam, *Kingdom of Snow*, 5.

36. Ibid., 2–3.

appeared in comparison with them ignorant and illiterate."[37] Nazianzen praised those who had gone before him and recognized that he was building on their foundation. "Others have benefited themselves and us, as we too have benefited them, by systematic studies here."[38] Following the death of Basil, Nazianzen and Basil's brother, Gregory, both attended the ecumenical council of Constantinople in 381. Nazianzen also served, for a brief and rather unpleasant period of time, as the bishop at Constantinople.[39]

Gregory of Nyssa

Gregory of Nyssa was the youngest of the three, and was a younger brother to Macrina. He was born as a third-generation Christian into a household of considerable wealth.[40] There is no clear record of Gregory's education; however, "from the weakness of his health and delicacy of his constitution, it was most probably at home."[41] This means that Macrina more than likely had a great influence on his education. Schaff states, "The daughter, called Macrina, from her grandmother, was the angel in the house of this illustrious family. She shared with her grandmother and mother the care and education of all its younger members. Nor was there one of them who did not owe to her religious influence their settlement in the faith and consistency of Christian conduct."[42]

While he was the younger sibling, he did not allow his age to be an obstacle when it came to theological debates. He was "more inclined to daring speculation and to what is usually called 'mysticism' than were his colleagues."[43] Hans Urs von Balthasar describes Nyssen: "Less brilliant and prolific than his great master Origen, less cultivated than his friend Gregory Nazianzen, less practical than his brother Basil, he nonetheless outstrips them all in the profundity of his thought, for he knew better than anyone how to transpose ideas inwardly from the spiritual heritage of ancient Greece into a Christian mode. And he accomplishes this in that fundamentally Hellenistic spirit that allows him to translate religious experience seamlessly

37. Socrates Scholasticus, *Ecclesiastical Letter* 4.26.

38. Nazianzen, *Or.* 31.2 (SC 250) (SC 250), trans. Wickham, 117.

39. Van Dam, *Kingdom of Snow*, 2–3.

40. *NPNF2* 5:1.

41. *NPNF2* 5:2.

42. *NPNF2* 5:1–2.

43. Meyendorff, from the preface to Gregory of Nyssa's *DVMo*, trans. Malherbe and Ferguson, *Life of Moses*, xii.

into its conceptual expression."[44] Nyssen had a more philosophical mind than that of Basil or Nazianzen and probably realized more than they the "significance of the great issues at stake."[45] "But it is also true that Gregory of Nyssa, as the youngest and last of the Cappadocians, inherited the great bulk of his ideas and problems from his two predecessors. He did not think of himself as an originator so much as a faithful disciple."[46] He accepted the appointment by his brother to the small see of Nyssa in 371/372. While this town was one of little distinction, it was Basil's hope that Gregory's presence and acumen would not only bring recognition to the city but also assure Basil an additional vote in Episcopal elections.

After Basil's death in 379, Gregory became "one of the foremost champions of the orthodox faith against Arianism."[47] Building upon the foundation of his older brother Basil, he played a major role in the second ecumenical council at Constantinople in 381.[48]

Theosis—defined

While theosis is a major theme of the early church writers, rarely is the term defined. There seems be an underlying assumption that the term is understood within the Christian context.[49] McGuckin states that when the two Gregories, Nyssen and Nazianzen, are compared, one recognizes the "bold language of *deification*" utilized by Nazianzen, while "Gregory of Nyssa is more intent on the wider implications of assimilation theory.[50] Both, however, emerge in their respective teachings as entirely absorbed by the same overall task: the rereading of Origen on how to Christianize Plato, as part and parcel of the evangelization of the educated classes of their day."[51] Gregory of Nazianzus uses the term deification more frequently than Nyssen or Basil. Winslow states, "No Christian theologian prior to Gregory [Nazianzen] employed the term *theosis* (or the idea contained in the term) with as much consistency and frequency as did he; both terminologically and conceptually Gregory went far beyond his predecessors in his sustained

44. Balthasar, *Presence and Thought*, 15–16.

45. Otis, "Cappadocian Thought," 97.

46. Ibid.

47. Nyssen, *DVMo*, trans. Malherbe and Ferguson, 1.

48. Ibid., xv.

49. Russell, *Doctrine of Deification*, 1. See also Finlan and Kharlamov, *Theosis*, 5.

50. This is the concept that man is assimilated into God. See McGuckin, "Strategic Adaptation of Deification," 102, and Gross, *Divinization of the Christian*, 197.

51. McGuckin, "Strategic Adaptation," 99.

application of *theosis*."[52] F. W. Norris comments on Nazianzen's use of the term theosis:

> The use of theosis was daring. Non-Christians employed it to speak of pagan gods deifying creatures. The philosophers Iamblichus and Proclus, the poet Callimachus and the dreaded Julian the Apostate had used *theoo* in that way. It was not first a Christian word nor always employed by only Christians after they made it central. From within his deep contemplative life and from previous Church Tradition the Theologian picked it up, cleaned it up and filled it up with Christian sense. He and his fellow theologians took it captive and used it to speak about Christian realities.[53]

While in later centuries there would be further development of the language of theosis,[54] for the Cappadocians there appears to have been an assumption that the language of theosis was understood within the Christian community and a formal definition was not necessary. Apparently, the concept of deification was part of the accepted fiber of Christian life, and the Cappadocians had a foundational understanding which brought them to this point.

Gregory Thaumaturgus and Origen

One cannot understand the Cappadocians and their theology without understanding their relationship to Origen, and this by way of Thaumaturgus. We learn of Thaumaturgus from Nyssen in *In Praise of Gregory Thaumaturgus*[55] and from Basil in *Epistle 28, To the Church of Neocaesarea*[56] as well as *Epistles* 204 and 207.[57] They were consistently bound to him, not only in a theological but also in a very personal and physical sense. Basil and Nyssen's maternal grandmother, Macrina the Elder, provided this link to

---

52. Winslow, *Dynamics of Salvation*, 179.

53. Norris, "Deification," 415.

54. In the sixth century, Pseudo-Dionysius finally provided a definition of the term deification: "Now the assimilation to, and union with, God, as far as attainable, is deification. Pseudo-Dionysius, *Complete Works*, bk. 2, *Ecclesiastical Hierarchy*, 1.3. In the century following Pseudo-Dionysis we find Maximus the Confessor, who, according to Russell seems to be the first to discuss theosis as a "theological topic in its own right." Russell, *Doctrine of Deification*, 1.

55. *Gregorii Nysseni opera* X.1.3–57.

56. Basil, *Ep.* 28 (PG 32:34) (Deferrari, LCL).

57. Ibid., 204 (PG 32:745) (Deferrari, LCL); and 207 (PG 32:759) (Deferrari, LCL).

Origen by way of Gregory Thaumaturgus. While hiding out during the persecutions they came under the leadership of Gregory Thaumaturgus, a disciple and friend of Origen, who was serving as bishop of Neocaesarea. Meredith comments, "Origen's influence, everywhere present in the writings of Gregory of Nyssa, is doubtless due in no small measure to Gregory Thaumaturgus."[58] As a young man, Gregory Thaumaturgus had traveled to Palestine to study under Origen, who was renowned for his "great learning and fame as an interpreter of Scripture."[59] Basil wrote about his connection to the teachings of Gregory in *Epistle* 204, *To the Neocaesareans*. Noteworthy, Neocaesarea is where Gregory served as bishop and is the town to which Basil's grandmother fled during the persecutions.

> And what indeed could be a clearer proof of our faith than that we were brought up by our grandmother, a blessed woman who came from amongst you? I mean the illustrious Macrina, by whom we were taught the sayings of the most blessed Gregory (as many as she herself retained, preserved to her time in unbroken memory), and who moulded and formed us while still young in the doctrines of piety . . . And even to this hour, by the grace of Him who summoned us with a holy calling to the knowledge of Himself, we are conscious of having received into our hearts no doctrine inimical to sound teaching, nor of having at any time defiled our souls by the abominable blasphemy of the Arians.[60]

This "blessed Gregory" was Gregory Thaumaturgus, which translated means "Wonderworker," so named because when he spoke stones were moved, the sick were healed, and demons cast out.[61] His own life had been greatly influenced by his teacher, Origen. Intellectual study or knowledge was not to be the entire focus for the students of Origen. Rather, they were to focus on the philosophical or spiritual life because for Origen the imitation of Christ was to be realized daily, both in his own life and in the lives of his students. Gregory Thaumaturgus in his *Oration and Panegyric Addressed to Origen*[62] comments on the encouragement students received from Origen:

> Those only live a life truly worthy of reasonable creatures who aim at living an upright life and who seek to know first of all

58. Meredith, *Gregory of Nyssa*, 2.

59. Wilken, *Spirit of Early Christian Thought*, 267.

60. Basil, *Ep.* 204 (PG 32:745) (Deferrari, LCL).

61. *ANF* 6:3.

62. Thaumaturgus, *Oration and Panegyric* (PG 10:1049) (SC 148), trans. Salmond. See also *ANF* 6:21.

themselves, what manner of persons they are, and then the things that are truly good, which man ought to strive after, and then the things that are really evil, from which man ought to flee. . . . I cannot recount at present all the addresses of this kind which he [Origen] delivered to us, with the view of persuading us to take up the pursuit of philosophy.[63]

This spiritual life, which Origen referred to as the philosophical life, had to be understood in light of a dynamic relationship with the Father through the operation of the Son and Holy Spirit.[64]

Origen urged Gregory not to seek secular life but rather to serve the church. The result was that he became bishop in Neocaesarea. In Origen's letter to Gregory, he urged him to follow the life of spirituality and eventually to become a partaker of Christ and God:

Do you then, my son, diligently apply yourself to the reading of the sacred Scriptures. . . . And applying yourself thus to the divine study, seek aright, and with unwavering trust in God, the meaning of the holy Scriptures, which so many have missed. Be not satisfied with knocking and seeking; for prayer is of all things indispensable to the knowledge of the things of God. . . . My fatherly love to you has made me thus bold; but whether my boldness be good, God will know, and his Christ, and all partakers of the Spirit of God and the Spirit of Christ. *May you also be a partaker, and be ever increasing your inheritance, that you may say not only, "We are become partakers of Christ," but also partakers of God.*[65]

Gregory passed this teaching on to his disciples who followed him into the wilderness of Pontus during the persecutions. It is this teaching that his disciple, Macrina the Elder, continued to pass onto the generations that followed.

Origen—the man

The Cappadocians spent much of their adult lives surrounded by the theology of Origen. Their theological understanding was consistently defined in light of Origen, whether in agreement or making correction. When Basil and Nazianzen went to Annesi to test out the ascetic life, they created the

63. Thamauturgus, *Oration and Panegyric* (PG 10:1049) (SC 148) (*ANF* 6:21).

64. Russell, *Doctrine of Deification*, 12.

65. Origen, *Letter from Origen to Gregory* (PG 11) (*ANF* 4:393), emphasis mine.

Philocalia, the spiritual works of Origen. Schaff tells us, "Together they prosecuted their prayer, studies, and manual labor; made extracts from the works of Origen, which we possess, under the name of *Philocalia*, as the joint work of the two friends."[66] While they did not sit under the leadership of Origen, they certainly seem to be his direct disciples. Therefore, to understand the Cappadocians, one must understand Origen.

Origen was born to a Christian family in the city of Alexandria around 185. As a Christian, Origen was educated in the Scriptures; however, he also studied philosophy under Ammonius Saccas, the founder of the Neoplatonist, or Middle-Platonic school, in Alexandria.[67] Once Origen became a teacher, "he attempted a synthesis on a grand scale between the gospel and philosophy."[68] Some critics would claim that he was more Greek than Christian in his thinking. The mature years of his life were spent at Caesarea in Palestine, where he was imprisoned in 250 during the persecutions of Decius. He died in 254 after a period of prolonged torture.[69]

Origen's Platonic influence

One cannot discuss Origen without discussing the influence of Platonic thought on his understanding of theosis. Christian as well as Greek academics studied the writings of Plato well into the late fourth century.[70] The Cappadocians themselves constantly struggled with the tension between their *Christian* understanding of theosis and that of the Greek world around them. Although the Cappadocians drew upon Platonic thought, they vigorously argued for a biblically based view of Christianity because they believed philosophy aided them in understanding and communicating the Scriptures.[71]

66. Schaff, *History of the Christian Church*, 901.

67. Clarke, *St. Basil the Great*, 28. See also Russell, *Doctrine of Deification*, 123. Middle Platonism being the "modern term for a theology, Stoic ethics, and Aristotelian logic that school Platonism had been since the time of Eudorus of Alexandria. The goal of this Platonism was to become like God so far as possible. Clement's pursuit of it brought him to Christianity . . . [it is] likely that Clement had a close relationship with Ammonius Saccas."

68. Clarke, *St. Basil the Great*, 28.

69. Wilken, *Spirit of Early Christian Thought*, 11. See also, Meredith, *Gregory of Nyssa*, 59.

70. McGuckin, "Strategic Adaptation of Deification," 99.

71. Limberis, *Architects of Piety*, 160. Not all authors would agree with this evaluation of the Cappadocians. In contrast Limberis argues that "Platonism serves as a subordinate hermeneutic for the Genesis account of creation." This is in the examination of the place of gender. She does later see in the Cappadocians the ability of humankind to

The "philosophical thought of Plato is dominated by the mind-matter and being-becoming dualisms,"[72] and we see Origen struggling with this concept. Plato, a student of Socrates, had a concept of the *ideal*, or of the *good* being perfection. He believed in a world that existed without beginning and without end. Within this idea of the *good*, was above all else the concept of the soul, or the νοῦς, which was actually the superior part of the soul. The body and the soul could be separated, and it was only the soul which could imagine the ideal and become immortal. Plato writes, "And in every point of view the soul is the image of divinity and immortality, and the body of the human and mortal. And whereas the body is liable to speedy dissolution, the soul is almost if not quite indissoluble."[73]

For Plato, the goal of humanity, or at least the νοῦς, was to continuously reach to higher levels. "So one climbs . . . from Idea to Idea, to that which governs them as their highest reason and that which gives them their completion, the mind finally grasps the highest Being; it sees God."[74] Important in this climb is the desire to reach a level of purity. However, one's ability to reach purity is hindered by the fact that "the soul is in the body just as in a 'jail.'"[75] In other words, to be in the flesh is to keep one from reaching purity, from reaching the Ideal, or God. Therefore, one must go through purification. The soul and the body must be kept as separate as possible. One must concentrate on withdrawing and living detached from the physical body.[76] The soul sets its mind on things above and eventually makes its way to the good. "In brief, it divinizes the soul in the sense that it releases it from any obscuring and restores to its original state the divine element which is in it."[77] The final goal is for the νοῦς to escape; "and to escape is to become like God, so far as this is possible; and to become like God is to become righteous and holy and wise."[78] The ultimate goal for Plato is to become like God, ὁμοίωσις τῷ Θεῷ.[79]

Upon closer examination, it appears that this journey to become like God is not available for all. Rather, only a select number of souls will be able to reach this level of divinization or θεοποίησις. For Plato, this divinization

---

rise above "gender" as the individual moves toward sainthood.

72. Gross, *Divinization of the Christian*, 39.

73. Plato, *Phaedo*. 80a–b; *Resp.* 611e C, in *Dialogues*, trans. Jowett.

74. Gross, *Divinization of the Christian*, 39–40.

75. Ibid., 41.

76. Ibid.

77. Ibid.

78. Plato, *Theaetetus*, 176b (original Greek version).

79. Gross, *Divinization of the Christian*, 48.

is "an inner assimilation of the soul to God, owing to the vision of the divine Reality."[80] In this way, Plato is able to summarize "the most profound intuitions and lofty aspirations of the Greek soul. The divinization that he proposes as the aim of human activity is unquestionably the most sublime ideal ever to have been conceived of outside of Christianity."[81] However, in his understanding, all of humanity is lost or absorbed in the process of becoming a god. There are, according to Gross, "grave deficiencies"[82] in this understanding. In this dualistic understanding, there is no unity of the human being's nature. Instead, according to Gross, his ideas are "based on a much too abstract idea of divinity and on an exaggerated optimism concerning the strength of the νοῦς, which too often appears as the unique agent of salvation."[83] The result is a diminished emphasis on the role of the Divine in the entire process.

The development of Platonic contemplation, as defined by the Neoplatonic thought of Plotinus, eventually provides the framework and terminology for Christian mysticism.[84] Plotinus was born in 205 in Alexandria and, while a few years his junior, is a contemporary of Origen. He follows Origen as a student of Ammonius Saccus. Plotinus is regarded as "the last truly great philosopher of Greece"[85] and is also considered the most religious. He began a period of "reverent criticism and reconstruction of traditional Platonism."[86] His *Ennaeds* became the template for understanding Neoplatonism.[87] This Neoplatonic thought was "a synthesis of Greek and Hellenistic philosophy . . . as well as of mystical aspirations of eastern origin."[88] He viewed the Supreme Being, the One, or God, as "being both the first principle and the final goal of all things."[89] The main theme of Plotinus'

---

80. Ibid., 43.

81. Ibid.

82. Ibid.

83. Ibid.

84. Ibid., 44. One must be cautious here in connecting Origen with Plotinus. Nearly twenty years separated their study under Ammonius Saccas. Dillon, *Middle Platonists*, 382, states, "Attempts have been made to abstract common and distinctive body of doctrine from a comparison of Plotinus' *Enneads* and Origen's *De Principiis* (his most Platonist work). This was a good idea, but it does not in fact lead to the discovery of any distinctive doctrines."

85. Meredith, *Gregory of Nyssa*, 59.

86. Ibid.

87. Plotinus, *Ennaedes* (original Greek); English trans. MacKenna and Page.

88. Gross, *Divinization of the Christian*, 50.

89. Ibid.

Neoplatonimism was "the return, or the ascension, of the soul to the One."[90] It is by way of personal will and the desire of the mind that a soul can be separated from the physical body and, ultimately, be united with the Divine.[91]

For Plotinus, the universe was conceived as a system of hierarchy. The pinnacle of this system was "the One, the Being, the Origin . . . He is even beyond being, also beyond action and beyond νοῦς and thought."[92] The soul must ascend through this system of hierarchy, through these different levels, until it finally reaches God. For Plotinus, this ascension is completed in two stages: "purification [κάθαρσις] and union."[93] The journey of purification occurs through virtue because, "by the practice of virtue, 'the soul separates from the body,' and becomes 'absolutely passive' [πάντως ἀπαθῶς ἔχουσα] and 'pure' of all passions, no longer letting itself go toward the disorderly enticements of the flesh."[94] The individual must put forth great effort with the final goal, "being without fault" but also, "being God."[95]

The human desires to be released from this body, and this is accomplished by utilizing the νοῦς. Whereas, in classical Greek understanding, the νοῦς simply identified with the One, Plotinus recognized a "genuine mystical cognition of the One involving *ekstasis*."[96] In this way the person was in a passionless state (ἀπαθής), governed by reason and intelligence, able to make his flight to the *homeland* where the Father stays. "It is a state which can be called, in all truth, likeness with God (ὁμοίωςιν πρὸς Θεόν)."[97] Having reached this pinnacle, the person became "purely and simply a god, one of those gods who come after the First."[98] This union, as was the case in Plato's teaching, appeared to obliterate all of the humanity that remained within the human, resulting in an absorption of the "soul into the One."[99]

We have already noted Plato's definition of theosis, becoming "like God, as far as possible."[100] For those who came after Plato, the question truly became: *How far is it possible to become like God?* By the fourth century, the

---

90. Ibid.

91. Ibid.

92. Gross, *Divinization of the Christian*, 51. Original, "ἐπέκεινα οὐσίας. ἐπέκεινα καὶ ἐνεργείας καὶ ἐπέκεινα νοῦ καὶ νοήσεως." *Enneaeds* 1.7.1.19–20.

93. Gross, *Divinization of the Christian*, 53.

94. Ibid. See also *Enneaeds* 1.2.5.1–25.

95. Plotinus, *Enneaeds* 1.2.6.2–3. Original, "ἔξω ἁμαρτίας εἶ ναι, ἀλλὰ θεὸν εἶ ναι."

96. Bartos, *Deification in Eastern Orthodox Theology*, 49.

97. Gross, *Divinization of the Christian*, 54, from *Enneads* 1.2.3.15–22.

98. Plotinus, *Enneaeds* 1.2.6.6–7. Θεὸς μόνον. Θεὸς δὲ τῶν ἐπομένον τῷ πρώτῳ. Trans. Gross, *Divinization of the Christian*, 54.

99. Gross, *Divinization of the Christian*, 56.

100. Plato, *Theaetetus*, 176b.

modified Origenistic tradition greatly differed from the Irenaean tradition, which had focused almost exclusively on the flesh.[101] The emphasis was no longer on the flesh, but rather "on the liberation of the immortal soul from the flesh."[102] This was because the flesh, for Plato, had become the "locus of passion, change, evil, death."[103] At the same time, sin became very "closely equated with flesh."[104] What remained was salvation for the soul, which was no longer connected to the flesh.

Origen's theological influence on the daily life

Origen was a man who embodied his great faith and it was because of his faith and lifestyle that people found it difficult to argue against him. The philosophy of Origen must be understood not simply as theory but as way of life that infused every part of a person's being.[105] The way of life for Origen was a way back to God. That is, a return to the *telos* of humanity made in the image and likeness of God.

One of Origen's theological understandings was the theory of the *pre-existence* of the soul. That is, he believed that the soul of man existed before, in another world. It was only in this regard that he was able to explain the current fallen state of humanity.[106] Schaff discusses Origen's difficulty in finding biblical sources for his understanding.[107] "Origen himself allowed that the Bible does not directly teach the pre-existence of the soul, but maintained that several passages, such as the strife between Esau and Jacob in the womb, and the leaping of John the Baptist in the womb of Elizabeth at the salutation of Mary, imply it."[108]

According to Origen, the human soul, born into the flesh, was in need of being restored to the divine likeness. This action was to be the result of the works of man. "If Adam was in the image of God because of his reasoning soul, he still had to acquire the divine likeness by means of his free activity, by the 'imitation of God.'"[109]

---

101. Otis, "Cappadocian Thought," 100.

102. Ibid., 101.

103. Ibid.

104. Ibid.

105. Wilken, *Spirit of Early Christian Thought*, 267.

106. Gross, *Divinization of the Christian*, 142–43.

107. This concept of Origen's was later condemned as heresy under Justinian.

108. Schaff, *History*, 831.

109. Gross, *Divinization of the Christian*, 143.

Now the expression "In the image of God created He him," without any mention of the word "likeness," conveys no other meaning than this, that man received the dignity of God's image at his first creation; but that the perfection of his likeness has been reserved for the consummation,—*namely, that he might acquire it for himself by the exercise of his own diligence in the imitation of God*, the possibility of attaining to perfection being granted him at the beginning through the dignity of the divine image, and the perfect realization of the divine likeness being reached in the end by the fulfilment of the (necessary) works."[110]

Although man is fallen, he has the ability, through *intelligence and free will*, to return to the Creator and obtain the divine likeness. However, this is not possible "without the assistance of God."[111]

But now we see that he has associated with the soul what is censurable, . . . because it has waxed cold from the fervour of just things, and from participation in the divine fire, and yet has not lost the power of restoring itself to that condition of fervour in which it was at the beginning . . . "Return, O my soul, unto thy rest." From all which this appears to be made out, that the understanding, falling away from its status and dignity, was made or named soul; and that, if repaired and corrected, it returns to the condition of the understanding.[112]

The "assistance of God" is found in the form of the *logos* or incarnated Christ. Christ's role is to be the mediator for human-kind:

The only-begotten Son, therefore, is the glory of this light, proceeding inseparably from (God) Himself . . . [and] renders them capable of enduring the splendour of the light, being made in this respect also a sort of mediator between men and the light.[113]

In his *Commentary on John*, Origen also referred to this action of Christ's, which is able to work the process of transformation. "Hence he is a great High-Priest, since he restores all things to his Father's kingdom, and arranges that whatever defects exist in each part of creation shall be filled up so as to be full of the glory of the Father."[114]

---

110. Origen, *De Principiis* 3.6.1 (PG 11:333c) (*ANF* 4:344), emphasis mine.

111. Gross, *Divinization of the Christian*, 144.

112. Origen, *De Principiis* (PG 11:222) (*ANF* 4:287).

113. Ibid. (PG 11:135c) (*ANF* 4:246).

114. Origen, *Commentary on John* (PG 14:39) (*ANF* 9:319).

The final result for Origen is that the human nature is absorbed into the Divine. "In Him the divine nature and the human nature have begun to be closely joined together in order that, by its closeness with what is more divine, the human nature might become divine, not only in Jesus, but also in all those who, with faith, embrace the life which Jesus taught and which leads to friendship and closeness with God."[115] For Origen, this divinization is salvation. The process may be equated to one's passing through different areas of the temple, until finally reaching the holy of holies. The process is accomplished through gnosis, but only with the "assistance of God"[116] and comes to final fulfilment in the vision of God.[117] While Origen's process included Divine intervention, the result was the same as for Plato: there is no longer any humanity and all that is human is absorbed into the Divine. This becomes one of the major points of controversy for those who would come after him.

Origen's explanation of Christ's role as a mediator was also not without its concerns. The ascent of the soul toward theosis is "mediated by agents who are, so to speak, at home in both worlds: as less than God they can meet man; as more than man they can meet God . . . [the mitigation] is by the Origenist notion of the eternal begetting of the Son."[118] According to Kannengiesser:

> The whole salvific work of the incarnate Logos in Origen's un-
> derstanding shapes up as a pedagogical undertaking. The Soul-
> joined-with-the-Logos operates in the flesh by addressing other
> souls. His exemplary action calls for imitation. His message
> dissipates ignorance. He rekindles the spark of noetic transcen-
> dence that enables human souls to become again irradiated with
> the divine Logos, in order to recover their original integrity as
> images of the image of God who is the Logos himself.[119]

The result is that imitation of Christ by way of a life of asceticism becomes foundational for the further development of Christian theological
thought in the following centuries. Athanasius in the next century would
bring the corrective which was needed, placing Christ in the flesh *and* the
human soul.[120] It becomes quite clear that Origen's thinking was not without

---

115. Origen, *Against Celsus* 3.28 (PG 11:956). This translation by Gross, *Divinization of the Christian*, 145. See also Origen, *Against Celsus* (ANF 4:475).

116. Gross, *Divinization of the Christian*, 144.

117. Ibid.s, 149.

118. Otis, "Cappadocian Thought," 101.

119. Kannengiesser, "Christology," 77.

120. Ibid., 78.

its errors and controversy. According to Otis, the Origenist tradition which remains is: "Origen's highly influential allegorical method of scriptural exegesis, his teaching about the 'eternally begotten' Son, and his general conception of the body-soul dualism with salvation thought of in spiritual or non-physical terms."[121]

Because of his great education and his "honest search after truth," Origen's doctrine eventually provoked others to "new investigation."[122] Followers of Origen, including the Cappadocians, "drew from his writings much instruction and quickening, without committing themselves to his words."[123] For centuries his views were seen as being "too Platonizing" and he was deemed a heretic.[124] However, recent scholarship has been more generous in regard to Origen. Kannengiesser reminds us:

> One must only keep in mind that, when he first conceived his Christology, in the first half of the their century, Origen ventured into a conceptual no-man's-land. The time was hardly ripe for a systematic treatise on Christ. However, in his whole written legacy the Alexandrian pioneer exhibits a consistent Gospel-based Christology, whose richness still amazes many historians of Christian thought.[125]

On the Soul and the Resurrection
—the voice of Macrina responds

One of the greatest challenges for the Cappadocians was to Christianize theosis and also to correct some of the understandings of Origen. Gregory of Nyssa's *On the Soul and the Resurrection* became an example of the synthesis of this Greek understanding of deification, while at the same time placing it within a Christian context. Gregory very cleverly utilized the same literary structure of Plato in his *Symposium*.[126] Here, Plato used the voice of a female, Diotima, to engage in an instructive conversation. Diotima was the teacher who was able to "point the way to this direct perception of the ultimate Good."[127] In the case of Nyssen's text, his sister Macrina became

121. Otis, "Cappadocian Thought," 104.

122. Schaff, *History*, 699.

123. Ibid.

124. Ibid.

125. Kannengiesser, "Christology," 74.

126. Plato, *Symposium*; English trans. Jowett.

127. Cameron, "Sacred and Profane Love," 12.

the female voice, the teacher. While Macrina was modeled after Diotima, her "words in the dialogue *On the Soul and the Resurrection* owe much to Plato's *Phaedo*."[128]

The majority of scholars agree that the words found in *On the Soul and Resurrection* are not the actual words of Macrina; rather, her voice serves as "a trope for Gregory."[129] Macrina had recently died, and it appears that Gregory wished to esteem his sister. While the text was written in the style of Plato's dialogue, it must be noted that Macrina played a much larger role in the conversation than did Diotima in the *Symposium*.[130] Within the argument, Macrina constantly utilized the Scriptures as support. This, of course, Christianized the argument but also leads one to believe that the real Macrina may have been much more influential in this document than previously thought. Macrina, while not having been schooled in Athens, was deeply educated in the Scriptures. Nyssen himself tells us of her passion for Scripture:

> For she thought that it was shameful and altogether unfitting to teach the soft and pliable nature either the passionate themes of tragedy (which are based on the stories of women and give the poets their ideas and plots), or the unseemly antics of comedy, or the shameful activities of the immoral characters in the *Iliad* defiling the child's nature with the undignified tales about women. Instead of this, whatever of inspired Scripture was adaptable to the early years, this was the child's [Macrina's] subject matter, especially the Wisdom of Solomon and beyond this whatever leads us to a moral life. She was especially well versed in the Psalms, going through each part of the Psalter at the proper time; when she got up or did her daily tasks or rested, when she sat down to eat or rose from the table, when she went to bed or rose from it for prayer, she had the Psalter with her at all times, like a good and faithful traveling companion.[131]

In keeping with her character, *On the Soul and the Resurrection* is itself "free of quotation from classical pagan authors, mirroring Macrina's own Bible-based education, although some of its philosophical discourse contains echoes of Plato."[132] Not only did Macrina know the Scriptures well herself, but she had been the teacher for her younger siblings, including

128. Clark, "Lady Vanishes," 24.

129. Ibid., 27.

130. Smith, "Just and Reasonable Grief," 61.

131. Nyssen, *DVM* (SC 178) (GNO VIII.I) (FC, 165).

132. Kruger, "Writing and the Liturgy," 496.

Peter, about whom Nyssen remarked that Macrina had "reared him herself and led him to all the higher education, exercising him from babyhood in sacred learning so as not to give him leisure to incline his soul to vanities."[133] This little brother, Peter, went on to become the bishop of Sebaste in Armenia and was later canonized as a saint.

The personality of Macrina is quite noticeable within the document when Gregory includes what appears to be a reprimand from Macrina. She tells Gregory,

> "You have tried nobly to attack the dogma of the resurrection by means of the so-called art of rhetoric. You have circumvented the truth with such persuasively destructive arguments that a person not examining the truth of the mystery would feel that the objections are reasonable and the suggested doubts not justified. But," she said, "this is not the truth, even if we are unable to match the rhetoric in word."[134]

That this is a flashback to earlier years when Macrina served as his his teacher in the home is highly plausible. In the De Vita Macrinae, Nyssen gives us a glimpse of Macrina's ability to deflate the great Basil as well.

> The distinguished Basil, came home from school where he had had practice in rhetoric for a long time. He was excessively puffed up by his rhetorical abilities and disdainful of all great reputations, and considered himself better than the leading men in the district, but Macrina took him over and lured him so quickly to the goal of philosophy that he withdrew from the worldly show and began to look down upon acclaim through oratory and went over to this life full of labours for one's own hand to perform, providing for himself, through his complete poverty, a mode of living that would, without impediment, lead to virtue.[135]

While we do sense Macrina's personality within the document, we also recognize that Gregory has utilized Macrina as a tool, giving him a place where he can think out loud, so to speak, and in this way Macrina becomes the spokesperson for his "revised Origenist theology."[136] Some scholars have suggested this may have been simpler for Nyssen to do because he may have wanted to express some aspects of his developing theology which may have

---

133. Nyssen, *DVM* (SC 178) (GNO VIII.I) (FC, 171–72).

134. Nyssen, *DAR* (FC, 265).

135. Nyssen, *DVM* (SC 178) (GNO VIII.I) (FC, 167–68).

136. Clark, "Lady Vanishes," 27.

been untenable in his role as a bishop.[137] By utilizing the voice of his sister, a woman, he may have been able to avoid some direct criticism. However, that the theological reflections in *On the Soul and the Resurrection* share deep similarity to those expressed by Nyssen in *On the Making of Man* should be noted. Therefore, one may equally argue he is not hiding behind the voice of his sister, for it was not necessary.

We can agree that Gregory utilizes Macrina's voice to make statements regarding his theology. Gregory disagreed with Origen's thoughts regarding the separation of the soul from the human body and thus argued against "Origen's theory that it is a spiritualized body which will rise."[138]

> Thus the soul knows the individual elements which formed the body in which it dwelt, even after the dissolution of those elements. Even if nature drags them far apart from each other and, because of their basic differences prevents each of them from mixing with its opposite, the soul will, nevertheless, exist along with each element, fastening upon what is its own by its power of knowing it and it will remain there until the union of the separated parts occurs again in the reforming of the dissolved being which is properly called "the resurrection."[139]

According to Nyssen the resurrected body is not a spiritual body which has been separated from the physical, but rather the entire human with all of its elements will be reunited in the resurrection. "Origen held that the two bodies will have different natures; St. Gregory insists that the body will be the same, but the two states of the body different, the risen body being the last of a series of transformations which the body of man goes through from infancy to the resurrection."[140] *Apokatastasis* is a concept in which there is "a return to a former state of perfection, and the idea was a familiar one in Greek mythology and philosophy."[141] For Gregory, "the resurrection is nothing but the restoration of our nature to its original state."[142] This means that ultimately there will be "a restoration of all things in Christ."[143] For Origen, the "doctrine of *apokatastasis* was part of his belief that the souls would

---

137. See Burrus, "*Begotten, Not Made*," 112–22; and Roth, "Platonic and Pauline Elements."

138. Nyssen, *Ascetical Works* (FC, 196).

139. Nyssen, *DAR* (FC, 229).

140. Nyssen, *Ascetical Works* (FC, 196).

141. Ibid.

142. Nyssen, *DAR* (FC, 270).

143. Nyssen, *Ascetical Works* (FC, 196).

return to a purely spiritual condition at the time of the resurrection."[144] The fifth Ecumenical council would eventually condemn this doctrine of apokatastasis, or universal salvation, and other concepts of Origen.[145]

It may never be known whether Macrina is the true voice heard in *On the Soul and the Resurrection*; nevertheless, her presence in the text is important and plays the role of correcting Origen's theology. This was a major task in the time of the Cappadocians. Her voice brings us a Christian understanding of Greek concepts. Many authors scoff at the idea that Macrina can truly be found in *On the Soul and the Resurrection*. It is interesting to note that Meredith, the great biographer of Nyssen, never claims one way or another.[146] We are able to affirm that there was much to learn from the words given to her voice and that her presence within Nyssen's writings have expanded the Christian understanding of deification.

Influence of Athanasius

Although the Cappadocians were greatly influenced by Origen, one must recognize they lived when the opportunity to engage in direct conversation with Athanasius was a fortunate circumstance of their reality. Basil corresponded with Athanasius, sending him five letters within one year's time.[147] Nazianzen visited Alexandria and may have come into personal contact with Athanasius; however, had there been such an encounter, it is curious that there is no mention of this in Gregory's *Oration 21, On Athanasius of Alexandria*.[148] The Cappadocians built upon the foundation Athanasius laid in regard to the Trinity. This, in turn, had to be reinterpreted into their understanding of deification. Historically, it has been thought that Athanasius had a strong influence on Basil and his theology. However, more recent historians are questioning this influence of Athanasius on Basil. Lewis Ayres states, "Modern scholarship has failed to demonstrate with certainty any detailed engagement with Athanasius' theology on the part of Basil."[149] What Basil does owe to Athanasius is an understanding that the power to deify comes from the divinity of the Spirit himself. Where they differ is in their understanding of the transformation of the flesh, and specifically, "the

144. Ibid.

145. Ibid.

146. Meredith, *Gregory of Nyssa*.

147. See *Epistles* 66, 67, 69, 80 and 82.

148. Nazianzen, *Or.* 21 (PG 35:1081) (SC 270).

149. Ayres, *Nicaea and Its Legacy*, 221.

Athanasian manner does not appear in Basil's writings."[150] Politics may have been the greater reason for Basil's correspondence with Athanasius. Basil was hoping that Athanasius would lend his political influence to help unify the church. In *Epistle* 66 he writes:

> What is more venerated in the entire West than the white hair of your majestic head? Most honoured father, bequeath to the living some memorial worthy of your polity. By this one work embellish those innumerable labours which you have performed for the sake of the true faith. Send forth from the holy church under your care to the bishops of the West a number of men who are mighty in the true doctrine. Describe to these bishops the misfortunes which afflict us. Suggest a method of assistance. Become a Samuel to the churches. Share in the sufferings of our people who are feeling the miseries of war. Offer prayers for peace. Ask as a grace from the Lord that He may send upon the churches some memories of peace.[151]

Basil was trying to defeat the Arians and was hoping that Athanasius would agree to his Trinitarian language, thus condemning Marcellus and recognizing Paulinus as bishop of Antioch. We find no record of a response by Athanasius, and this "lack of response indicates what he thought of Basil's plan."[152]

Gregory of Nazianzus, developing Athanasius' thoughts found in the *Life of Anthony*, agreed that the incarnation makes the deification of human nature possible. The role of humanity is to accept baptism and struggle to "live the moral life."[153] It is thus that we find a connection between the Cappadocians and Athanasius and a connection to the monastic life. In Nazianzen's *Oration* 21, *On Athanasius of Alexandria*, we find this description of deification, applied to Athanasius:

> Whoever was permitted to escape by reason and contemplation from matter and this fleshly cloud or veil (whichever it should be called) and to hold communion with God, and be associated, as far as man's nature can attain, with the purest Light, blessed is he, both from his ascent from hence, and for his *deification* (θεώσεως) there, which is conferred by true philosophy, and

---

150. Russell, *Doctrine of Deification*, 212.

151. Basil, *Ep.* 66 (PG 32:425) (Deferrari, LCL).

152. Hildebrand, *Trinitarian Theology of Basil*, 26.

153. Russell, *Doctrine of Deification*, 225.

by rising superior to the dualism of matter, through the unity
which is perceived in the Trinity.[154]

Nazianzen does not develop Athanasius' doctrine of participation but leaves
this to Nyssen.[155]

Meredith argues that Athanasius is Nyssen's instructor in Christology.
Borrowing from Athanasius Nyssen focuses on the incarnation of Christ
and the importance of the incarnation for deification.[156] For Nyssen, deification is more about participation in the divine attributes,[157] and among
the attributes "beatitude is the property of God par excellence."[158] One is,
therefore, to participate in the beatitudes, the result of which is communion
or fellowship with the Godhead.[159] The Cappadocians utilized the doctrine
of deification from Alexandria and adapted it to a Platonic "understanding
of Christianity as the attainment of likeness to God as far as is possible for
human nature."[160] The Alexandrian's terminology (Θεοποιέω) was rarely
used by the Cappadocians, with Nazianzen "preferring to use θεόω and his
own coinage, θέωσις."[161] Athanasius' work in the development of Trinitarian
language made it possible for the Cappadocians to develop their Christianized understanding of deification or theosis.

154. Nazianzen, *Or.* 21 (PG 35:1082) (SC 270) (*NFNP2* 7:269–80).

155. Russell, *Doctrine of Deification*, 225.

156. Meredith, *Gregory of Nyssa*, 86.

157. Russell, *Doctrine of Deification*, 226.

158. *De Beat.* 5. Russell, *Doctrine of Deification*, 227.

159. Russell, *Doctrine of Deification*, 227.

160. Ibid., 233.

161. Ibid.

CHAPTER 3

Christocentric Development

THE CHRISTIANIZATION OF THEOSIS was a difficult task, but one which the Cappadocians were able to address because of their education and skill in theology. John Meyendorrf, a twentieth-century Orthodox theologian, reflects on the Cappadocians' influence on the understanding of theosis or deification. He states that under the Cappadocians, theosis became "a Christocentric and eschatological concept, expressed in Platonic language but basically independent of philosophical speculation."[1] Norman Russell suggests that the Cappadocians move the language more toward that of *participation* rather than deification.[2] That is, they attempt to make clear that the human is not completely absorbed into the divine, with this concept becoming more developed in Nyssen than in the other two Cappadocians. Brooks Otis suggests that the Cappadocians faced a rather ominous task, one in which they were to "reconstruct the entire Origenist or anti-Irenaean position on the basis of the *homoiousian* theology."[3] According to Gross, Nyssen's "conception of deifying ecstasy . . . is clearly influenced by the unitive gnosis of his master Origen, but also by the mysticism of Philo and Plotinus. Indeed, following the latter, he accepts that the ecstatic union is accomplished not by the νοῦς, as Origen thinks, but outside of or beyond the νοῦς by means of a mysterious contact of a spiritual nature."[4] Socrates Scholasticus explains the way in which Basil and Nazianzen responded:

> Having had some slight taste of philosophical science from him who then taught it at Antioch, they procured Origen's works, and drew from them the right interpretation of the sacred

1. Meyendorff, "Theosis in the Eastern Christian Tradition," 471.

2. Russell, *Doctrine of Deification*, 235.

3. Otis, "Cappadocian Thought," 106–7. The homoiousian theology of the day provides the backdrop for the arguments of the Cappadocians. Otis saw two major traditions in conflict, the Origenist and the Irenaean-Athanasian.

4. Gross, *Divinization of the Christian*, 188–89.

Scriptures; for the fame of Origen was very great and wide-spread throughout the whole world at that time; after a careful perusal of the writings of that great man, they contended against the Arians with manifest advantage. And when the defenders of Arianism quoted the same author in confirmation, as they imagined, of their own views, these two confuted them, and clearly proved that their opponents did not at all understand the reasoning of Origen.[5]

For a brief period, Basil was a member of the *homoiousian* party, along with his friend Eustathius of Sebaste. It is against this backdrop that the Cappadocians' Neo-Nicene theology was developed. It will be noted that in the later years of Cappadocian theological development, the fathers, specifically Basil, created more distance between themselves and the *homoiousians*. Basil eventually condemned the errors of the *homoiousians* and "vindicated the doctrine of the *homoousion*."[6] Rousseau notes that while Basil was willing to utilize the term ὅμοιος, this was only if "it was taken to mean ὅμοιος χατ᾽οὐσίαν, 'like in substance,' and provided he was allowed to add yet another word, ἀπαραλλάχτως, 'without variation.' Those phrases together, he said, amounted to the ὁμοούσιος of Nicaea."[7]

Otis referred to the contemporaries of the Cappadocians as being rather "narrow-minded" forcing the Cappadocians to go to the "great minds of the past; to Origen, Clement, and the pagan Platonists"[8] to develop their theology. Srawley, in his introduction to Nyssen's *Catechetical Oration*, reminds us that Origen's theological system, "though not accepted in its entirety, was the only adequate form of Christian scientific thought known to that age."[9] Gregory of Nyssa, in *The Life of Moses*, suggests that those seeking virtue must also equip themselves

> with the wealth of pagan learning by which foreigners to the faith beautify themselves. Our guide in virtue commands someone who "borrows" from wealthy Egyptians to receive such things as moral and natural philosophy, geometry, astronomy, dialectic, and whatever else is sought by those outside the Church, since these things will be useful when in time the divine sanctuary of mystery must be beautified with the riches of reason.[10]

---

5. Socrates Scholasticus, *Ecclesiastical Letter* 4.26 (*NPNF2* 2:110).

6. Ibid.

7. Rousseau, *Basil of Caesarea*, 102.

8. Otis, "Cappadocian Thought," 106–7.

9. Nyssen, *Catechetical Oration*, trans. Srawley, x.

10. Nyssen, *DVMo* (PG 44:360B) (*SC* 1), trans. Malherbe and Ferguson, 63.

One major flaw in Origen's doctrine was that Origen viewed the *logos* as "neither God nor man but an intermediate being."[11] Crouzel would argue that this was a misunderstanding or misreading of Origen, for his Trinitarian doctrine was not yet fully developed.

> Origen would then be read in the context of heresies other than the ones he had in mind: as he had not foreseen these, some of his expressions or speculations could, with a bit of a push, be made to look as if he embraced these heresies, especially when no trouble was taken to look in other parts of his work for the key to his assertions. The main one was Arianism. Origen, whose Trinitarian vocabulary was not yet sufficiently precise, might seem opposed to the unity of nature defined at Nicaea, although he held its equivalent in a dynamic rather than ontological mode. Some expressions could draw his subordinationism, which is in terms of origin and "economy," towards the Arian subordinationism of inequality using texts which assert nothing more than a hierarchy of origin. Besides, he is constantly accused, for reasons of vocabulary . . . of making the Son and the Holy Spirit creatures of the Father. In this detractors take no account of his speculations on the eternal generation of the Word in the *Treatise on First Principles* itself and of the celebrated formula attested as being in Origen by Athanasius himself: "*ouk en hote ouk en*—there was not a moment when He (the Word) was not."[12]

The Cappadocians were able to work out some of the linguistic difficulties found in Origen, and building on Athanasius, they obliterated any distinction between the natures of God and Christ. Therefore, for the Cappadocians, "the life of the Redeemed becomes the infinite pursuit of an ever pursuable God: the creature never overcomes his separation from the creator (*theosis* thus loses its Neoplatonic and Origenist senses of the loss of creatureliness in the divine unity), but achieves a constantly increasing satisfaction in the infinite process of approximation to God."[13] This becomes the theological framework for the Cappadocians' spiritual doctrine of theosis.

The changes made to Origen's doctrine were quite significant, and the doctrine of the Cappadocians began to become clear. Nyssen replaced Origen's concept of *static unity* with that of *continued progress*.[14] Origen's spirituality was governed "by the omnipresent possibility of temptation

11. Otis, "Cappadocian Thought," 107.

12. Crouzel, *Origen*, 171–72.

13. Otis, "Cappadocian Thought," 108.

14. Nyssen, *DVMo*, trans. Malherbe and Ferguson, 13.

and sin" while Gregory of Nyssa was "concerned almost exclusively with the sinless life of the saved or blessed."[15] The two Gregories were able to develop and focus this doctrine more fully than Basil. Much of Basil's writing was the result of defending his theology while debating his contemporaries. The two Gregories, both younger, had the privilege of building upon Basil's theological foundation and arguments. Therefore, it is the synthesis of this understanding which we find in the later writings of Nyssen and Nazianzen. Nyssen describes what occurs in the following manner:

> All heavenly bodies that receive a downward motion, even if they receive no further impulse after the first contact are rapidly carried downward of themselves, provided that any surface on which they are moving is graded and sloping, and that they meet no obstacle to interrupt their motion. So too, the soul moves in the opposite direction, light and swiftly moving upwards once it is released from sensuous and earthly attachments, soaring from the world below up towards the heavens. And if nothing comes from above to intercept its flight, seeing that it is of the nature of Goodness to attract those who raise their eyes towards it, the soul keeps rising ever higher and higher, stretching with its desire for heavenly things *to those that are before*,[16] as the Apostle tells us, and thus it will always continue to soar ever higher. For because of what it has already attained, the soul does not wish to abandon the heights that lie beyond it. And thus the soul moves ceaselessly upwards, always reviving its tension for its onward flight by means of the progress it has already realized.[17]

This framework for their doctrine of deification may be defined as a kenosis-theosis parabola, for which Christ becomes definitive. Nazianzen expresses it in this manner: "I must be buried with Christ, rise with Christ, be joint heir with Christ, become the son of God, even God Himself."[18] He expounded on this, saying:

> This is the intent of God, who for our sake was made man and became poor,[19] in order to raise our flesh[20] and restore His image

15. Otis, "Cappadocian Thought," 108, 115.

16. Phil 3:13.

17. Nyssen, *DVMo* (PG 397D–405A); ed. Daniélou, ii.219–39, in *From Glory to Glory*, 144.

18. Nazianzen, *Or.* 7.23 (PG 35:755) (SC 406) (FC, 24).

19. 2 Cor 8:9.

20. Rom 8:11.

and remake man,[21] that we might all become one in Christ,[22] who was perfectly became in all of us all that He is Himself,[23] that we might no longer be male and female, barbarian, Scythian, slave or freeman,[24] the distinctions of the flesh, but might bear in ourselves only the stamp of God by whom and for whom we were made,[25] so far formed and modelled by Him as to be recognized by it alone.[26]

F. W. Norris identifies this kenosis-theosis pattern in his doctoral dissertation. "Nazianzen intends the self-emptying—divinizing figure to be the primary organizing principle of his theology."[27] Meyendorf presents suggestions for a kenosis-theosis parabola. The pattern is similar to that suggested by Winslow.[28] For the purposes of this study the kenosis-theosis parabola is utilized with the following points:

1. Humankind is made in the image of God and is a reflection or mirror of that image.

2. The image is tarnished by the fall into sin.

3. Christ assumes the human nature in order to restore humanity to its original nature.

4. In conversion one's capacity to reflect the divine nature is once again restored.

5. The Christian life becomes one of "incessant transformation into the likeness of God as man stretches out with the divine infinity."[29]

6. Throughout this journey there is an "ever-greater participation in God."[30]

Paul reminds us in the christological hymn found in Phil 2 that humanity is to desire to have the same mind as that of Christ. Christ, having seen the corrupted state of humankind poured himself out for the salvation

---

21. Col 3:10.
22. Gal 3:28.
23. 1 Cor 15:28.
24. Col 3:11.
25. Rom 11:36.
26. Nazianzen, *Or.* 7.23 (PG 35:755) (SC 406) (FC, 24).
27. Norris, "Gregory Nazianzen's Doctrine," 132.
28. Winslow, *Dynamics of Salvation.*
29. Nyssen, *DVMo*, trans. Malherbe and Ferguson, 12.
30. Ibid. This entire outline is adopted from Meyendorff's comments here.

of humanity. The result, however, was that Christ did not remain in this state. God exalted the Son and lifted him up. Origen made the connection between the kenosis of Christ and the resulting possibility of theosis for humanity: Michael Christensen notes, "Human *deification* is possible, according to Origen, because of God's humanization in Christ. In the descent of divinity into the body of humanity, an historic mutation occurred—'human and divine began to be woven together, so that by prolonged fellowship with divinity, human nature might become divine.'"[31] This same theme is heard in Nazianzen:

> The Son's "coming down from heaven not to do his own will, but the will of him who sent him."[32] Certainly had these words not been spoken by the very one who "came down" we should have said the language bore the stamp of a mere man like us, not that of the Saviour we know. *His* will is not in the least degree opposed to God, is totally dependent upon God. Our merely human will does not always follow the divine; it often resists and struggles against it.[33]

Later, in the same *Oration*, Nazianzen states, "Walk like God through all that are sublime, and with a fellow feeling through all that involve the body; but better, treat all as God does, so that you may ascend from below to become God, because he came down from above for us."[34] Meyendorff sees Nyssen's *Life of Moses* as "a parabola of the Christian spiritual ascent," when, through baptism man begins a relationship with God, which is followed by a life of virtue, which enables the human to "acquire 'spiritual senses,' which allow him to perceive, through communion in Christ and the Holy Spirit, the One who is beyond creation."[35]

Humankind is made in the image of God and is a mirror reflecting that image

Plato had provided a unique understanding of image to the Greek world. Under his influence both Plotinus and Christian theologians used the word

31. Christensen, "Theosis and Sanctification," quoting Origen, *Contra Celsum*, 3.238.

32. John 6:38.

33. Nazianzen, *Or.* 30.12 (PG 36:103) (SC 250), trans. Wickham, 102–3.

34. Ibid., 30.21 (PG 36:103) (SC 250), trans. Wickham, 112.

35. Nyssen, *DVMo*, trans. Malherbe and Ferguson, xiii. Meyendorff provides the introduction here.

image to "define the metaphysical status of living beings and the visible entities of the natural world in relation to God."[36] Plotinus' utilization of this concept of image in his understanding of metaphysics influenced the Christian understanding of the creation account of humanity "in the image and likeness of God."[37] It was Origen who provided the concept of image for the Cappadocians. Origen limited his understanding of image to the soul, and the Cappadocians expanded that understanding of image to include the whole person. Significantly, Origen provided them with the concept of restoration, and that the restoration of the image was dependent upon "the Christian's conscious imitation of Christ, God's first image."[38] This concept became formative in the Cappadocians' understanding of theosis.

Among the three Cappadocians, it was Nyssen who provided the clearest anthropological teaching on the nature and destiny of man.[39] According to Nyssen, it was God's desire from the very beginning for human nature to be "unbroken and immortal. Since human nature was fashioned by the divine hands and beautified with the unwritten characters of the Law, the intention of the Law lay in our nature in turning us away from evil and in honouring the divine."[40] It is in this way that humanity is made in the image of God, and according to Nyssen, "this is the same as to say that He made human nature participant in all good; for if the Deity is the fullness of good, and this is his image, then the image finds its resemblance to the Archetype in being filled with all good."[41] Here again we see a modification of the Neoplatonic concepts of Plotinus in the Cappadocian understanding of the image. That is, the image in humankind is dependent upon its relationship to the original, or the Archetype. Plotinus writes, "It is like the reflection in the mirror, depending upon the original which stands outside of it."[42] This image is not the reproduction of an artist; rather, it is an image which is created by the original. The focus must be on the "making of image as we see in water or in mirrors or in a shadow; in these cases the original is the cause of the image which, at once, springs from it and cannot exist apart from it."[43] The Cappadocians took this mirror imagery and placed it within a Christological context. The human was created in the image of the

---

36. Miles, "Image," 160.

37. Ibid., 161.

38. Ibid., 163.

39. Ladner, "Philosophical Anthropology," 61.

40. Nyssen, *DVMo*, II.215, trans. Malherbe and Ferguson, 110.

41. Nyssen, *DHO* (PG 44:184b) (*NPNF2* 5:404).

42. Plotinus, *Enneades* 6.2.22.

43. Ibid., 6.4.10.

Archetype, with the intent that it would be a reflection of the original. Christ is the Archetype, or original likeness of God, and humans are created to be a reflection of him. "And as we said that the mind was adorned by the likeness of the archetypal beauty, being formed as though it were a mirror to receive the figure of that which it expresses, . . . so to say, a mirror of the mirror."[44] Therefore, the Christian life is to be one in which you are "constantly growing more and more to be, a real unspotted mirror of God and divine things."[45]

The Cappadocians wrestled over the concept of the image. One specific concern seemed to be whether or not the image was gender specific, because male language is used in the scripture.[46] Gross believed that the Cappadocians developed a concept of the "ideal humanity" which "possessed the perfect likeness with God to the point of not being sexed, 'sexual difference being unknown to the divine nature.'"[47] Nyssen's understanding was that full humanity was expressed in the first creation account, where he saw that *man* was made in the image of God. It is this total humanity which is the expression of God.

> In saying that "God created man" the text indicates, by the indefinite character of the term, all mankind; for was not Adam here named together with the creation, as the history tells us in what follows? Yet the name given to the man created is not the particular, but the general name: thus we are led by the employment of the general name of our nature to some such view as this—that in the Divine foreknowledge and power *all humanity is included in the first creation*; for it is fitting for God not to regard any of the things made by him as indeterminate, but that each existing thing should have some limit and measure prescribed by the wisdom of its Maker.[48]

Basil also made the argument that the image of God was not only male but also female. This is made in a text whose source was considered controversial until the 1970 edition of *Sources Chrétiennes*, which deemed it an authentic work of Basil's. Here, Basil specifically created a dialogue with a

---

44. Nyssen, *DHO* (PG 44:156) (*NPNF2* 5:398).

45. Nazianzen, *Or.* 2.7 (PG 35:413c) (SC 247) (*NPNF2* 7:206). (Latin, *speculum*; Greek, εσοπτρον). See last two sentences of 413c.

46. Gen 1:26–27.

47. Gross, *Divinization of the Christian*, 177. Nyssen, *DHO* (PG 44:181b, 185d) (*NPNF2* 5:405).

48. Nyssen, *DHO* (PG 44:184b) (*NPNF2* 5:405), emphasis mine.

woman in which they discuss whether the image of God might be present in a woman.

> God created man in his image. "Man?" asked the woman. "How does that relate to me? Man was created," she continued, "but God didn't just say, 'There only exists a man.' In addition to *man*, he revealed that the conversation was in regard to the creation of humankind . . . " Do not misunderstand what is meant by a *man*, that it refers only to the male gender, for the [Scriptures] add, *male and female* he created them.[49] The woman is equal with the man and has the honour to be created in the image of God. The creation of each is equal; equal in good deeds, equal in honour, and identical in reward. May [the woman] not say, "I am weak." Weakness comes from the flesh, but strength is in the spirit (soul). Since the image of God is identical in each of them, may there be equal honour and equal good works done by both. . . . There is no excuse for bodily (fleshly) weakness. Is a body like this weak? . . . How can the male gender compete with the female, when it comes to the personal life? How can a man emulate the endurance of a woman during times of fasting, through her persistence in prayer, the strength of her tears, and her diligence in good works?
>
> I have been witness to the good intentions of women who have been willing to work in secret. They have not received any praise, but simply work for the joy of the man and children, and the good of her home. . . . She does not work for a reward, but works for the one who sees what we do in secret.[50]
>
> The good works of the woman are those which are possessed on the inside; which are within the image. Do not pay attention to the exterior or visible appearance of a person. The spirit may appear to be hidden beneath a weak body but the true person is revealed within the spirit.[51]

Nyssen further developed Basil's concepts related to image and, in doing so, made it clear that all of humanity is included in the first creation, and the image is for the whole human.

---

49. Gen 1:26.

50. Matt 6:4.

51. Basil, *Homily 10 & 11* or *Or. 1 On the Human Condition*, from the Russian, Святитель Василий Великий. *Творения. Том Первый. Догматико полемические творения экзегетические сочинения беседы. В Полное собрание творений святых отцов церкви и церковных писателей в русском переводе.* Сибирская Благозвонница: Москва, 2008. «Беседы о сотворении человека» 18. Russian translation of the Greek which is not found in Migne, but rather in SC 160, published 1970.

For the image is not in part of our nature, nor is the grace in any one of the things found in that nature, but this power extends equally to all the race: and a sign of this is that mind is implanted alike in all: for all have the power of understanding and deliberating, and of all else whereby the Divine nature finds its image in that which was made according to it: the man that was manifested at the first creation of the world, and he that shall be after the consummation of all, are alike: they equally bear in themselves the Divine image.[52]

Nyssen also rejected Origen's concept of the preexistence of souls,[53] for Nyssen saw the human soul and body fused into one. "Thus this doctrine of theirs, which maintains that souls have a life by themselves before their life in the flesh, and that they are by reason of wickedness bound to their bodies, is shown to have neither beginning nor conclusion: and as for those who assert that the soul is of later creation than the body, their absurdity was already demonstrated above."[54] Origen believed in the preexistence of the souls and that at birth they were deposited into human flesh to begin a journey upward throughout life to be freed from the flesh. According to Nyssen, the mind was made in the image of God, and it is the mind which reflects God, as a mirror, but in the same way, the physical part of the human "is made beautiful by reflecting this human reflection of the supreme beauty as a mirror's mirror."[55] Nazianzen describes it in this way, "What God is to the soul, that the soul becomes for the body: it trains (παιδαγογήσασα) the body's matter, which is its servant, and adapts the fellow servant to God."[56] It is in this way that the physical body or natural life becomes a reflection of the person's "spiritual resemblance to God."[57] The result is that the person is transformed into the likeness of the image, not only in mind, but in every facet of his or her being.

Nyssen believed that God, in foreknowledge, knew that humanity would sin, and consequently procreation would be necessary, which resulted in the differentiation of male and female.[58] "Our whole nature, then, extending from the first to the last, is, so to say, one image of him who is;

---

52. Nyssen, *DHO* (PG 44:188) (*NPNF2* 5:405).

53. Ibid. (PG 44:229) (*NPNF2* 5:418).

54. Ibid. (PG 44:229–30) (*NPNF2* 5:419).

55. Ladner, "Philosophical Anthropology," 77. Nyssen, *DHO* (PG 44:161c) (*NPNF2* 5:396).

56. Ladner, "Philosophical Anthropology," 77. Nazianzen, *Or.* 2.17 (PG 35:428a) (SC 247).

57. Ladner, "Philosophical Anthropology," 66.

58. Nyssen, *DHO* (PG 44:177–88) (*NPNF2* 5:405, 406).

but the distinction of kind in male and female was added to his work last."[59] Interestingly, while some may see this in a negative light, the result of this line of thinking became an emphasis on the equality of men and women, rather than the traditional view of the subordination of women to men.[60] Basil wrote, "The creation is of equal honour for both, and so the reward for both is the same."[61] In *The Life of Moses* Nyssen said, "Human nature is divided into male and female, and the free choice of virtue or evil is set before both equally. For this reason the corresponding example of virtue for each sex has been exemplified by the divine voice, so that each, by observing the one to which he is akin (the men to Abraham and the women to Sarah), may be directed in the life of virtue by the appropriate examples."[62] The development of the different monastic movements in the region of Cappadocia, in which, at times, males and females served together, may have influenced the Cappadocians' understanding in this area. Their older sister, Macrina, was more than likely also an example to them.[63] The final result was that for the Cappadocians, the image "represents the universal nature of humanity, not the differentiated 'Adam,' a thing of the earth."[64] This universal nature of humanity included all of humanity, both male and female, and the image was fully present in both.

The image is tarnished by the fall into sin

All of humanity was marked with the image of God; "purity, freedom from passion, blessedness, alienation from all evil, and all those attributes of the like kind which help to form in men the likeness of God: with such hues as these did the Maker of his own image mark our nature."[65] Sadly, humanity sinned, and the result was not that the image was lost, but rather, that the image in humanity became corrupted. Referring to fallen man, Nyssen said, "preserving his resemblance to the Deity as well in other excellences as in possession of freedom of the will, yet being of necessity of a nature subject

---

59. Ibid. (PG 44:177) (*NPNF2* 5:405).

60. Beagon, "Cappadocian Fathers," 166.

61. Basil, *Homily On Psalm 1* (PG 29:216D–217A), trans. Beagon, 166.

62. Nyssen, *DVMo* (GNO VII 1, p. 5, 1.16f.), trans. Malherbe and Ferguson, 32.

63. Beagon, "Cappadocian Fathers," 166.

64. Clark, "Lady Vanishes," 28. Nyssen, *DHO* 16 (PG 44:181, 185) (*NPNF2* 5:405). Note Verna Harrisons's summation: "Gregory argues that there is no gender in the eternal Godhead since even within the human condition gender is something temporary" ("Male and Female in Cappadocian Theology," 441.)

65. Nyssen, *DHO* (PG 44:137a–b) (*NPNF2* 5:390).

to change."[66] Nyssen related free will to the image, and free will is never lost in humanity. However, because of the choices made as a result of free will, the reflection of the image changes. No longer is the human a perfect reflection of the original for the mirror has become stained or marred. "We see this happen also on earth in the case of a mirror or water or anything that has the power of reflection because of its smoothness. For, when these receive the beam of the sun, they create another beam from themselves, but this would not occur if their clean and shiny surface became dirty."[67] This dirty or marred mirror has become, according to Nazianzen, a foul mirror. "For neither can a soiled mirror receive the reflections of images, nor can a soul that is already beset with the cares of life and darkened by the passions due to the arrogance of the flesh receive the rays of the Holy Spirit."[68]

The Cappadocian understanding of free will is essential to understanding the corruption of humanity and the presence of evil. Nyssen, agreeing with Origen, believed that evil was not caused by some type of external matter but "by the act of this free will of man; in other words, by sin."[69] However, Nyssen firmly believed that God created humanity so that humanity could participate in God's goodness and that the image included all the instincts necessary for everything that was excellent. Included in this instinct was free will. "[God] would never have deprived him of that most excellent and precious of all goods; I mean the gift implied in being his own master, and having a free will. For if necessity in any way was the master of the life of man, the image would have been falsified in that particular part, by being estranged owing to this unlikeness to its archetype."[70] Nyssen explained that it is the person's "departure of the better state" which becomes "the origin of its opposite."[71] "Since then, this is the peculiarity of the possession of a free will, that it chooses as it likes the thing that pleases it, you will find that it is not God who is the author of the present evils, seeing that he has ordered your nature so as to be its own master and free; but rather the recklessness that makes choice of the worse in preference to the better."[72] In other words, it is the human's will which is "swept away by deceit"[73] that becomes the

---

66. Nyssen, *OC* (PG 45:47) (GNO III.4) (SC 453) (*NPNF2* 5:490).

67. Nyssen, *DV* (PG 46:364) (SC 119) (GNO VIII.I) (FC, 41).

68. Basil, *Ep.* 210 (PG 32:768) (Deferrari, LCL).

69. Schaff, *Gregory of Nyssa*, 15.

70. Nyssen, *OC* 5 (PG 45:19) (GNO III.4) (SC 453) (*NPNF2* 5:476).

71. Ibid.

72. Ibid.

73. Nyssen, *DV* (PG 46:369) (SC 119) (GNO VIII.I) (FC, 43).

"inventor of evil."[74] It was not something that the human simply discovered "after it had been invented by God. Nor did God create death; man, in a way, is the founder and creator of evil."[75] Nyssen puts this creation of evil juxtaposed against virtue; evil is the result of turning away from virtue.[76]

Free will includes the desire to practice virtues and to participate in the gracious acts of God. Nyssen sees "human freedom as moral freedom, the freedom to become what we are made to be."[77] It means that humankind can make the choice to return to the Creator and obtain the "divine likeness, but not, however, without the assistance of God."[78] It is this synergy which helps to bring healing through theosis to humanity and restores the image in humankind. This fallen state is a state of illness, not of wellness, and humanity is in need of a cure. Lossky tells us, "Unless man turns towards God of his own free will and with all his longing, unless he cries to him in prayer with complete faith, he cannot be cured."[79] It is not a magical activity, instead, it is a human life in which, "grace and free will work together."[80] Nyssen states,

> For the grace of God does not naturally frequent souls which are fleeing from salvation, and the power of human virtue is not sufficient in itself to cause the souls not sharing in grace to ascend to the beauty of life. . . . What does this mean? It means that the Lord from on high enters into an alliance with the doers, and, at the same time, it means that it is not necessary for men considering human efforts to think that the entire crown rests upon their struggles.[81]

It is this synergy which is found within the Cappadocian understanding of the restoration of humanity. The gift of grace is not the result of the acts of the free will. This activity of God and people has a cooperative property, or a "synergy of the two wills, divine and human, a harmony in which grace bears ever more and more fruit."[82] However, it must be made very clear that this understanding of free will does not result in what would eventually become known as Pelagianism. Pelagianism considered free will

74. Ibid.

75. Ibid.

76. Ibid.

77. Wilken, *Spirit of Early Christian Thought*, 153.

78. Gross, *Divinization of the Christian*, 144.

79. Lossky, *Mystical Theology*, 206. See also St. Macarius of Egypt, *Hom. Spir.* XXXII (PG 34:741s).

80. Norris, "Deification," 417, referring to Maximus the Confessor, *To Thalassius* 61.

81. Nyssen, *De Instituto Christiano* (PG 46:289c) (FC, 131–32).

82. Lossky, *Mystical Theology*, 198.

an innate human ability, whereas the Cappadocians (and the majority of Christians in church history) believed that people's free will is enabled by divine grace, preveniently given by God. As such, people cannot merit or earn salvation (or growth in spirituality); yet, God voluntarily self-restricts power over people in order that they have sufficient power to choose freely to receive the gift of eternal life, and to live Christ-like lives.

Free will becomes a way of ordering one's life by choosing to focus on virtue and the imitation of Christ. It is then that the human begins to flourish, delighting in participation with the original image or good. Here we see that free will is relational, and it cannot stand on its own but is always measured by its relationship to God, the Creator. To be fully human one must turn toward God and allow divine love to fully form a reflection within the human.[83] Without this response, the corrupted image within humanity will not reflect what God intended originally for humanity, and the result that one is not fully human. It is in the process of deification or theosis that we become truly human.

Christ assumes human nature in order to restore humanity to its original nature

Because free will and acts of virtue alone were not sufficient to restore the image in humanity, God sent the Son, assuming human nature so that humanity could be restored. It is Christ's kenosis which provides the possibility for theosis or deification for humankind; through Christ, God initiated the means by which people may be saved by grace through faith, and to grow in Christ-likeness. Nazianzen believed humanity was carrying about the shame which came from the transgressions of the first man and that humanity needed to be delivered from this shame so that the glory of the Lord could be seen "as though reflected in a mirror."[84]

Christ's assumption of humanity had huge implications for the Cappadocians' understanding of the potential for deification as well as their understanding of the nature of Christ. In the Eastern Church tradition, it is believed that which has been assumed[85] is that which has been saved; therefore, humanity could only be saved through Christ's assumption of the human nature. Nazianzen said, "He remained what he was; what he was

---

83. Wilken, *Spirit of Early Christian Thought*, 153–54.

84. Nazianzen, *On the Mysteries III, Lecture* 21.4 (*NPNF2* 7:150). 2 Cor 3:18 NRSV.

85. Through Christ's assumption of humanity there is a restoration of all things "from the one who has assumed, that is to say, what 'came down.'" Nazianzen, *Or.* 30.12 (PG 36:103) (*NPNF2* 7:314).

not, he assumed."[86] Probably Nazianzen's most recognized statement on this topic comes from his *Epistle* 101 in which he states, "For that which he has not assumed he has not healed."[87] The Cappadocians were arguing against Apollinarianism; therefore, for them it had to be made clear that Christ assumed the entire person. Christ was completely divine and at the same time entirely human. "On earth he has no father, but in heaven no mother."[88] Because of the incarnation, it is the entire person that is saved, and ultimately, "it will be the whole person, in all constituent parts, that will attain to the heavenly state."[89] Nazianzen described it in this way:

> He assumed the worst that he might give us the better; he became poor that we through his poverty might be rich; he took upon himself the form of a servant that we might be exalted; he was tempted that we might conquer; he was dishonoured that he might glorify us; he ascended that he might draw us to himself, who were lying low in the fall of sin.[90]

Therefore, it is the whole human which has the possibility of restoration in the image because of the incarnation of Christ. Nyssen tells us that Christ "became the image of the invisible God because of his love for mankind, in order to make you again the image of God. By his own change which he assumed, there was a change effected in you so that you also might be refashioned through him to the beauty of the Archetype into the character which was from the beginning."[91] The image of God had been lost to humanity. By Christ's assumption of humanity, Christ restored the image to humanity, setting again the possibility for man and woman to be in the image and likeness of God. The incarnation was and is indispensible for the salvation and restoration of humanity.

It is especially important to note that this assumption is for all of humanity. Nazianzen made it clear that both men and women had sinned and were in need of a Savior.

> The Woman sinned, and so did Adam. The serpent deceived them both; and one was not found to be the stronger and the other the weaker. But dost thou consider the better? Christ saves

86. Nazianzen, *Or.* 29.19 (PG 36:100) (SC 250), trans. Wickham, 86. John 1:1.

87. Ibid., 101 (*NPNF2* 7:839).

88. Ibid., 29.19 (PG 36:100) (SC 250) (*NPNF2* 7:308), trans. Wickham, 87. Matt 1:20; Ps 2:7.

89. Winslow, *Dynamics of Salvation*, 174.

90. Nazianzen, *Or.* 1.5 (PG 35:398) (SC 247) (*NPNF2* 7:204).

91. Nyssen, *DP* (PG 46:269c–d) (GNO III.I), trans. Keenan, "De Professione Christiana," 195.

both by his Passion. Was he made flesh for the Man? So he was also for the woman. . . . He is called of the seed of David; and so perhaps you think the Man is honored; but he is born of a Virgin, and this is on the Woman's side.[92]

This emphasis on the "Woman's side" bears significance for the salvation of the feminine, especially in light of deification and the potential salvation of that which is assumed. One of the more difficult Pastoral texts can be found in 1 Tim 2:14–15: "The woman was deceived and became a transgressor. Yet she will be saved through childbearing, provided they continue in faith and love and holiness, with modesty" (NRSV). For centuries this text has been a puzzle to those individuals attempting to comprehend the intention of the author, especially considering the emphasis on remaining single. Must every woman bear a child to be saved? Rather, one could consider that this understanding of assumption resulting in salvation may have influenced the Apostle Paul as well. Was it possible that women were saved through the physical assumption of Christ into the womb of a female?[93] Therefore, because Mary bore a child, women are saved. Nyssen hints at this as well:

> Just as she who introduced death into nature by her sin was condemned to bear children in suffering and travail, it was necessary that the Mother of life, after having conceived in joy, should give birth in joy as well. No wonder that the angel said to her, "Rejoice, O full of grace!"[94] With these words he took from her the burden of that sorrow which, from the beginning of creation, had been imposed on birth because of sin.[95]

Eve's punishment for sin was to give birth in pain, but God through grace in Christ, assumed his place in the womb of a woman, setting the order of humanity aright through the very avenue in which the punishment began. God's first step in the restoration of the image to humanity was to reach out to a woman. What we witness is the grace of God reaching to the one who had been the object of blame for the sinfulness of all humanity. No longer is a woman sinful and without hope, unable to be a part of the process of deification, but rather, the woman is to participate in the synergistic effect of theosis by living a life of virtue, which may be seen in faith, love,

---

92. Nazianzen, *Or.* 37.6–7 (PG 36:262) (SC 318) (*NPNF2* 7:340).

93. Harrison, "Gender, Generation, and Virginity," 50.

94. Luke 1:28.

95. Nyssen, *On the Song of Songs* 13 (PG 44:1052–53B) (GNO VI); trans. Gambero, *Mary and the Fathers of the Church*, 159.

holiness and modesty. The result is that deification in the life of a woman was not only possible but also expected by the Cappadocians.

The incarnation is the first step in the restoration of the image in humanity. In Nyssen this idea of return or restoration to the original image is placed against his doctrine of endless progress. It is in this return to the beginnings that we find the "possibility of the release in us of the drive upward."[96] For the knowledge of God does not begin with the upward drive of the mind, but rather with God's descent into humanity.[97] This activity of God, descending toward the human, is seen as an act of grace.[98] For in this act, Christ took upon himself the curse and was willing to become sin for us: "No—look at this fact: the one who releases me from the curse was called 'cursed' because of me; 'the one who takes away the world's sin' was called 'sin' and is made a new Adam to replace the old."[99] Through the incarnation Christ provided a new pathway for humanity, a path of restoration. "After he wiped away our infirmities, he again returned to his own bosom the hand which had been among us and had received our complexion."[100]

It is Christ's kenosis which opened the pathway toward theosis for all of humanity. Humankind would have to learn about Christ's participation in the process so that humans too, could experience deification. "Walk like God through all that are sublime . . . but better, treat all as God does, so that you may ascend from below to become God, because he came down from above for us."[101] However, the prerequisite is for the human to learn once again how to reflect the divine nature.

In conversion one's capacity to reflect the divine nature is once again restored

For the Cappadocians, conversion was to be experienced graciously through faith and baptism. Interestingly, the word conversion came originally from Plato, where he utilized this terminology when one adopted the philosophical life and ensuing change of lifestyle.[102] Obviously, the term was Christianized throughout the early period of Christianity and the Cappado-

96. Meredith, *Gregory of Nyssa*, 89.

97. Wilken, *Spirit of Early Christian Thought*, 12. Origen, *Against Celsus* 7.42.

98. Wilken, *Spirit of Early Christian Thought*, 19.

99. Nazianzen, *Or.* 30.5 (PG 36:108) (SC 250), trans. Wickham, 96. Gal 3:13; John 1:29; 2 Cor 5:21; 1 Cor 15:22, 45.

100. Nyssen, *Life of Moses* II, trans. Malherbe and Ferguson, 30.

101. Nazianzen, *Or.* 30.21 (PG 36:131) (SC 250), trans. Wickham, 112.

102. Jaeger, *Early Christianity and Greek Paideia*, 10.

cians themselves added to the definition. Nyssen said, "It is prayer and the invocation of heavenly grace, and water, and faith, by which the mystery of regeneration is accomplished."[103] Christ himself had been baptized; therefore, his incarnation or assumption was a restoration and his life served as an example, one which was to be imitated if a person were to experience deification. "As man he was baptized, but he absolved sins as God; he needed no purifying rites himself—his purpose was to hallow water."[104] Everything about his life pointed one back toward restoration. As a result, we are to imitate Christ though the practice of virtue, but "we also imitate him by clothing ourselves in Christ."[105] This sacrament of baptism was seen as a means of God's grace reaching out to humanity, liberating from sin and death in a desire for restoration "of the original human destiny, which consists in being the 'image of God.'"[106] Nyssen expressed it in this way:

> So the one who falls into the mire of sin no longer is the image of the incorruptible God, and he is covered through sin with a corruptible and slimy form which reason advises him to reject. However, if, purged by the water, so to speak, of this way of life, the earthly covering can be stripped off, the beauty of the soul may reappear again.[107]

The Cappadocians recounted conversion experiences within their own families or their own personal lives. Basil gives this account:

> Having lavished much time on the vanity, and having consumed almost all my youth in the futility, which were mine while I occupied myself with the acquirement of the precepts of that wisdom made foolish by God, when one day arising as from a deep sleep I looked out upon the marvellous light of the truth of the gospel, and beheld the uselessness of the wisdom "of the princes of this world that came to naught," bemoaning much my piteous life, I prayed that there be given me a guidance to the introduction to the teachings of religion.[108]

---

103. Nyssen, *OC* 33 (PG 45:84d) (*NPNF2* 5:499).

104. Nazianzen, *Or.* 29.20 (PG 36:100) (GNO III.4) (SC 453) (*NPNF2* 7:309). Matt 3:16; Luke 3:21; John 1:29; Matt 9:2.

105. Russell, *Doctrine of Deification*, 13.

106. Meyendorff, "Theosis in the Eastern Christian Tradition," 472. See also Damascene, "Way of Spiritual Transformation."

107. Nyssen, *DV* (PG 46:369) (SC 119) (GNO VIII.I) (FC, 44).

108. Basil, *Ep.* 223.2 (PG 32:820) (Deferrari LCL).

Nonna, the mother of Nazianzen, prayed for years for the conversion of her husband, Gregory the Elder. Schaff refers to her as "one of the noblest Christian women of antiquity, [who] exerted a deep and wholesome influence. By her prayers and her holy life she brought about the conversion of her husband."[109] Nazianzen, while sailing from Alexandria to Greece found himself in the center of a bad storm. It was after this experience that he decided to dedicate himself to God and contemplate baptism.[110]

> Despairing of all hope here below, I turned to you, my life, my breath, my light, my strength, my salvation, the source of terror and affliction, but the benign healer, too, ever weaving good into the dark pattern. . . . Yours, I said, I have been formerly; yours am I now. Please accept me for a second time, the possession of your honored servants, the gift of land and sea, dedicated by the prayers of my mother and by this unparalleled crisis. If I escape a double danger, I shall live for you.[111]

This was a promise from Nazianzen to not only seek baptism, but also "focus his future completely on God's service."[112]

The Cappadocians' understanding was that through baptism they would recover the lost likeness to God and would then be able to participate "in the divine life which that likeness entailed."[113] Baptism was a very physical act on the part of the individual.[114] It was this human response that led to participation with the resultant ability to again look upon the face of the Son and in this way become a reflection of him. "For just as one, perceiving in a bright mirror the reflection of a shape that appears therein, receives a definite knowledge of the imaged face, so he who recognizes the Son, through his knowledge of the Song receives in his heart the 'figure of His (the Father's) person' or 'hypostasis.'"[115] The corruption has been removed, and the mirror again becomes a smooth surface on which the reflection is made clear.[116] Once the corruption has been removed through grace, it is

---

109. Schaff, *History*, 910–11.

110. Van Dam, *Families and Friends*, 91.

111. Nazianzen, *On His Own Life*, trans. Meehan in FC, 75. See Daley, *Gregory of Nazianzus*, 191n29.

112. Daley, *Gregory of Nazianzus*, 6.

113. Russell, *Doctrine of Deification*, 12.

114. Nyssen, *CC*, sermon 5 (PG 44:865a–868a) (GNO VI), trans. Musurillo, in Daniélou, *From Glory to Glory*, 185.

115. Basil, *Ep.* 38.8, *To His Brother Gregory, concerning the difference between* οὐσία *and* ὑπόστασις (PG 32:325) (Deferrari LCL).

116. Nyssen, *DAR* (PG 46:11–160).

the responsibility of the individual to imitate the life of Christ, and through this synergistic activity, the individual is ever transformed into the likeness of God.

The Christian life becomes one of "incessant transformation into the likeness of God as man stretches out with the divine infinity"[117]

Once humanity has been restored graciously in the incarnation and through conversion, the life of the Christian is one in which he or she is to be an imitator of God. At this point it would be easy to consider this Pelagianism; however, the concept of the Cappadocians is truly one of synergy—people partnering with God, enabled by grace. It is the divine action of God, or grace, which works on the life of the individual. The Cappadocians utilize the parables of the lost sheep, the lost coin and the lost son to demonstrate their understanding of grace. The image is only lost in humanity because humanity is no longer facing in the direction of God. By free will the human may respond to the grace of a loving God who has never neglected humanity but is constantly seeking the lost. It is through cooperation with God's divine nature through imitation of Christ that humanity is continuously transformed into a clearer reflection of the likeness of God. God's original plan for humanity was a likeness to God which is found in the image.

This synergism, human participation in God, is vital because it is representative of free will. It is the freedom found in free will, enabled by grace, which brings us closest to God or can lead us to become betrayers. For Nyssen the practice of virtue was vitally important in relation to spiritual progress. This practice of virtue was the result of free choice. Meredith describes the aim of the Christian life for Nyssen as likeness to God, this likeness being "seen as largely a matter of the informed will, ever striving to realize within itself that greater assimilation to God who, being by nature infinite, always permits further efforts."[118] This is not necessarily a simple task, and Nazianzen reminds us, "What is gained by effort is usually kept; what is lightly gained is quickly spurned because it can be gained anew."[119]

This activity of the free will, becoming imitators of God, must be seen within a Christological context.[120] St. Seraphim of Sarov, a Russian

---

117. Nyssen, *DVMo*, trans. Malherbe and Ferguson, 12.

118. Meredith, *Gregory of Nyssa*, 24.

119. Nazianzen, *Or.* 28.12 (PG 36:40) (SC 250), trans. Wickham, 45.

120. Meredith, *Gregory of Nyssa*, 8.

Orthodox Saint reminds us of the Christological tradition handed down through Orthodoxy. He speaks of the importance of prayer, fasting, vigils, alms and other good works that are done in the name of Christ. This is the important feature, for all must be done in the name of and for Christ. Lossky makes this point clear, "Note well that it is only those good works which are done in the name of Christ that bring us the fruits of the Holy Spirit. Other actions, even good ones, not done in the name of Christ, can neither procure us a reward in the life of the present age to come, nor win us the grace of God in this present life."[121] As we are imitators of God, we are ascending toward Christ, the one who has provided the possibility of our theosis through his kenosis and theosis. The words of Paul in Phil 3:14, "I press on toward the goal for the prize of the heavenly call of God in Christ Jesus," provide us with ascent language which calls us onward. In Nyssen's *Commentary on the Song of Songs*, he uses this Pauline language but also expresses this kenosis-theosis principle. "It is evident that she who moulds her own beauty in accordance with this grace imitates Christ himself in her endeavours and so becomes that to others, which Christ himself became to human nature."[122] In *On the Life of Moses*, Nyssen calls us ever upward on this journey.

> This is the reason why we say that the great Moses, moving ever forwards, did not stop in his upward climb. He set no limit to his rise to the stars. . . . He constantly kept moving to the next step; and he continued to go ever higher because he always found another step that lay beyond the highest one that he had reached.[123]

Basil utilized this kenosis-theosis language when describing the life required of an ascetic: "submitting himself to the excellent yoke of the Lord, conducting himself in imitation of Him who became poor and endured flesh for our sake, and by running with an eye to the prize of his high calling, he may obtain acceptance with the Lord."[124]

The Apostle Paul was often a template for the Cappadocians. They frequently utilized his language of knowing Christ, and this process of knowing Christ was seen as an ascent. "Paul found no way through, no stopping-place

---

121. Lossky, *Mystical Theology*, 197.

122. Nyssen, *CC*, Homily 15 (PG 44:443.6) (GNO VI), trans. Meredith, *Gregory of Nyssa*, 115. Song 6:4.

123. Nyssen, *DVMo* (PG 44:397d–405a), trans. Musurillo, 144.

124. Basil, *Ep.* 23, *To a Solitary* (PG 32:294) (Deferrari LCL). 2 Cor 8:9.

in his climb, since intellectual curiosity has no clear limit and there is always some truth left to dawn on us."[125] Nazianzen went on to say,

> This is the "maturity" towards which we speed. Paul himself is a special witness here. What he predicates of "God" without further specification in this passage, he elsewhere assigns clearly to Christ. I quote: "Where there is neither Greek nor Jew, circumcision nor uncircumcision, Barbarian, Scythian, bond nor free; but Christ is all in all."[126]

It is humans, and humans alone, whether Jew or Greek, or male or female, who are created in the image of God and who may be restored. "This faculty belongs to a living thinking being, one with more wisdom than any other and on the way to being something heavenly."[127] Nazianzen encourages us in the journey and tells us of a bright future.

> If you have traversed the air and reckoned up all it involves, come now with me, touch heaven and things celestial. . . . If so, it follows that you will not be a wholly earthbound thinker, ignorant of your very ignorance.[128]

Instead, according to Nazianzen, humanity will be on a journey toward God. "'God,' according to bright students of Greek etymology, is derived from words meaning 'to run' or 'to burn'—the idea being of continuous movement and consuming of evil qualities hence, certainly, God is called a 'consuming fire.'"[129] The goal for the human is to run toward God, toward this consuming fire in which the impurities of humanity will be destroyed in a continuous and on-going process. Nazianzen reminds us, "We do not stay exactly the same for one day, let alone a lifetime."[130]

On this journey one "discovers God through the beauty and order of things seen, using sight as a guide to what transcends sight without losing God through the grandeur of what it sees."[131] Therefore, life is viewed as a spiritual journey in which incessant transformation occurs. This transformation draws one closer to God, and in this nearness one is able to actually

125. Nazianzen, *Or.* 28.21 (PG 36:54) (SC 250), trans. Wickham, 53.

126. Ibid., 30.6 (PG 36:110) (SC 250), trans. Wickham, 98. 1 John 3:2; 2 Pet 1:4; Col 1:28; 3:11.

127. Nazianzen, *Or.* 28.24 (PG 36:58) (SC 250), trans. Wickham, 56.

128. Ibid., 28.28 (PG 36:66) (SC 250), trans. Wickham, 60.

129. Ibid., 30.18 (PG 36:124) (SC 250), trans. Wickham, 108. Deut 4:24.

130. Ibid., 30.15 (PG 36:150) (SC 250), trans. Wickham, 106.

131. Ibid., 28.13 (PG 36:41) (SC 250), trans. Wickham, 47.

see God. Nyssen grounds his spirituality in Matt 5:8: "Blessed are the pure in heart, for they shall see God."

> The promise is so great that it vastly exceeds the highest bound of blessedness. What could anyone possibly desire after such a good as that, since he already has everything possible in what he has seen? In scriptural usage, *seeing means the same as possessing.* . . . Therefore, whoever has seen God has possession through that sight of whatever is contained in the list of good things, that is, life without end, . . . and kingdom that knows no end . . . the complete good.[132]

This statement is vitally important in understanding the Cappadocians. While humanity could not share in the substance of God, they did believe that humanity could be *deified.* This helps to clarify their mirror imagery because "seeing means the same as possessing." The spiritual life is one in which the person draws ever closer to the original and in this process becomes a complete reflection of the image. In this way, seeing the image becomes the same as possessing the image.

Nazianzen describes the spiritual journey as one without end. It is a journey in which we continue to climb, as if ascending a mountain in our minds, in which we will finally see God.[133] However, it is interesting to note that while they described a spiritual journey in which one draws closer to God and has a desire to see God, they also developed *apophaticism.* The idea that the actual nature of God is not comprehendible to humans develops from this *ousia* of God which is not knowable.[134] Gregory of Nyssa asserts the infinity of perfect being, something that we cannot possibly know. However, in making this assertion, he departs from Origen and Plato, who argue that knowing God may be difficult, but at the same time, they "regard absence of limit and form as a defect. For Plato, indeed, the absence of form or shape was something indicative of failure and evil, and matter which awaited the imposition of form from the divine architect."[135] While God may be infinite and not completely knowable, throughout the process of deification, continual revelation raises human awareness of the Godself. The narrative of Elijah exemplifies this. He experiences God in the light breeze, "which gave outline to the presence, but not the nature of God."[136] Nazianzen reminds

132. Nyssen, Homily 6, (*PG* 44:1264B) (*GNO* VII.I.136–48), trans. Meredith, 92, emphasis mine.

133. Nazianzen, *Or.* 28.3 (PG 36:30) (SC 250), trans. Wickham, 38–39.

134. Papanikolaou, "Divine Energies," 373.

135. Meredith, *Gregory of Nyssa*, 13.

136. Nazianzen, *Or.* 28.19 (PG 36:50) (SC 250), trans. Wickham, 51. 1 Kgs 19:11–12.

us that God is infinitely greater than humankind and greater than what humankind can experience in this lifetime. He says, "Even a vision of God is too much for men let alone God's nature."[137] He affirms John's writing in his gospel that the Word is "beyond the present world's power to contain."[138] "The substance of God is what belongs to him particularly and uniquely."[139]

Finally, it is in the voice of Macrina we find words drawing us nearer to the final level where beauty is discovered. "For Beauty has in its own nature an attractiveness for everyone who looks at it. So, if the soul becomes clean of all evil, it will exist entirely in beauty. The divine is beautiful by its own nature. The soul will be joined to the divine through purity, adhere to that which is proper to it."[140] It is in this state of beauty that we become partakers of the divine nature.

Throughout this journey there is an "ever-greater participation in God"[141]

It is only because of the work of Christ, his kenosis and theosis, that humanity can participate in God. The synergistic pattern of divine-human interaction leads to an ever-increasing participation in God, initiated, enabled, and completed by grace. For the Cappadocians this was the result of a daily walk with God and the practice of virtues. All of this had to be understood in light of their Trinitarian theology and, therefore, must be seen relationally, because for them, the *telos* of all of creation was communion with God.[142] As humans, we are invited to participate in what God does, in a relational manner, but not in what God is, for the substance or nature of God is unique to the Trinity alone.

Nyssen affirms "that humility and patience, virtues which were most conspicuous in his Passion, are the dominant colours to be used in our copy of the Image. 'So that we may become the Image by true imitation of the beauty of the Archetype, as Paul did, who by his virtuous life became an imitator of Christ.'"[143] Christ is the One who manifests all the virtues, and he is the Archetype as well as the Head. "Thus it follows that the other notions

---

137. Ibid., 28.19 (PG 36:50) (SC 250), trans. Wickham, 51.

138. Ibid., 28.20 (PG 36:52) (SC 250), trans. Wickham, 52.John 21:25.

139. Ibid., 29.10 (PG 36:85) (SC 250), trans. Wickham, 44.

140. Nyssen, *DAR* (PG 46:89D).

141. Nyssen, *DVMo*, trans. Malherbe and Ferguson, 12.

142. McCormick, "Theosis in Chrysostom and Wesley," 31.

143. Nyssen, *DP* (PG 46:272a–b) (GNO III.I), trans. Keenan, "De Professione Christiana," 196.

ascribed to the Head: peace, holiness, truth, and all such virtues, should be observed in the members. For through the Son these and similar virtues are revealed in the members when they testify that they belong by nature to the Head."[144] For this reason, one is to practice patience while gazing upon the image, because it is through this patience that one is transformed into the "image of the invisible God."[145]

Love is to be the rule of humanity's relationship with the Trinity. This is made possible through *perichoresis*, which is found within the Trinity. F. W. Norris tells us that it was Nazianzen who first took up *perichoresis* "as a Christological term. It often meant only 'to go around something' or 'to rotate something.' He filled it up with the meaning of 'interpenetration.' He wanted a word to express how the divinity and the humanity in Jesus Christ coinhered."[146] Nazianzen utilizes the term "when speaking of the titles of Christ with regard to his humanity and divinity."[147] It is because of this interpenetration of the human and the divine that humans are invited to become a part of the loving relationship which is found in the Trinity. With the restoration of the image in humanity, "created being mirrors the Uncreated."[148] According to Stramara, "Perichoresis is the basis for the believer's experience of the indwelling Trinity."[149] Nyssen responds to one desiring communion with God, "I and the Father will come and we will make our abode with him (of course, the Holy Spirit had already been dwelling there)."[150] It is precisely in this manner that we are invited to become partakers in the divine nature.

The cornerstone of this understanding is the Petrine passage, "Thus he has given us, through these things, his precious and very great promises, so that through them you may escape from the corruption that is in the world because of lust, and may become participants of the divine nature" (2 Pet 1:4 NRSV). The Authorized Version renders it, "partakers of the divine nature." The Cappadocians utilized Petrine language on several occasions. Nazianzen stressed the importance of the humanity of Christ and his incarnation in the process of theosis. "Even at this moment he is, as man,

---

144. Ibid. (PG 46:273b–c) (GNO III.I), trans. Keenan, 170.

145. Keenan, "De Professione Christiana," 196–97.

146. Norris, "Deification," 416. He is referring to Nazianzen, *Or.* 18.42; *Or* 22.4; *Ep.*101.31; and finally Athanasius, *Discourse Against the Arians* 3.1, 17, 19, 24–25.

147. Stramara, "Gregory of Nyssa's Terminology," 257. Nazianzen, *Ep.* 101.6 (SC 208:38).

148. Stramara, "Gregory of Nyssa's Terminology," 263.

149. Ibid.

150. Nyssen, *De Beatitudinibus* 4 (GNO VII.2 122, 23–25). *Gregory of Nyssa: Homilies on the Beatitudes*, 129.

making representation for my salvation, until he makes me divine by the power of his incarnate manhood. 'As man' I say, because he still has with him the body he assumed, though he is no longer 'regarded as flesh.'"[151] Nyssen, utilizing Petrine language, saw this goal present from the beginning, in creation. "The Logos created humankind 'in the superabundance of His love . . . in order to make them partakers of the divine benefits.'"[152]

But while humans are invited to be "partakers of the divine benefits," humanity will never become God. This is primarily because of God's *ousia* and an understanding that God in his nature is infinite. Humans are creatures and thus are finite. Brooks Otis found the distinctive note in Cappadocian mysticism to be the doctrine "of the infinite pursuit and of the infinite progress in the never completed journey to God."[153] For Nyssen, seeing God as infinite meant there was no rest or attainment creating a profound effect on the individual participating in God.[154] "Since, then, those who know what is good by nature desire participation in it, and since that good has no limit, the participant's desire itself necessarily has no stopping place but stretches out with the limitless."[155] Our desire, according to Nazianzen is to return "to the pattern it now longs after."[156] Man's longing is manifest in the desire to make progress toward God. This progress is inspired "by the image of God in himself as clarified and fortified by Christ."[157]

While the longing may exist, a total vision of God will never be possible in this lifetime. "Yet neither he [Jacob], nor any other after him to this day from the twelve tribes, whose Father he was, could boast of this: that he had taken in the nature, the total vision, of God."[158] The good news for humanity is the discovery that the life ever stretching out limitlessly is a life perpetuated with new beginnings.[159]

The Cappadocians certainly lived lives filled with numerous new beginnings. They were continually challenging themselves and those who surrounded them to explore the meaning of what it is to become more like Christ. Nyssen encouraged followers to go on to perfection in their Christian

151. Nazianzen, *Or.* 30.14 (PG 36:121) (SC 250), trans. Wickham, 105. 2 Cor 5:16.

152. Nyssen, *OC* 5 (PG 45:21c) (*NPNF2* 5:476). English trans. Onica from the French by Gross, *Divinization of the Christian*, 177.

153. Otis, "Cappadocian Thought," 115. See Nyssen, *DVMo* (PG 44:403C and following).

154. Meredith, *Gregory of Nyssa*, 22.

155. Nyssen, *DVMo*, prologue section 7.

156. Nazianzen, *Or.* 28.17 (PG 36:48) (SC 250), trans. Wickham, 50.

157. Otis, "Cappadocian Thought," 116–17.

158. Nazianzen. *Or.* 28.18 (PG 36:49) (SC 250), trans. Wickham, 51.

159. Meredith, *Gregory of Nyssa*, 22.

walk. "This, therefore, is in my judgment the perfection of the Christian life, that in thought, in speech, and in all the pursuits of life there be a participation in all the names by which the name of Christ is made known so as to preserve perfectly in the entire body, mind, and spirit, without admixture of evil, the holiness praised by Paul."[160] The life of the individual was to be completely and entirely devoted to service to God. The trajectory of this reasoning, following its natural course, led to the expansion of how the Cappadocians understood asceticism, particularly in regard to celibacy and the monastic movement of their time.

160. Nyssen, *DP* (PG 46:285a) (GNO III.I), trans. Keenan, "De Professione Christiana," 205.

CHAPTER 4

The Development of Monasticism and the Role of Virginity in the Cappadocian Understanding of Theosis

THE DEVELOPMENT OF THE Cappadocians' theology of theosis has been explored. Throughout their lives the Cappadocians worked toward this *telos*, reasoning the realization of this goal was through synergistic activity between God and people. This theological development occasioned from within their unique context. This included the social and historical context of their day combined with their relationships. Shape was given to the life of asceticism or monasticism through the milieu in which they lived and the people with whom they came into contact. Their understanding of theosis cannot be divorced neither from their development of monasticism nor their writings on the mystical life. Therefore, the historical context of the Cappadocians: the outside influences, and the internal influences, will be explored in relation to their development of monasticism. Finally, these factors will be analyzed in the light of Nyssen's mystical writings. All of these are vital in terms of understanding their usage of women within their story or plot and as examples of theosis.

All three of the Cappadocian Fathers were raised in homes which directed them toward a life of piety. The women in those homes nurtured them and instructed them in the need for a life of virtue. One might describe this training as a part of what was later known as the *Domestic Ascetic Movement*. This movement developed in households where the parents, usually with the wife in the lead, "chose an early adult baptism and took its implications seriously."[1] Considering that this occurred during the Constantinian era when many postponed baptism, this was a significant development.

1. Silvas, *Macrina the Younger*, 3.

This resulted in entire families committing themselves to "pursuing a life of Christian piety."[2] It is in this nurturing domestic environment that the Cappadocians explored the importance of monasticism or the ascetic life to the development and/or restoration of the image of God in people. It was not the more famous Cappadocians alone who sought out this way of life. Naucratius, the second-born son (younger brother of Basil and older brother of Gregory Nyssen), who died at a young age, "was in fact the first of the brothers to dedicate himself to God in the ascetic life."[3] *De Vita Macrinae* reveals that Peter, the younger brother, is the one who remained at the family monastery for many years as the leader before leaving to become the bishop of Sebaste. It is Basil, however, the prolific writer, who left us with his rules for the coenobitic monastic life and is today revered as the "originator of the monasticism of the Eastern Church."[4] Ultimately, the Cappadocians were reformers of the "existing organizational models of ascetic life," and their new model was "better suited to the demands of contemporary society."[5]

In this fourth century, cataclysmic societal changes fostered the ascetic ideal. Major societal changes meant marriage had become rather unattractive and the natural desire for a wife and family had become quite weak.[6] These circumstances helped to prepare the way for the type of monasticism that was to be developed by Basil. However, Clarke warns us, "it would be a mistake to lay too much stress on social influences,"[7] because there were also moral factors at work. One of the greatest was the institutionalization of Christianity within the Roman Empire. The persecutions had come to an end, and a sudden flood of new converts poured into the church. This flood created a deterioration in the standard of church life but also brought with it new individuals who were truly seeking holiness. Those frustrated with the secularization of the church were drawn to monasticism.[8]

Basil may have been the one who gave the people of the region of Pontus their monastic constitution, but it would be his brother Gregory who

---

2. Ibid.

3. Ibid., 2.

4. Clarke, *St. Basil the Great*, 2, 29. Coenobites are the ones known as followers of the *common life*. See also Wagner (FC, ix), "Perhaps it may safely be asserted that the creation of true coenobitical monachism, receptive of both sexes and all classes, was substantially the work of St. Basil." See also Keenan, "De Professione Christiana," 171–72.

5. Elm, *"Virgins of God,"* ix.

6. Clarke, *St. Basil the Great*, 13.

7. Ibid., 14.

8. Ibid.

provided the spiritual form for the monastic life.[9] The foundation for the faith of the Cappadocians was laid out in the Nicene Creed. The theological battle for Nicene Orthodoxy, for which they fought, defined much of their lives and writings. Gregory built on this Nicene foundation and presented "the Christian religion as culminating in the contemplation of the divine Being and its eternal Will. The sanctification of man was interpreted as a process of purification of the soul and as its gradual ascent and return to divine Being."[10] This was their understanding of theosis.

The relationships among the Cappadocians were intertwined; they influenced one another and their desire for the holy life. In Athens, both Basil and Nazianzen sought after the holy life, this being their greatest concern. However, while still in Athens, Basil came under the influence of Eustathius of Sebaste, whose reputation for piety was well known. While Basil's *First Epistle* would suggest that Eustathius was the impetus for his return to Caesarea and his exploration of monasticism, debate exists over whether it was Eustathius of Sebaste or Basil's sister, Macrina, who had the greatest influence on his interest in the life of asceticism. Basil's brother, Gregory of Nyssa, credited their sister Macrina with the change in Basil. She was frustrated by Basil's behavior when he returned from Athens; she chastised him and called him to the life of philosophy through the practice of virtue.[11]

Scholars who have studied the life of Macrina give her clear credit for Basil's monasticism.[12] The problem with this account by Gregory in *De Vita Macrinae* is that it does not fit well with Basil's own account of his spiritual development. Gregory fails to mention Eustathius of Sebaste in the *De Vita Macrinae*; however, it would have been politically incorrect to have done so. *De Vita Macrinae* is written soon after the death of Macrina but a good two years after the death of Basil, and by this time the family had broken all ties with Eustathius. A new family history would not have wanted to record any previous connections between Basil and Eustathius.[13]

Eustathius was a colorful figure in "fourth century ecclesiastical politics,"[14] and Basil had great admiration for his ascetic character. It was Eustathius who introduced the monastic system into the region of Pontus, home to grandmother Macrina. The novel feature of his asceticism was that

---

9. Jaeger, introduction to *Two Rediscovered Works*, 23.

10. Ibid., 23.

11. Nyssen, *DVM* (PG 46:965b), trans. Clarke.

12. These include Sister Mary Emily Keenan, Averil Cameron, Daniel F. Stramara Jr., Verna E. Harrison, and Susanna Elm.

13. Beagon, "Cappadocian Fathers," 168.

14. Ibid.

it was of the coenobetic type. However, because of Eustathius' politically charged activities later in life, coenobetic monasticism has historically been tied to Basil. We learn of the extreme nature of Eustathius' monasticism from Sozomen. Later, the "canons of the Council of Gangra condemn the ascetic excesses of the Eustathians."[15] Unfortunately, as the years went by, Eustathius signed nearly every creed that was sent through the region. Schaff concludes by saying that Eustathius "was consistent only in inconsistency."[16] This criticism may be unfair and it is important to note that Basil himself was not always consistent. It is Basil who makes his way through the development of his thought regarding the homoiousians and the homoousians. In retrospect it may have been simpler to place blame with Eustathius in an effort to maintain the dignity of Basil's name.

During the time that Basil was influenced by Eustathius, Macrina was already busy establishing her community in Annesi. Her betrothed husband died when she was only twelve years of age. Against the requests of her family she adopted a life of virginity while still living in the family home.[17] After her father's death, she persuaded her mother, Emmelia, to join her in a life of asceticism. They moved to the family estate at Annesi in the Pontus, taking with them their female servants. The servants were treated as equals, and other devout women from the community began to gather about Macrina and Emmelia.

Basil was the eldest son of the family; Naucratius was the second, followed by Gregory and Peter. Naucratius followed Macrina's example and turned his back on the world in 352.[18] Naucratius, wanting to live the ascetic life, lived in Pontus, about three days' journey from the family home. He lived there with a servant for nearly five years, surviving by hunting and fishing, giving their excess to neighbors and needy individuals. Sadly, in 357, Naucratius died in a hunting accident. This was near the time Basil decided to leave the practice of rhetoric in Caesarea and begin his travels to the East. While the dates are not certain, it is more than likely that the death of Naucratius contributed to Basil's desire for the ascetic life.[19]

15. Ibid., 168, Sozemen (3.14.31–37).

16. Schaff, prolegomena on Basil, section 8, Basil and Eustathius, 30–31.

17. Nyssen, *DVM* (PG 46:964c; 965a) (SC 178) (GNO VIII.I).

18. Elm, *"Virgins of God,"* 91.

19. Clarke, *St. Basil the Great,* 23.

External influences on Basil's monasticism

Basil departed on a journey to search out the monastic life. He headed to Alexandria and other areas of Egypt, as well as Palestine, Coele-Syria, and Mesopotamia. Egypt was a natural choice because "the Christian Church was eminent both for orthodoxy and asceticism and here also was to be found the cradle of Christian eremitical or semi-eremitical life in its two lines of development: the Antonian and Pachomian systems."[20]

About the same time that Basil traveled to Egypt, Athanasius wrote *De Vita St. Antoni.*[21] There is no evidence that Basil met with Athanasius during his visit to Egypt. Anthony, a Coptic solitary who attracted numerous disciples, was the originator of the Antonian system. However, Basil was attracted to the system led by Pachomius, who was a "younger contemporary of Anthony."[22] While the Pachomian system "also involved an element of voluntary, individual effort, especially as regards personal interior life, in its external framework it represents the earliest systematic effort toward a corporate and stable monasticism."[23] Purpose and meaning was found in continual prayer and work while living within a community of faith.

Basil was impressed with the steadfast lives and *continence* of the ascetics that he saw on his journeys. He prayed that God would help him to emulate these men.[24] Unfortunately, when he first endeavored to live the life of asceticism on his return to Cappadocia, he attempted to practice the severe asceticism of the eremitic saints of Syria and Arabia. This severe asceticism and its physical results also caused him to rethink his plans for monasticism. Clarke warns us, "Much as Basil derived from Pachomius, his eloquent vindication of the superiority of the common life was not a product of his Egyptian visit."[25] Therefore, Pachomian coenobitism was a model for Basil, but the system that he eventually developed came with considerable correction and modification.[26]

After a little over a year of travel, Basil returned home to begin his own life of asceticism in the region of Pontus. His friend, Eustathius of Sebaste, had already established monasteries in Pontus, as well as in Roman

---

20. Basil, *Ascetical Works* (FC, viii–ix).

21. Athanasius, *Life of Saint Anthony*, trans. Ellershaw, in *NPNF2* 4.

22. Basil, *Ascetical Works* (FC, viii–ix).

23. Ibid.

24. Ibid. (FC, viii).

25. Clarke, *St. Basil the Great*, 40. See *Ep.* 223.

26. Basil, *Ascetical Works* (FC, viii–ix).

Armenia and Paphlagonia.[27] Basil succeeded in encouraging his friend from Athens, Gregory Nazianzen, to come and join him in prayer, studies, and manual labour. Together they studied and made extracts from the work of Origen which would eventually become the *Philocalia*. They also began to write monastic rules for the foundation of further developing regulations applicable to the coenobitic way of life.[28] Unfortunately, the severe asceticism which they practiced was detrimental to his health. Nazianzen was not pleased with Basil. He complained to his friend on a regular basis until, at last, he left Basil in Pontus. The long-term effects of this first round at asceticism are believed to have contributed to Basil's premature death at the age of fifty. However, until that time, he continued to work and adapt his life and develop his rules for monastic living.

Union with God by imitating Christ

Monasticism had a single, primary goal. This goal was union with God, or theosis. By intention it was to be lived out in the routine and mundane activities of life, seen as the imitation of Christ, which might include prayer, meditation, physical labour or acts of benevolence. This became known as the practice of virtues. The practice of living daily in God's presence was to result in continuous prayer, and in this prayer, seeking the face of God. In seeking God's face, one is assured that Christ is ever before, providing the example for life, which is to be imitated.[29] Brooks Otis comments: "Man's progress toward God is, so to speak, inspired by the image of God in himself as clarified and fortified by Christ.[30] Basil, referring to John 15:13, tells us, "Moreover, be not cast down at having divested yourself of friends and relatives, since you are thereby united with Christ who was crucified for you; and what greater proof of love could be conceived of than this?"[31] Basil is encouraging those embracing the life of philosophy to live life as an imitator of Christ.[32] For Basil, asceticism was not the end but the means. The goal of the true Christian was to be union with God. Through asceticism one could fix his or her eyes on the goal and remain true throughout life.[33] Basil found

27. Ibid.

28. Schaff, *History*, 901.

29. Morison, *St. Basil and His Rule*, 27.

30. Otis, "Cappadocian Thought," 116–17.

31. Basil, *Ascetical Discourse and Exhortation on the Renunciation of the World and Spiritual Perfection* in *Saint Basil* (PG 31), trans. Wagner (FC, 19).

32. Basil, *Ascetical Discourse* (FC, 30–31).

33. Morison, *St. Basil and His Rule*, 22.

it important that the specific type of asceticism must be appropriate for the goal. One should not practice a type of asceticism that might not keep the "great end in view."[34] If extreme forms of asceticism removed the focus from Christ and put the focus on the suffering of people, this became a distraction to the *telos*.

The life of the ascetic was not reserved for men, but was available for all. Basil broaches the subject of female ascetics in his *Introduction to the Ascetical Life*.

> But our discourse is not addressed to men only; for members of the female sex are not rejected because of physical weakness, but, chosen for the army of Christ by reason of their virility of spirit, they also battle on the side of Christ and fight no less valiantly than men. Some even win a greater renown. . . . Indeed, women as well as men followed after the Lord during his life on earth and both sexes ministered to our Savior.[35]

The ascetic life allowed men and women to practice the uninterrupted "presence of God and of the imitation of Christ."[36] Basil presented a model for this practice in his rules, which could be utilized by men and women alike.

Coenobitic monasticism as expression of love of God and love of neighbor

Basil's monastic doctrine was based on the Scripture.[37] The great commandment became foundational to his understanding of coenobitic monasticism. This form of monasticism provided the manner in which one could live out the true Christian life. The chief motive for the Christian life was love of God and love of neighbor.[38]

> Every man, indeed, will be asked for the fruits of his love of God and neighbor and he will pay the penalty for his violation of these as well as of all the commandments, as the Lord declares in the Gospel, saying: "He that loveth father or mother more than me is not worthy of me."[39]

34. Ibid.

35. Basil, *Ascetical Works* (FC, 12).

36. Morison, *St. Basil and His Rule*, 27, SR 195.

37. Basil, *Ascetical Works* (FC, viii–ix).

38. Morison, *St. Basil and His Rule*, 22–23.

39. Basil, *Ascetical Discourse* (FC, 17). Matt 10:37.

The love of God becomes the central focus for all of Basil's religious and moral activity. However, Basil sees that there can be no distinction between love of God and love of neighbor. He sees them inextricably bound together because he views love within a relational framework. "It is possible, therefore, through the first commandment to fulfil the second also, and through the second to return again to the first; and so he who loves the Lord, loves in consequence of his neighbor."[40] For Basil, this understanding led him to believe that love of God could only find fulfillment in community and not in a life of solitude. The coenobitic life actually refers to the *common life* or *κοίνος*. "Love of God and neighbor find full expression only in community life where all cooperate in their efforts toward perfection. . . . This enthusiasm for the principle of the common life rests upon his [Basil's] conviction that a life of seclusion from one's fellow men offers no scope for the practice of humility and obedience and is plainly opposed to the law of charity."[41] Basil's *ascesis* is not solely a call to moral perfection but integrates a relationship to God and others. The inevitable outcome is social action.[42]

The result for Basil is a type of monasticism which is no longer isolated from society. His *coenobia* are established in or near towns, not out in the desert. The ascetics are to live in the midst of society so that they can become a model for true Christian living.[43] They are to be the image of Christ present in a society. The Apostle Paul had said, "Be imitators of me, as I am of Christ."[44] Nyssen believed that it was through imitation of Christ that one became a reflection of the image.[45] These ascetics, or images of Christ, were to be spread throughout the community. Therefore, we come to understand why Basilian monasticism is coenobian while that of Pachomius really was not. "The Pachomian monasteries were cenobitic only in outward appearance; their inner essence was individualist."[46] Basil made coenobism a reality.

This love of God and love of neighbor had many expressions for Basil including the establishment of a hospital or hospice in Caesarea. The famine of 369 precipitated the formation of the *Basileidos* by Basil and his monks, which Gregory of Nazianzus referred to as the *soup kitchen*. Once again we see the influence of Eustathius, because the *Basileidos* was actually

---

40. Morison, *St. Basil and His Rule*, 26. See Basil LR 3.2.

41. Basil, *Ascetical Works* (FC, viii–ix).

42. Bassett, *Holiness Teaching*, 126.

43. Basil, *Ascetical Works* (FC, viii–ix).

44. 1 Cor 1:11 NRSV.

45. Nyssen, *DP* (PG 46:272a–b), trans. Keenan, "De Professione Christiana," 196.

46. Clarke, *St. Basil the Great*, 120.

inspired by one of his earlier ventures.[47] Basil's status and his family's wealth were of considerable assistance in helping him to complete numerous social projects. The purpose of urban ministry was twofold for Basil: he wanted to minister to the people of the city and to provide an outlet for the *common life* of his monks.[48] His influence was felt throughout Cappadocia and beyond.[49]

The first four of the *Long Rules* in the *Great Asceticon* express Basil's emphasis on love of God and love of neighbor found in the evangelical commandments.[50] In the *Long Rules* Basil quotes the Gospel of John, "By this everyone will know that you are my disciples, if you have love for one another."[51] In this regard, Basil sees love as the sign of the true disciple.[52] Lossky says,

> In love directed towards God each human person finds his per-
> fection; nevertheless, individual persons cannot arrive at per-
> fection without the realization of fundamental unity of human
> nature. Love of God is necessarily bound up with love of one's
> fellow-man. This perfect love will make a man like Christ, for,
> in his created nature he will be united to the whole of humanity,
> while in his person he will unite the created and the uncreated,
> the human complex and deifying grace.[53]

Ultimately, it is love of God and love of neighbor which becomes the focal point for all of humanity. When humanity is united with God, then God's uncreated love, the true nature of God, is poured out into humanity. Love brings human nature into perfection with the divine nature. This occurs in the life of one who is focused on the goal of unity with God.

Basil's coenobitism had a profound impact on the future of the ascetic life in the East as well as in the West. It is believed that St. Benedict based many of his ideas on the *Rules* of St. Basil.[54] Basil's monasticism was receptive of both sexes and all classes of individuals.[55] The influence was felt for centuries as Basil was able to establish numerous monasteries throughout every part of Pontus.

47. Tredget, "Basil of Caesarea," 4.
48. Clarke, *St. Basil the Great*, 62.
49. Tredget, "Basil of Caesarea," 9.
50. Ibid., 7.
51. John 13:35 NRSV.
52. Tredget, "Basil of Caesarea," 8.
53. Lossky, *Mystical Theology*, 214–15.
54. Clarke, *St. Basil the Great*, 2.
55. Basil, *Ascetical Works* (FC, viii–ix).

Nyssen's influence

While Basil was foundational to the development of monasticism, it was his younger brother Gregory who built upon that foundation and brought a greater depth to the understanding of monasticism and its θεορία. The life of asceticism was a common ideal for all of the Cappadocians. Though Basil was the one who put it into practice, it was Nyssen who became the great theoretician. On the other hand, "Nazianzen embraced both πρᾶξις and θεορία, but in a very personal way, which was neither that of the hierarch Basil nor that of Gregory of Nyssa, who, though a mystic, was also a systematic thinker."[56] Therefore, it becomes vital that one examine the Cappadocian perspective through the lens of Gregory of Nyssa, because only here does Cappadocian anthropology reach its fullness.[57] Gregory wrote a number of ascetical treatises.[58] In writing the biography of his beloved sister, *De Vita Macrinae*,[59] Gregory's emphasis is also on the ascetical life.

To understand Nyssen's perspective, one must understand his anthropology. In *De Hominis Opificio* this is readily discovered.[60] For Nyssen it is important to refute Origen's concept of the preexistence of the soul,[61] because Nyssen believed the human soul and body were fused into one. Therefore, the life in the flesh has a direct affect upon the soul, and vice versa.[62] The goal of all of humanity, union with God, leads toward perfection, and that perfection is seen in the renewing of the image.[63] Nyssen was developing a new anthropology in regard to the terms and concepts εἰκόν (image) and ὁμοίωσις (likeness) found in Gen 1:26. "Then God said, 'Let us make

---

56. Ladner, "Philosophical Anthropology," 77. This is in no way to underestimate the influence of Nazianzen, but this is specifically in regard to the mystical or ascetic life.

57. Ibid., 78. After the death of Basil, Nyssen became a very powerful leader, especially in the Arian controversy. He is one of 150 bishops summoned by Theodosius to the second Ecumenical Council of Constantinople in 381. We don't know much of his later life but we know that he was at the Synod of Constantinople in 394. He probably died in 395.

58. Nyssen, *De Professione Christiana* (PG 46:237) (GNO III.I), *DP* (PG 46:252) (GNO III.I); *De Instituto Christiano* (PG 46:288) (GNO III.I); *De Castigatione* (PG 46:308) (GNO III.I); and *DV* (PG 46:317) (GNO III.I).

59. Nyssen, *DVM* (PG 46:949) (SC 178) (GNO III.I).

60. It has been questioned whether these sections are from Nyssen or unfinished works of Basil. SC has placed them as *Homilies X* and *XI* of Basil. The newest Russian translation (2008) also places this as the work of Basil.

61. Nyssen, *DHO* 28 (PG 44:229) (*NPNF2* 5:418).

62. Ibid., 28.7 (PG 44:229–30) (*NPNF2* 5:419).

63. Ibid., 30.33 (PG 44:256) (*NPNF2* 5:426).

humankind in our image, according to our likeness'" (NRSV). He refused to accept the earlier understanding held by Irenaeus, Clement of Alexandria, Origen and Basil, who had seen *homoiosis* "as the perfection of the original image relation" so that "in creation this God-likeness existed only in a germinal state."[64] Gregory believed that this *homoiosis* existed completely and fully in the created human or *eikon*, though it was lost through original sin and must be regained. "Gregory could therefore, use the words 'image' and 'likeness' interchangeably, and use the static terms ὁμοίωμα (that which is alike) or ὁμοιότης (being alike) beside the more dynamic term ὁμοίωσις (which means both becoming alike and likeness)."[65]

The initial creation of the human becomes foundational and gives hope that through God's grace, together with the virtuous activity of humanity, one may become similar to God again.[66] His own personal twist on the parable of the woman with the lost coin is that the coin represents the "image of the King" and that image "is not entirely lost, but it is hidden under the dirt."[67] We must look for it and clean it up, and in this is the hope of renewal or restoration for all of humanity. We must find that which has been lost, which is the "divine image which is now covered by the filth of the flesh."[68] "Now may we all return to that Divine grace in which God at the first created man, when He said, 'Let us make man in our image and likeness'; to Whom be glory and might for ever and ever. Amen."[69] The Cappadocians believed that the *best* way for this image to be recovered was through the life of asceticism or virginity.

Nyssen's *De Virginitate* was his seminal work on the ascetic life. Interestingly, it is believed to be his earliest work on the ascetic life, written around 372.[70] According to Meredith *De Virginitate* was "probably designed as a rational account of the monastic ideals of his brother, Basil."[71] While Basil and his friend Nazianzen had their early experience with extreme asceticism, it is the community of his sister Macrina at Annesi which became the model for Basil's monasticism. By 372 Nyssen would have had the monastery at Annesi as a model and his brother's rules as a foundation for his theological work. While it appears that this document is a defense of

---

64. Ladner, "Philosophical Anthropology," 63–64.

65. Ibid.

66. Ibid.

67. Nyssen, *DV* 12 (PG 46:39) (SC 119) (GNO VIII.I) (FC, 45).

68. Ibid.

69. Nyssen, *DHO* 30.3–4 (PG 44:256) (*NPNF2* 5:426).

70. Meredith, *Gregory of Nyssa*, 88.

71. Ibid.

virginity, "it becomes clear as it progresses that it is not primarily concerned with physical virginity, but rather virginity of the soul which is available to all Christians, married or otherwise."[72] This concept may have been uniquely important to Nyssen, for it seems that he is the only one of the three Cappadocian Fathers ever to have married. In *De Virginitate* Nyssen writes,

> Blessed are they who have the power to choose the better things and those who are not cut off from them by having chosen the common life previously, so that we are kept as if by an abyss from the boast of virginity to which one cannot return once he has set his foot upon the path of the worldly life. On account of this, we are only spectators of the beauty belonging to others and witnesses of the blessedness of others. And even if we gain some special knowledge of virginity, we have the same experience as cooks and servants who season the delicacies of the rich, but do not themselves partake of what is prepared.[73]

It appears that he is referring to himself and his own marriage, lamenting that he cannot experience physical virginity as a path toward theosis.

Asceticism as prolepsis

The life of asceticism is proleptic, looking forward toward eschatological perfection, but Nyssen's *De Virginitate* is also protreptic,[74] in that it is written to persuade his listeners to the life of virginity. Nyssen makes this very clear from the beginning stating, "The aim of this discourse is to create in the reader a desire for the life of virtue."[75] For Nyssen, "virginity is the central virtue through which man perfects himself and reaches his goal, which is participation in the purity and incorruptibility of God. It is the mediating force which brings God down to man and lifts man to God."[76]

> What greater praise of virginity is there than its being proved that in some way those who have a share in the pure mysteries of virginity become themselves *partakers* of the glory of God, who

---

72. Ibid.

73. Nyssen, *DV* 3 (PG 46:325) (SC 119) (GNO VIII.I) (FC, 12–13).

74. This is a form of rhetoric utilized to persuade listeners, a type of propaganda speech, as it were. *Merriam-Webster.com*, s.v. "protreptic."

75. Nyssen, *DV* (PG 46:317) (SC 119) (GNO VIII.I) (FC, 6).

76. Callahan from the introduction to *DV* (FC, 4).

alone is holy and blameless, since they participate in His purity and incorruptibility?[77]

Virginity is then the "supreme attribute of God which deifies those who participate in it."[78] Nazianzen described it as "the first fruits of the life to be."[79]

For Nyssen the individual who inaugurates this concept as its first role model is Miriam, the sister of Moses and Aaron.[80] He sees her leading the chorus of women, playing the tambourine after they crossed the Red Sea, and refers to her as the first Mary. Miriam, therefore becomes "the prototype of (Θεοτόκον) Mary."[81] Mary, however, becomes the ultimate prototype for those who would come after her. Nazianzen writes:

> But after Christ was born of a chaste and virgin Mother, not bound by carnal chains and like unto God (for it was necessary that Christ should come into the world without marital relations and without a father), virginity began to sanctify women and drive away the bitter Eve. It took away the laws of the flesh, and, through the preaching of the gospel, the letter gave way to the spirit, and grace entered in.
>
> Then virginity shone out clearly before mortals; it appeared in the world freely, as the liberator of a helpless world. It is as superior to matrimony and to the conditions of life as the soul is superior to the body and as the wide heavens are superior to earth, as the lasting life of the blessed is superior to the fleeting life of earth, as God is superior to man.[82]

With this model in mind, a woman (and ultimately a man as well) has the possibility of entering into a new lifestyle, one in which the individual prepares for becoming the bride of Christ. Nyssen believed that the cares of this world were the greatest distraction to the philosophic or ascetic life and that it was only by ridding oneself of "idle bodily desire," that one could attain to the good.[83] The virgin's desire was to be pure and to have great

---

77. Nyssen, *DV* 1 (PG 46:320) (SC 119) (GNO VIII.I) (FC, 9).

78. Russell, *Doctrine of Deification*, 226. Nyssen, *DV* 1 (PG 46:321C) (SC 119) (GNO VII.I); Methodius of Olympus, *Symposium* 9.4, where chastity is similarly presented as deifying.

79. Nazianzen, *De vita sua* (PG 37:1029–166), in *Saint Gregory of Nazianzus: Three Poems*, trans. Meehan, 456–57.

80. Nyssen, *DV* 19 (PG 46:396) (SC 119) (GNO VIII.I) (FC, 60).

81. Ibid. (PG 46:396b) (SC 119) (GNO VIII.I) (FC, 60–61).

82. Nazianzen, *Moral Poems* I, 189–208 (PG 37:537a–538a), trans. Gambero, *Mary and the Fathers of the Church*, 165.

83. Nyssen, *DV* (PG 46:317) (SC 119) (GNO VIII.I) (FC, 6).

"zeal for incorruptibility," resulting in an "ability to see God, for the chief and first and only beautiful and good and pure is the God of all, and no one is so blind in mind as not to perceive that even by himself."[84]

Understanding virginity beyond the physical

While fighting for Nicene Orthodoxy, the Cappadocians wrote a large number of documents, sermons and letters on the Holy Trinity. Interestingly, it is within the relationship of the Holy Trinity that Nyssen finds his image of the original virgin. He does note that it is a paradox "to find virginity in a Father who has a Son whom He has begotten without passion, and virginity is comprehended together with the only-begotten God who is the giver of incorruptibility, since it shone forth with the purity and absence of passion in His begetting."[85] However, this becomes the hope for all of humanity, that this virginity is possible for all of humankind, whether they have been married or not. With the Trinity as his example, Nyssen explains the incorporeal nature of virginity, which "through the kindness of God, it has been granted to those whose life has been allotted through flesh and blood, in order that it may set human nature upright once more after it has been cast down by its passionate disposition, and guide it, as if by the hand, to a contemplation of the things on high."[86] Thus, the reason Jesus was not born of a married woman, but rather a virgin, so that he could demonstrate "that purity alone is sufficient for receiving the presence and entrance of God."[87]

> For what happened corporeally in the case of the immaculate Mary, when the fullness of the divinity shone forth in Christ through her virginity, takes place also in every soul spiritually giving birth to Christ, although the Lord no longer effects a bodily presence.[88]

The power for the life of virginity, then, does not reside within the self but resides in heaven with the Father.[89] It is this life of virginity which "brings God down to a sharing in human life and lifts man up to a desire of heavenly things, becoming a kind of binding force in man's affinity to

84. Ibid., 11 (PG 46:364) (SC 119) (GNO VIII.I) (FC, 42).

85. Ibid., 2 (PG 46:321) (SC 119) (GNO VIII.I) (FC, 10).

86. Ibid. (PG 46:321) (SC 119) (GNO VIII.I) (FC, 11).

87. Ibid.

88. Ibid. John 14:23.

89. Nyssen, *DV* (PG 46:321) (SC 119) (GNO VIII.I) (FC, 11).

God."[90] For Gregory, it is marriage and the distractions of that life, including children, which keeps one from having one's "thoughts on high" and making one's "way up to God."[91]

Nyssen did not view the life of virginity as negative; rather, he believed that this life brought freedom. It brought freedom from the cycle of life and death to which women were tied. The natural order was for a young woman to be betrothed at a young age, possibly by ten to twelve years of age, and married by fourteen. More than likely the age of fourteen was selected because of the onset of menses and, therefore, a woman's ability to bear a child. While a young woman may have begun menstruating her body may not have completely developed physically, making it difficult to deliver a newborn. The result was pregnancy always brought with it the possibility of death, for the child, the mother, or both. Nyssen argued that on a very human level the future of a married woman was nothing to compare "against the freedom of virginity."[92]

Virginity brought freedom to women, not only freedom from the cycle of death but also from the misfortunes of marriage, which were many. "Thus manifold and varied is the supply of evils that come from marriage. Children born and not born, living and dying, are alike the source of pain."[93] Nyssen became passionate as he discussed the problems in marriage and suggested that a young woman should go to the law court and "read the marriage laws" for there she will discover "the abominations of marriage."[94] Albrecht notes that the "marriage of late antiquity was meaningless."[95] The pagan woman had little to look forward to in her rather mundane lifestyle filled with attending the theatre while dressed in finery and flirting with men. Should she be married, she would be thrown into the cycle of death in terms of pregnancy and childbirth. The hope for most women was "escape from the world."[96] Female ascetics, then, "were emancipated precisely by their asceticism—that is, by the withdrawal of their bodies from the roles usually imposed on them by society."[97] Gregory believed those women who chose the life of virginity were more intelligent because they fully understood the

---

90. Ibid.

91. Ibid., 20 (PG 46:338) (SC 119) (GNO VIII.I) (FC, 21).

92. Ibid., 3 (PG 46:329) (SC 119) (GNO VIII.I) (FC, 17).

93. Ibid. (PG 46:338) (SC 119) (GNO VIII.I) (FC, 19).

94. Ibid.

95. Albrecht, *Das Leben der heiligen Makrina*, 17.

96. Ibid.

97. Ludlow, *Gregory of Nyssa*, 205.

consequences of their choices.[98] Asceticism offered women a completely new life without the rule of patriarchy. They could live in female run communities with the freedom to study, protected from unwelcomed advances of certain men. It was in these protected environments where women began to experience the eschatological hope of equality found in the spiritual kingdom. Asceticism allowed them the freedom to be the liberated "career" women of their day.

Transformation—the virgin,
a reflection of the image

Nyssen describes the virgin as a mirror, one which has been cleaned and is shiny and reflective. She is also the lost coin which, found in a dirty room, has been cleaned and polished. This being the case, "we leave behind earthly darkness, and become light-like there, because we are near the true light of Christ, or the true Light shining in the darkness comes down to us and we are made light."[99] Each of the Cappadocians use this mirror imagery to help explain that part of the process in theosis is the restoration of the original image in the human. This restoration is available for men and women alike. But the original image is only visible when the mirror has been cleaned so it can be a pure reflection. "In this way, reflecting as the mirror does, when it submits itself to the purity of God, it will be formed according to its participation in and reflection of the prototypal beauty."[100] This is an interesting statement because it not only produces the imagery of reflection but speaks of participation. This participation is the result of uniting oneself with God by way of crucifixion "with him and living with him and sharing his glory and his kingship; offering yourself to God means transforming human nature and worth into the angelic."[101] The virgin was to live a life fixed upon Christ, without any of the world's distractions, and thereby participate with God and God's interaction in the world. She was to be the reflection of Christ to this needy world.

---

98. Nyssen, *DV* 14 (PG 46:381) (SC 119) (GNO VIII.I) (FC, 48).

99. Ibid., 11 (PG 46:364) (SC 119) (GNO VIII.I) (FC, 41).

100. Ibid.

101. Ibid., 23 (PG 46:405) (SC 119) (GNO VIII.I) (FC, 74).

Participation in God changes
perspective and behavior

For Nyssen, children were not necessarily a distraction from the holy life for his concern was childbirth. Gregory saw childbirth as a path to death, most likely a result of the number of young mothers whose deaths he had experienced in his day. He saw the married life as having "death as a consequence,"[102] because of the resultant pregnancy, as it was the function of the wife to bear children. For the virgin, on the other hand, the joy came in bearing spiritual children. He said that virgins birth "immortal children through the Spirit,"[103] and this does not lead to death. The virgin has chosen a path where there is no longer any "unlawful pregnancy or conception in sin";[104] instead, there is new birth through the life-giving Spirit, and in this way "it is possible for everyone to become a mother."[105] This reasoning suggests being a mother is not a distraction from the holy life in imitation of Christ. Rather, being a mother to a needy world means that one is participating in God and God's love pours out in motherly tenderness.

This participation in God begins to change the virgin's perspective on everything. Beauty takes on a new meaning. It is no longer defined by the world's standards, but by God's, for God is beauty. "By a participation in this beauty, the other beautiful things come into being and are identified."[106] These other beautiful things are much higher than our human comprehension, and when our desire is to know Christ, then our desire leads us to a new level where human perception does not reach. One is then "led to a desire for that beauty of which the heavens tell the glory and the firmament of all creation proclaims the knowledge. In this way, the soul, rising and leaving behind all notice of unimportant things, arrives at a knowledge of the grandeur beyond the heavens."[107]

Nyssen reminds us that this does not occur because of our own power or resources. It occurs because one becomes "equipped with heavenly wings" so that he or she may be "borne upwards because of his lofty way of life."[108] Here one experiences the synergism between the practices of virtue, the life of purity, and the power of God. The result is that one's self

102. Ibid., 13 (PG 46:376) (SC 119) (GNO VIII.I) (FC, 48).
103. Ibid.
104. Ibid., 14 (PG 46:381) (SC 119) (GNO VIII.I) (FC, 50).
105. Ibid.
106. Ibid., 11 (PG 46:364) (SC 119) (GNO VIII.I) (FC, 39).
107. Ibid.
108. Ibid. (PG 46:364) (SC 119) (GNO VIII.I) (FC, 40).

becomes beautiful through participation with beauty, and this beauty is true light. Therefore, through "participation in the true light, he will himself be in a state of brightness and illumination."[109] This is the same light which shone from Moses' face after he has been spending time with God. Nyssen believed the same was true in regard to his sister Macrina, and he vividly described the illumination of her body after death.[110] For Gregory, all of this represented the *telos* of the final participation in God. This is God's light shining through those who have been united with Christ.

The practice of virtue

Virginity becomes a tool or an ally in the development of the life of virtue in an individual. It is through the life of virginity that certain "skills are devised for the perfection of each of the things sought after . . . the pursuit of virginity is a certain art and faculty of the more divine life, teaching those living in the flesh how to be like the incorporeal nature."[111] One of the ways in which a virgin can remain pure is to remain "aloof from every evil which in any way touches the soul and to keep herself pure for the Bridegroom legitimately suited to her, having no stain or spot or any such thing."[112] Human passions can lead one astray therefore one must be careful to restrain the passions or risk going too far in the opposite direction. For while one is to control the passions, the paradox is that the ascetic is to *be passionate* about God. These passions for God are "beyond human feelings, in fact *apathes*. The classic ascetic virtue of *apatheia* turns logic on its head by claiming that passionlessness is reached through passion and desire."[113] This passion and desire is for the bridegroom, Christ.

The spiritual discipline of virginity also applied to physical discipline and not just in the area of sexual relations. Rather, the virgin was warned not to allow her "soul to come near any temptation to pleasure."[114] Interestingly, Nyssen warned against the following:

> The pleasure of taste, because somehow this seems to be the most forbidden. Pleasures connected with eating and drinking abound in immoderate consumption, create in the body the

109. Ibid.

110. Nyssen, *DVM* (PG 46:976) (SC 178) (GNO VIII.I) (FC, 174) and (PG 46:992) (SC 178) (GNO VIII.I) (FC, 186).

111. Nyssen, *DV* 4 (PG 46:338) (SC 119) (GNO VIII.I) (FC, 27).

112. Ibid., 16 (PG 46:385) (SC 119) (GNO VIII.I) (FC, 53).

113. Cameron, "Sacred and Profane Love," 13.

114. Nyssen, *DV* 21 (PG 46:400) (SC 119) (GNO VIII.I) (FC, 65).

> necessity for a surfeit of undesirable evils, and this begets many
> similar sins among men.[115]

He suggested self-control in the area of eating by setting boundaries of in-take in direct proportion only to what was needed. Gregory consistently encouraged moderation in the life of the ascetic. Gregory was witness to the damage which could be done by those who went to extremes. By damaging the human body, one could actually hinder the spiritual growth of the indi-vidual.[116] The virgin was encouraged to do all he or she could to maintain good health.[117] Gregory made it clear that the goal was not "suffering of the body" but "the efficient working of the instruments of the soul."[118]

As this practice of asceticism spread throughout Cappadocia there were certain ascetic practices which were rather unsavory, and this was one of the reasons that Gregory felt he needed to speak about the extremes.

> We know also those who starve themselves to death on the
> grounds that such a sacrifice is pleasing to God, and again, oth-
> ers, completely opposite to these, who practise celibacy in name,
> but who do not refrain from social life, not only enjoying the
> pleasures of the stomach, but living openly with women, call-
> ing such a living together "brotherhood," and thinking that they
> are avoiding suspicion by this pious term. Because of them, this
> revered and pure way of life is blasphemed by the pagans.[119]

Different models of monasticism were developing which included a spiritual "father" who would gather around him his spiritual "children," including women. These would live in the same household with him. They might even share the same bed attempting to prove their dedication to celi-bacy and self-discipline. Understandably, they became the laughing stock of the pagan world who saw all of this as ridiculous. Basil had already ad-dressed this issue by using the type of double monasticism seen at Annesi as a template. Here the women answered to Macrina and the men to Peter. Interestingly, we do not see misogyny in Basil's understanding of monasti-cism. However, there was a real problem of cohabitation of celibate men and

115. Ibid.

116. More than likely this idea of moderation may have been the result of his brother Basil's early experiment at asceticism which was rather extreme.

117. Nyssen, *DV* 22 (PG 46:401) (SC 119) (GNO VIII.I) (FC, 67).

118. Ibid., 23 (PG 46:405) (SC 119) (GNO VIII.I) (FC, 68). This would not be the case today of Russian Orthodoxy which values suffering as equaling holiness. To be canonized in the Russian Orthodox church one must prove that the individuals have suffered. For example, this led to the sainthood of the entire family of the last czar. They were not necessarily holy people, but they had suffered and therefore were made saints. This early concept of moderation on the part of Gregory has been often ignored.

119. Ibid. (PG 46:405) (SC 119) (GNO VIII.I) (FC, 71).

women during this period, and obviously it was not working. The problem was so great that Nazianzen, in reaction to the situation, wrote the following poem *Against Celibate Co-habitation.*

It is a dangerous thing	Πῦρ ἐγγὺς καλάμης,
To hold fire near straw.	οὐκ ἀσφαλές.
And so it is, O monk,	Οὐδὲ γυναῖκα Παρθένον,
To let a virgin share your house.	ὦ μοναχὲ,
Better by far	κτᾶσθαι 'ομωρόφιον
To keep the sexes separate.	Αρσενα, καὶ θήλειαν ἐχώρισεν
For human nature harbours a	ἐλπὶς ἀμείνων
weakness inside.	Ἡ δὲ φύσις κρυπτὴν τὴν
However separate you become	νόσον ἔνδον ἔχει.
The glowing embers are still there.	Ἡν ἀπέχῃς μαχρὰν,
Draw close together again	σπινθὴρ μένει εἰ δ᾽ἀναμίσγῃ
And even a breath of air	Αψεις πυρκαῖὰν
can raise a fire.[120]	πνεύματος ἐξ ὀλίγου.

Gregory reiterated that the model at Annesi was their model for understanding the ascetic life. Basil based his *Rules*, which have continued to influence Eastern monasticism to this day, on Annesi as well.[121] Gregory frequently reiterated that virginity was not merely a physical attribute but was an attitude which should affix itself to every aspect of the individual's life. He admonishes the virgins to "seek out the good for themselves from all sides, so that their life will be secure in every respect."[122] He uses the analogy of a soldier who does not protect a singular part of his body, but takes care to be protected on every side. In this regard, he sees virginity as the foundation for the life wholly devoted to God, "but let there be built upon this foundation all the products of virtue."[123] The products of virtue include an orderliness to life. Gregory gives us a quick glimpse into daily life when he provides the following illustration of the unordered life. One finds the house "unsuitable and incongruous: the bed

120. Nazianzen, *Epigr.* 12 (PG 38:88) (Paton, LCL), in *Saint Gregory Nazianzen: Selected Poems,* trans. McGuckin, 19. "In nascent monasticism the custom of *Subintroductae,* or mixed-sex celibate community life, began to be introduced. In its origins it came about as a protection of Christian virgins by their brother monks, and as a mode of celibate companionship. Gregory is an inveterate opponent of the development, not only because of its evident moral dangers, which he mentions here, but also because in his opinion it obscured the sign-value of the Church's public witness to celibacy." McGuckin, *Saint Gregory Nazianzen,* 23n57.

121. Stramara, "Double Monasticism," 282.

122. Nyssen, *DV* 18 (PG 46:389) (SC 119) (GNO VIII.I) (FC, 55).

123. Ibid. (PG 46:389) (SC 119) (GNO VIII.I) (FC, 56).

overturned, the table full of dirt, valuable objects cast aside into filthy corners, vessels serving the needs of nature in full sight of those who come in."[124] But the life that is wholeheartedly committed to God has built a life of virtue on the foundation of virginity, but leading to a life which is "uniformly virtuous" where purity is "evident in every aspect."[125]

To becomes brides of Christ

Nyssen felt that the life of the virgin was certainly one of freedom but it was not a life without a bridegroom. Rather, it was a life in which the virgin was "always accompanied by an incorruptible Bridegroom,"[126] and in this was peace and security. While the young women were not marrying physically, they were preparing their hearts, lives and minds to be the brides of Christ. This was to be seen in the final goal of theosis, which would result in unity with Christ. Therefore, the vow of virginity was seen as a marriage vow, with Christ as the groom. These vows were taken with the deepest solemnity for "a woman's initial profession must have been the equivalent of a marriage vow, a lifelong commitment on an individual and personal level, yet with its own legal consequences."[127] The popularity of this type of life grew rapidly at the turn of the fourth century, and the virgins were highly regarded in the congregations. However, "those who reneged on their promises suffered official retribution."[128] That was because, essentially, they were married to Christ. To leave this life and marry a man would be considered an act of adultery.

All of her life the virgin was to keep herself from distractions, in a type of spiritual marriage, which might keep her from being prepared for her groom. "The bold will dare to say that it is not beyond likelihood that the virginity of the body is the co-worker and sponsor of an inner and spiritual marriage."[129] One entering into a spiritual marriage should look at it just as seriously as she would a physical marriage, as if preparing oneself for a bridegroom. The bride would want to present herself as "youthful and intellectually rejuvenated" and "from a family that is rich in a way that is most desirable, a family not respected because of its earthly possessions, but because of the abundance of its heavenly treasures."[130] A woman entering

---

124. Ibid. (PG 46:389) (SC 119) (GNO VIII.I) (FC, 57).

125. Ibid. (PG 46:389) (SC 119) (GNO VIII.I) (FC, 59).

126. Ibid., 3 (PG 46:325) (SC 119) (GNO VIII.I) (FC, 18).

127. Elm, "*Virgins of God,*" 28.

128. Ibid., 29.

129. Nyssen, *DV* 20 (PG 46:397) (SC 119) (GNO VIII.I) (FC, 62).

130. Ibid. (PG 46:397) (SC 119) (GNO VIII.I) (FC, 63).

into this spiritual marriage did not bring with her a dowry of corruptible things; rather, she brought with her the fruits of the spirit.[131]

Apokatastasis

Virginity assists humanity in reaching that final goal of union with God and the restoration of all things. The purpose of the journey is to purify the mind while on the journey of life. Pleasure is not to delay or impede the journey.[132] Comparatively, they are so focused on Christ, the *telos* of their existence, nothing on earth can become a distraction. Only by being singularly focused is one able to enter this journey, for "in proportion to the greatness of what is sought after, it is necessary to elevate the mind in thought and to lift it to the level of what we are seeking, so that we are not excluded entirely from participation in the good."[133] It is through this process of seeking after God that we become acquainted with God, and therefore, do not lose track of him during the journey. Nazianzen encourages the virgin, "so if you confine your desire, and be wholly joined to God, you will not fall downward; you will not be dissipated; you will remain entirely Christ's, until thou see Christ your Bridegroom."[134] For according to Nyssen, "The final goal of our journey is restoration (*apokatastasis*) to our original state or likeness (*homoisis*) to God."[135] It is in this apokatastasis that we find "a renewal of our original nature. There [human] nature cannot be renewed without the resurrection; it cannot take place without death preceding it which is the beginning and way leading to our betterment."[136] The goal ever before the virgin was physical death which would result in apokatastasis and ultimately union with the Bridegroom, for whom she had so long awaited.

The theological thought of the Cappadocians and their concept of deification was heavily infused with the feminine, specifically in regard to understanding virginity as a goal to becoming a bride of Christ. The female, in this regard, transcends gender and represents both male and female. In an era where some contemporary theologians are focusing on the masculinity of the church, one could argue the Cappadocians argued for femininity and certainly were not threatened by this metaphor. Reasonably, they encouraged all, male and female, to fall deeply in love with Christ and live a life of preparation as his virgin bride.

131. Nazianzen, *Or.* 37.11 (PG 36:295) (SC 318) (*NPNF2* 7:341).

132. Nyssen, *DV* 4 (PG 46:338) (SC 119) (GNO VIII.I) (FC, 24).

133. Ibid., 11 (PG 46:364) (SC 119) (GNO VIII.I) (FC, 38).

134. Nazianzen, *Or.* 37.11 (PG 36:295) (SC 318) (*NPNF2* 7:341).

135. Nyssen, *Homily of Consolation* (PG 46:864–77) (J.51), trans. McCambly, 6.

136. Ibid. (J.472), 12.

CHAPTER 5

The *Fallen Virgin*

THE WOMEN WHO WERE a part of the Cappadocians' lives provided the background and the environment for much of their theology, and to understand these men, one must look behind them to see the equally great women. While the men have left volumes of their writings (Basil alone has four volumes in *Patrologia Graeca* including 366 letters), we have no first hand writings from these women. Historically, many women's voices have been lost to us either because their stories were never told, or the men whom they influenced never mentioned them.[1] Correspondingly, for centuries there has been a vacuum in the matter of the role which women played in the development of theological thought. In the case of the Cappadocian Fathers, the Western church in the last half-century has, in a sense, rediscovered their theology, and concomitantly, there has been an unearthing of the women in their lives. While Basil in extant works never directly referred to his sister Macrina, he did mention the influences of his mother and grandmother. It is Gregory of Nyssa, the younger brother, who depicted the relationship between his two older siblings, Macrina and Basil. The friend, Nazianzen, provided reflections on Macrina, Emmelia and Theosebia from Basil's family and wrote orations for his own family members which give us insights into his home life and personal development.

Each of the women whose lives are detailed in the writings of the Cappadocians can be seen as models for a portion of the Cappadocians' theological development germane to deification. While the Cappadocians' understanding of theosis led to their theological conclusion that the life of virginity was best for one wanting to unite with God, the women who were associated with them presented illustrations of the stages of theosis. Derek Kruger observed, "For Nyssen memorializing the lives of holy men, like Gregory Thaumaturgus, and holy women, like Macrina, fills the gap between the present life and the heavenly reality they mediated—a gap left

---

1. Castelli, "Virginity and Its Meaning," 73–74.

empty by their passing."[2] The stories inform us about that which could not be found in their theological writings alone, and it is here the plot continues.

F. W. Norris believes that Nazianzen would applaud the use of narrative "as the proper form of theology" but would argue that too few of today's contemporary theologians "have yet moved beyond the stories themselves to the Theologian's drumbeat of narrative bits for the divine and human in Christ, a performance that depended upon those Gospel accounts but in some ways still has more ability to move hearers or readers than they do."[3] What we discover here is the women serve as the narrative threads which present the concept of deification, moving readers in a practical sense to join the narrative. Wilken reminds us, "Without examples, without imitation, there can be no human life or civilization, no art or culture, no virtue or holiness."[4] Van Dam comments, "Perhaps it is not too fanciful to suggest that treatises about virginity, especially women's virginity, were the complements of theological treatises about the doctrines of God the Father and the Son. Among churchmen an obsession with the paternity of the Son corresponded to an emphasis on the purity of women."[5] To understand the concepts of deification experienced in the lives of virginity and marriage which the Cappadocians desired to pass on to future generations, one must examine the women associated with them.

In chapter 3, we introduced the kenosis-theosis parabola. Six distinctive stages were noted giving clarity to the understanding of theosis. While the concepts of theosis seem to have been worked out in the Cappadocians' defence of Nicene Orthodoxy, one readily observes their arguments appear to have been highly influenced by personal experience and, specifically, by the women who were related to them. Each life is a story which illustrates their understanding of deification. Therefore, in each stage of this kenosis-theosis parabola, it is possible to overlay the story of a woman in the writings of the Cappadocians who exemplifies each stage *of* theosis. Moving through the parabola there are intersections which demonstrate that the women may have had significant influence on the development of the Cappadocians' theological thought.

The Cappadocians, quite distinctively for their era, left us with a large volume of work written about the women who were associated with them. Nazianzen's *Oration* 8, written for his sister Gorgonia, is the first female

---

2. Smith, "Just and Reasonable Grief," 82. See Kruger, "Writing and the Liturgy," 489. See also Clarke, *St. Basil the Great*, 49.

3. Norris, "Gregory Contemplating the Beautiful," 34.

4. Wilken, *Spirit of Early Christian Thought*, 262.

5. Van Dam, *Families and Friends*, 85–86.

panegyric which we have on record. Basil writes letters in which we find reference specifically to his grandmother, Macrina the Elder, and also to his mother, Emmelia. Nyssen writes the hagiographic document on the life of his sister, *De Vita Macrinae*, as well as *On the Soul and the Resurrection*, which is a philosophical document written in Macrina's voice. Nazianzen's panegyrics on his father and his brother also provide us with lengthy details on his mother, Nonna's, life. In these different accounts these men make reference to the influence of these women on their lives, whether in the development of their theological thought, or selection of a vocation. Therefore, not only did they write about the women, but the women have direct influence on their theological development. Lynda Coon comments, "The hagiography of female saints replicates the process of redemption. By transforming profane female flesh into a vehicle of grace, women's conversion extends the hope of universal salvation to sinful humanity."[6] Therefore, it is possible to place the female saints related to the Cappadocian Fathers into the framework of the kenosis-theosis parabola. While the world saw the Cappadocians arguing theology with some of the greatest minds of their day, undergirding such theological conversation was a foundation of experience within their own homes which moulded them into the theologians they became. We will demonstrate how the different women about whom they wrote became living illustrations of each stage within the parabola, therefore becoming theology by way of biography. The first two stages of this parabola: (1) Humankind is made in the image of God and is a reflection or mirror of that image, and (2) The image is tarnished by the fall into sin, may be illustrated within the life of a young lady known to us only as the *Fallen Virgin*.

Humankind is made in the image of God and is a reflection or mirror of that image

The female saint who most clearly illustrates the concept of the image and restoration was not originally included in the scope of this thesis. Found within Basil's *Letter 46, To a Fallen Virgin* is the description of a young woman who has walked away from her vows of celibacy. This rather esoteric document has led to speculation as to the nature of the letter. It is worth noting it formerly has not been given much consideration. Silvas's recent publication on *Macrina the Younger* includes a study of Basil's *Letter 46*. In her opinion this letter directly connects this young woman with

---

6. Coon, *Sacred Fictions*, xvii–xviii.

Basil the Great.[7] However, Elm in her extensive monograph on asceticism does not believe her to be a sister, but rather a description of another family member, possibly that of an aunt and a cousin.[8] Limberis, while referring to the letter does not provide any connection to the family of Cappadocians.[9] Elm does give us a possible dating of this letter to sometime after Basil's ordination in 370,[10] with the Benedictine editors placing it distinctly within the letters written during his presbyterate.[11] However, Silvas provides a compelling argument for a dating of 362–63 and the placement of this sister as one of the youngest, born perhaps just before Peter, who was born about 345. This would make the timing of her vows in the early 360s, coming at about the same time of the "final development of Annesi into a full-fledged monastery."[12] In late 362, "Basil travelled down to Caesarea for the death of Bishop Dianius, and in the aftermath of the election of the new bishop, was himself ordained to the presbyterate."[13] Silvas says, "One can well imagine the writing of this letter at just this period, that is 362–63."[14] Recently, there has been wider acceptance of the *Fallen Virgin* as a member of the household of Basil. The curious similarities of the details in the two families, that of Basil's and the one in the letter, make it highly likely this young woman is none other than a younger sibling of Basil the Great, and therefore one of the daughters of Emmelia.

If one agrees with Silvas, then this younger sister has demonstrable influence on the development of Basil's understanding of image and restoration. The first stage in the parabola is an understanding that "man," or humanity, is made in the image of God. As noted previously, the image of God in humanity was foundational to the Cappadocian understanding of deification. The Cappadocians develop a concept of in which all of humanity, both male and female, were included or created in the original image. Nyssen's understanding was that full humanity was expressed in the first creation account, where he saw that "*man*," or humankind, was made in the

---

7. For Silvas's extensive argument on the case of the younger sister, see *Macrina the Younger*, 62, on "*Letter 46, To a Fallen Virgin.*" The case for Theosebia will be discussed in greater detail in ch. 8.

8. Elm, "*Virgins of God*," 144, does not come to the same conclusion and seems to think that perhaps this relates to another branch of the family and a group of cousins who seem to have a similar family configuration.

9. Limberis, *Architects of Piety*, 172.

10. Elm, "*Virgins of God*," 142.

11. Silvas, *Macrina the Younger*, 62.

12. Ibid., 65.

13. Ibid.

14. Ibid.

image of God. It is this total humanity that is the expression of God, and it is gender neutral.[15] This meant that for Basil this younger sister was wholly and completely created in the image of God.

The image is tarnished by its fall into sin

Sin did not destroy the image but it was corrupted in the fall of humankind. While the Cappadocians used mirror imagery to comprehend the corruption of the divine design for personhood, they presented it in two different ways. One manner in which it was portrayed was as a corruption of the mirror itself. Because of the dirt or filth of the mirror, it could no longer clearly reflect the image. However in Nyssen's *Commentary on the Canticles*, he stated, "Indeed, man was once created in God's image, but became a wild beast, transformed into an irrational creature, becoming a lion and a leopard by reason of his sinful ways."[16] This second form is relational for we understand that the image in humankind is directly dependent upon its *relationship* to the original, or the Archetype. Therefore, as a result of sin, not only has the mirror become corrupted, but the human is no longer in relationship with God. The end result of both is that the image is no longer a reflection of God.

In *Letter* 46 we find a young woman who becomes for Basil the living illustration of one in whom the image has been lost. Her story represents a disruption in the relational aspect. She has turned her back on her bridegroom, Christ, to whom she was committed when she took her vows. Her behavior has changed and she is no longer living a life of virtue which would lead one on the progressive path toward deification. She has slipped backward and is showing an attitude of defiance. The image is no longer visible in this younger sister.

Basil comments that the young lady had been abducted; however, in the fourth century, abduction was not necessarily done against the will of a young woman, but with her blessing. More than likely what had occurred was an elopement, enacted completely at the will and consent of the young woman so that the family could not protest the relationship, for once the relationship was consummated, the couple was married.[17] According to the Cappadocians' understanding of sin, it is free will that allows one to make a choice which results in the corruption of the image. This is exactly what is illustrated by this comment about the sister's abduction. Basil knows and

---

15. Nyssen, *DHO* 16.16 (PG 44:184b) (*NPNF2* 5:405).

16. Nyssen, *CC, Homily* 8 (PG 44:944d–945d) (GNO VI), trans. Musurillo, 215.

17. See Silvas, *Macrina the Younger*, 67n23.

understands the culture of his day and recognizes that his sister would have been complicit in this act, thereby exercising free will which would result in the loss of the image.

Free will may lead one to the loss of image

The life of virginity was one with no outside distractions. The call of the world would have left an individual open to greater opportunities to fall into sin. However, even a woman living in the safe environs of the monastery would have been able to exercise free will. The Cappadocians understood that free will was available to all humans, male and female, slave and free. Therefore, temptations would have made all individuals vulnerable. One of the purposes of the life of asceticism was to reduce the number of distractions and/or temptations. The family monastery at Annesi should have provided a safe location from distractions. The vows taken by these young women were valued highly by the entire Christian community. The virgins were considered the actual bride of Christ, and for them to be coerced away from that vow was for them to be drawn into adultery. Nyssen had related free will with the image, and free will is never lost in humanity. However, because of the choices made as a result of free will, the reflection changes. No longer is the human a reflection of the original, for the mirror, so to speak, has become stained or marred.[18] This stained or marred mirror has become, according to Nazianzen, a foul mirror. In the case of the fallen virgin, she has fallen as a result of her free will, and the image is corrupted. Basil's response parallels the response of God, who is moved by the fall of humanity and the loss of the image. Basil writes, "We must not pass over so great a fall without a tear."[19] For Basil the fall is great, for sin has caused this once pure bride of Christ to sin and for the image to be lost. Basil recounts the command in Deut 5:21, "Neither shall you covet your neighbor's wife" (NRSV). In his opinion, the young man has coveted the Lord's wife, and the wife has succumbed to the advances of the other man. The fall of this bride of Christ was great, for it was very public. "They now behold the Bride of the Master yielding herself without fear to adultery."[20] For him this relationship was an "outrage" which touched "the holy bridal-chamber of the Lord."[21] Not only was she defiled, but she had been unfaithful to the object of all of their love and affection, Jesus Christ, himself.

---

18. Nyssen, *DV* 11 (PG 46:364) (SC 119) (GNO VIII.I) (FC, 38).

19. Basil, *Ep.* 46 (PG 32:369) 1a, trans. Silvas, 66.

20. Ibid.

21. Ibid., 1d, trans. Silvas, 67.

The virgins were taught a life of virtue which included humility. Nazianzen argued that the way to draw closer to the image was through "humble contemplation."[22] This is "something that went beyond the confidence or arrogance of most logical investigations."[23] It is in an attitude of arrogance that we see the development of the sin aspect of the tarnished image. As this sister continues to slip into sin, the corruption of the image continues and becomes visible in her defiant response to the situation. Basil describes her attitude as one of "bravado" and sees her behavior as "contemptuous" to the point that she denied her "very pact with the Bridegroom."[24] He reminds her of her vows, "You cry aloud that you neither are nor ever promised to be a virgin, and this though you accepted many pledges of virginity, and indeed offered many."[25]

The image was tarnished, and Basil evaluated the situation and what had brought her to this point. By contextualizing, Basil recognized the role of temptation which may have led to this sin. A moment of introspection brought Basil and the rest of the family to realize that they were a source of temptation to this younger sister. With most of the family being recognized as spiritual leaders within their respective communities, it would certainly have placed inordinate pressure on this younger sister. More than likely she felt pressured to take the vows for the sake of the family. It is unknown at what age this young woman would have taken her vows, but it has been suggested that it was not uncommon to submit young girls to the monastery at the age of twelve. It is interesting to note that five years later in *Epistle* 199.19, Basil writes that a young woman should be at least sixteen or seventeen years of age before taking her vows. This could very well have been in response to the situation with this younger sister whom he may have, in hindsight, felt was encouraged to take her vows at too young of an age. This may also have been an admission on Basil's part of responsibility for her actions and the role which he may have played in her fall.

The hope of restoration

In *Letter* 46 we also find illustrated the Cappadocian understanding of restoration. The optimism of the grace of God providing for restoration is seen not only in God's action but also in the action of the family. The family members themselves, through theosis and their own participation in God,

22. Norris, "Gregory Contemplating the Beautiful," 27.

23. Ibid.

24. Basil, *Ep.* 46 (PG 32:369)2b, trans. Silvas, 67.

25. Ibid.

respond to the loss of the image. All of those who were associated with the great Cappadocian family of Basil were considered faithful. History, as we have seen, has recorded that an extraordinary family was led and raised by the mother, Emmelia, and grandmother Macrina.

The optimistic faith of the Cappadocians did not point toward an image which was unrecoverable. Rather, their concept of theosis allowed for an image which was simply lost and in need of recovery. It was through the synergism of the one who had lost the image combined with God's activity that the lost image could again be restored. Nyssen sees "human freedom as moral freedom, the freedom to become what we are made to be."[26] It means that humankind can make the choice to return to the Creator and obtain the "divine likeness, but not, however, without the assistance of God."[27] It is this synergy which helps to bring healing through theosis to humanity and restores the image in humankind.

Of significance is that the Cappadocians, utilizing the three parables of the lost sheep, the lost coin, and the lost son in Luke 15, saw a loving God reaching out to humanity, desiring restoration. "Similarly too the lost drachma was found with the help of a lamp, and all the friends and neighbours were glad."[28] God never gives up on humanity. The Bridegroom sends out the angels, or friends of the Bridegroom who are looking for those who are lost, stating, "Thus it is a good thing for the soul to be found by the angels *that go about the city*."[29] While not specifically utilizing the language of grace,[30] we see the concept of a gracious God reaching out in a desire to return humanity to its original likeness and image. F. W. Norris describes Nazianzen's hopeful anthropology as "an understanding that however great was the influence of sin, the image of God in which humans were shaped was marred but still struggling."[31] The sister was struggling, but there was hope that she could be restored.

His theological understanding shapes Basil's response to this younger sister. One might expect a man of the stature of Basil to be embarrassed by the action of the sister. In this case it may have been easier to simply remove her from the community of faith and leave her to live with the consequences of her actions. At this juncture we see the intersection of Basil's theological

26. Wilken, *Spirit of Early Christian Thought*, 153.

27. Gross, *Divinization of the Christian*, 144.

28. Luke 15:9.

29. Nyssen, *CC*, Homily 12 (PG 44:1029a–1037c) (GNO VI), trans. Musurillo, 267.

30. The concept of grace is found throughout the Cappadocians. "The word Grace occurs as often in them [Cappadocians] as in Augustine" (*NPNF*2 5:54). See also Nyssen *Cont. Eun.* 2.9, 3.4, 4.3, *OC* 37.

31. Norris, "Gregory Contemplating the Beautiful," 23.

understanding and the reality of family. Whether it is Basil's theological thought which leads him to write a letter, or the love for a younger sister which drives him to have an optimistic faith of restoration, we cannot be sure. However, at this moment in history the two, theology and family, have become one, and Basil must become a participant in God's salvific activity for his sister.

Basil encourages this young woman to imagine the scene in which she took her vows and remember those who were present. It is in this description that we begin to hear the details of a family which has become familiar. "Recall your grandmother, grown old in Christ but still youthful and vigorous in virtue."[32] This description is reminiscent of the grandmother Macrina. He continues speaking of a mother who worked together with the grandmother. "Your mother vying with her in the Lord and struggling by strange and unfamiliar labours to break with the force of habit."[33] This certainly appears to be a description of his mother, Emmelia, who worked shoulder to shoulder with her mother-in-law to raise a household of godly children. It was this same mother who after the death of her husband struggled to give up the aristocratic life and became as a servant, living out the remainder of her days at the family monastery at Annesi. Finally, he says, "And your sister, who likewise imitates them both and yet strives even to surpass them, for indeed she, by the greater prize of virginity outstrips the achievements of her forebears. Both by her words and by her life, she earnestly summons you, her sister as she thought, to a rivalry of like effort."[34] This sounds very much like a description of the great Macrina, the daughter who was never married and had lived her entire life as a virgin. This is Macrina who was the teacher to her younger siblings and the one who was the leader of the monastic life in Annesi. It is interesting to note that if this letter is truly written in regard to Basil's own family, this becomes the only statement he ever makes praising or giving credit to Macrina. One can imagine the two older siblings in such a family always having just a touch of sibling rivalry and, therefore Basil neglects to give credit given to Macrina.

Going forth and searching

Just as the good shepherd utilizes all of his skill and talent to bring back the lost sheep, Basil now steps into the role of the shepherd to try and bring back his sister. If we understand that Basil himself was also undergoing

32. Basil, *Ep.* 46 (PG 32:369)2d, trans. Silvas, 67.

33. Ibid.

34. Ibid., 67–68.

deification, we can see his response in connection with his participation in God. He becomes a channel for God's action in the world. He himself steps into the role of the good shepherd in terms of his behavior here on the earth. He is the one who is reaching out in an effort to bring back the one who has been lost. This coincides with Basil's theological development in regard to coenobitic monasticism. It was the responsibility of the person who was being transformed into the image of God to become the *eikon* of Christ. This involved incarnational activity in the world. In this case, the incarnational activity was extended to a lost loved one. In an effort to bring her to her senses, Basil reminds her of the pleasant nature of the life in the monastery, and in doing so he gives us a glimpse of what daily life must have been like at the monastery, a life that was proleptic, where a bit of heaven existed on earth.[35] This is a holy place where those who are committed to a life of virginity, with the ultimate goal of theosis, can live out their days in anticipation of being united with Christ. Basil's physical description here also leads one to believe that he knew this young virgin very well, but it also helps us understand what may have been expected of her in terms of appearance.

> What has become of your dignified appearance, that reserved manner, that simple dress befitting a virgin, that beautiful blush of modesty, and that comely pallor which blooms through self-control and vigils and glows with a greater charm than any freshness of complexion?[36]

We have other physical descriptions of this family, including the rugged and handsome Naucratius, the beauty of Emmelia (who had to be saved from numerous suitors), and Macrina. Nazianzen was rather overwhelmed by this family, commenting that this was an instance where a family had children who are both "many and beautiful."[37] We can only imagine that this fallen girl was also quite beautiful, but she may have rebelled against the constraints placed upon her from the life of asceticism as described above. As the younger girl, she may have been raised almost exclusively in the more austere setting of Annesi, rather than in the city, as the older siblings would have been. When a young man gave her attention and possibly noticed her beauty, her instinct was to be set free of the confines that life had placed upon her and flee.

---

35. Ibid., 2e, trans. Silvas, 68.
36. Ibid.
37. Nazianzen, *Or.* 43, *Panegyric on Saint Basil* 9 (PG 36:494) (SC 384).

Continuing as an agent of God's redemptive activity, after reminding her of what she had been, Basil again shared his disappointment in this one whom he now saw as a child "of disobedience."[38] The father of all these children, the elder Basil, had died long before and the oldest son, Basil, was now the head of the family. As the earthly father of the household, Basil also played the role of the heavenly Father in this situation. The pain in Basil and the Father's voice may be heard as Basil responds, you "have exchanged that precious possession worth fighting for on every side, for a brief moment of pleasure, a pleasure which tickles your appetite for the moment but which you will one day find more bitter than gall."[39] It is this same disappointment which is found at the moment when the heavenly Father discovers that his children Adam and Eve have lost the image.

Basil is gravely concerned because he understands this behavior in light of the spiritual and the eternal consequences. The image has been gravely marred because this *bride of Christ* has become sullied. He compares her to the unfaithful Israelites, for faithfulness to God is constantly seen in light of fidelity, the fidelity of a relationship in which the two become one. It is in the fidelity of this relationship that one experiences theosis, which Basil sees as the goal of all of humanity. This bride has turned from the Bridegroom and united with another. The love of God is expressed in Basil's sudden change of tenor and his voice becomes tender as one can imagine an older brother reminiscing about his relationship with this little sister.

> For this reason I tried always to calm the turbulence of your passions by a myriad charms, and with a myriad safeguards to protect the Bride of the Lord. Always I tried to explain the life of the unmarried, that only *the unmarried woman cares for the things of the Lord, how her life may be holy in body and spirit.*[40] And I used to set forth the high worth of virginity and, address you as *the temple of God,*[41] gave wings as it were to your zeal, thus lifting you up to Jesus; and I tried to help you not to fall with the fear of the terrible possibility, saying *If anyone violates the temple of God, him shall God destroy.*[42]

He laments that all of these efforts have turned bitter. Basil again turns to the spiritual nature of this downfall, comparing it to Eve and the Serpent, only

---

38. Basil, *Ep.* 46 (PG 32:369)2i, trans. Silvas, 68.

39. Ibid.

40. 1 Cor 7:34.

41. 1 Cor 3:16.

42. Basil, *Ep.* 46 (PG 32:369)3d, trans. Silvas, 69. 1 Cor 3:17.

telling this little sister that her sin was even more bitter![43] "For not only *your thoughts* have been *corrupted,*[44] but with them your very body as well."[45] Obviously he feels the depth of the corruption when he states, "you *took the members of Christ and made them the members of a harlot.*"[46]

The corrupted image

The result of this action is the corruption of the image of God in the life of the individual. Restoration of the image comes in salvation, but now, this person who has an "indwelling soul made after the image of God"[47] has been marred. His language becomes strong as he compares what has happened to his little sister as someone engraving "the forms of unclean swine upon a royal image."[48] Basil is angry with the young man who has done this to his little sister. "How much more do you think he deserves worse punishment who has trampled underfoot the Son of God, and defiled his professed Bride and outraged the spirit of virginity?"[49] The excuses sound all too familiar, "*But she wanted it*, he says, *and I did not violate her against her will.*"[50] They remind us of Adam and Eve, who did not want to take responsibility for their own actions. In this case no one is willing to take responsibility for the corruption. Basil understands that the path to restoration involves acceptance of responsibility and admission of guilt. He recognizes that this is not an acceptable response and chastises the young man for not responding with the self-discipline of Joseph who ran from temptation. But the damage is done and the image has been lost, and he has taken her from Christ.

The image is only lost and may be recovered

The Cappadocians' optimistic hope of restoration goes beyond God's action in reaching out to humanity, becoming therapeutic. The image has been lost and the blemish is also referred to as a wound. The concern is whether the wound is too deep or the fall is too great, escaping the possibility

43. Ibid.
44. 2 Cor 11:3.
45. Basil, *Ep.* 46 (PG 32:369)3g, trans. Silvas, 69.
46. Ibid., 70. 1 Cor 6:15.
47. Ibid., 4a, trans. Silvas, 70.
48. Ibid.
49. Ibid., 4b, trans. Silvas, 70–71.
50. Ibid., 4c, trans. Silvas, 71.

of restoration. He asks, *"Is there no balm in Gilead; is there no physician there?"*[51] Hope is found in the parables of the New Testament, in the return of the "lost drachma, the lost sheep," and "the son who wasted his substance on harlots."[52] There is hope that the image can be restored when it has been lost. Basil uses the same illustration as his brother Gregory, the woman with the lost coin.[53] If it has been lost, we must seek for it, so that it can be recovered.[54]

Humanity's response to sin is repentance

The one who has lost the image is the one who must seek for the restoration of that image; and therefore, Basil turns to reminding this sister of the eternal results of her current status, for there is "that great journey beyond."[55] This is the synergistic action in restoration which has been referred to previously. Basil also believes in a day of judgment and punishment for those in whom the image has not been restored.[56] Basil's description of the punishment comes from a desire to move his sister to seek redemption and restoration. He tells her, "But it is possible to escape these things now."[57] Basil's understanding of the restoration of the image is a process which begins immediately, at the time of repentance and baptism. Basil believes that even from such a fall one can be completely and totally restored, for the focus is not on physical virginity but rather on an attitude of virginity. The attitude of virginity is a life with a singular purpose, which is to know Christ. In this way both those who are physical virgins and those who are married have the hope of restoration in the image and reconciliation of the relationship with the Bridegroom. Basil requests that she respond by bowing down and weeping before Christ in an attitude of repentance. He tells her "There is a way to salvation, if we are but willing."[58] He gently reminds her that God will wipe "away every tear from the face of all who repent."[59]

---

51. Ibid. Jer 8:22.

52. Ibid.

53. Nyssen, *DV* 12 (PG 46:369) (SC 119) (GNO VIII.I) (FC, 45).

54. Basil, *Ep.* 46 (PG 32:369)5b, trans. Silvas, 71.

55. Ibid.

56. Ibid., 5f, trans. Silvas, 72.

57. Ibid.

58. Ibid.

59. Ibid.

The Father continues to face in the direction of one who is lost

Basil's language helps us to understand that he believes in this restoration for all who are involved. "The great Physician of our souls is ready to heal your malady. From him come the words, it was his sweet and saving lips that said: *It is not the healthy who need a physician, but the sick, for I have not come to call the righteous, but sinners to repentance.*"[60] The Bridegroom does not turn his back on the fallen virgin; he continues facing in the direction of the one who is lost. Christ is represented as the physician offering healing for the wounds and a shepherd to guide the path home.

Again we find Basil in an incarnational role as he represents the Father standing on the path home, awaiting the return of the prodigal. He is still facing the one who is lost, just as God continues to be turned toward his lost children. It is the children who need to turn around, return in the direction of the Father, and in the process have the image restored.

> You have only to set out again, and while you are still afar off, he will run to you and cast himself about your neck. In loving embraces he will enfold you, cleansed already by repentance. And first he will put a robe upon you, a soul which has *put off the old man with all his works* (Col 3:9). . . . And he will announce a day of merriment and gladness for his own, both angels and human beings, and in every way celebrate your salvation.[61]

Here we begin to see Basil's eschatology. He understands that complete restoration is possible. The angels who accompany the Bridegroom represent the Cappadocian family, who is ready and willing to receive her back.

There is no focus on punishment for those in whom the image has been restored. Instead, there is a demonstration of the hope of rapid and complete restoration. Note how quickly they will celebrate her return. Let others be critical and think that this one must be punished; Basil's intent is not to punish but to welcome her home. "And if any of those who think they stand find fault because you have been received too quickly, the good Father himself will speak in your defense, saying: *it was fitting that we should make merry and be glad, for this* my daughter *was dead, and has come to life again, was lost, and is found.*"[62] Basil represents God as a loving, optimistic God who does not turn his back on his lost children and readily welcomes them back home.

---

60. Ibid., 6d, trans. Silvas, 73. Matt 9:12–13.

61. Ibid., 6f, trans. Silvas, 73.

62. Ibid. Luke 15:32.

Twenty years later Nazianzen writes his *Epigrams*,[63] in which he comments that Emmelia's children were "good children. . . . Three of her sons were illustrious priests, and one daughter the companion of a priest, and the rest were like an army of saints."[64] Also in his *Panegyric to Basil*, Nazianzen writes of the victorious spiritual lives of all of Emmelia's children: "This is evidenced by the enviable number of priests and virgins, and of those who in marriage did not in any way allow their union to be an obstacle to an equal repute for virtue, making the distinction between them consist in a choice of career rather than in conduct."[65] Evidently, the fallen one was restored and is remembered as being a part of the army of saints. Basil's optimism in terms of restoration would have reached as far as the young man who stole his sister. A few years following *Letter* 46, Basil wrote:

> He who holds a wife by secret or somewhat violent seduction must acknowledge the punishment for fornication. And punishment for four years has been prescribed for fornicators. In the first year they must be excluded from the prayers, and weep for themselves at the door of the church: in the second year they are to be admitted to the place of the "hearers:" in the third to penance: in the fourth to "standing" with the laity, abstaining from the oblation: then the communion with the Good is to be permitted them.[66]

Not only was the younger sister restored, but evidence would point to the fact that the man who abducted her was restored as well.[67] Basil used this experience as a reference point for the development of rules or principles which helped to govern his ministry.

Conclusions

For the Cappadocians, the concept of image was vital to their understanding of theosis and the *Fallen Virgin* provided them with an illustration of this theological concept. A theme within the writings of the Cappadocians is the optimism of a God who continues to face humanity in which the image is lost, seeks after that lost humanity, and rejoices at the time of restoration.

63. Silvas, *Macrina the Younger*, 79.

64. Nazianzen, *Epigr.* 161 (*Anthologia Graeca* 8:39), trans. Silvas, 81.

65. Nazianzen, *Or.* 43.9 (PG 36:504) (SC 384) (FC, 34).

66. Basil, *Ep.* 199.22 (PG 32:722) (Deferrari, LCL).

67. This evidence includes the positive statements from Nazianzen regarding Emmilia's married children being saints and the plans for restoration found in Basil.

For Basil, his personal experience and emotional connection with the *Fallen Virgin* resulted in his personal response being a reflection of and incarnation of God's response to humanity. Finally, in a very practical sense, Basil's experience with this younger sister directly influenced future decisions he made regarding his ministerial practice.

CHAPTER 6

Married Women as the New Eve:
Nonna and Gorgonia

THEOSIS IS THE FRAMEWORK for the Cappadocians' understanding of the spiritual life. Within it there is the goal for all of humanity to ever increasingly participate in God. The fallen virgin clearly represented the Cappadocians' theological understanding of image and the hope of restoration. Moving through the kenosis-theosis parabola, stages three and four include: (3) Christ assumes the human nature in order to restore humanity to its original nature, and (4) In conversion one's capacity to reflect the divine nature is once again restored. Two women within the family of Nazianzen serve, for him, as examples of restored humanity. The Cappadocians made it clear that it is Christ's very *kenotic* activity, his willingness to assume human nature that makes deification possible for humanity. Christ, then, replaces Adam as the new Man. His life becomes the model for the possibility of theosis in the lives of all who would be willing to follow his example. For Nazianzen, his mother Nonna and his sister Gorgonia become expressions of this restoration, and very specifically, they represent the Cappadocians' optimistic perspective that restoration in the original image is possible for all of humanity.

Christ assumes the human nature in order to restore humanity to its original nature

The optimistic perspective of the Cappadocians takes on a larger scale when their willingness to include women as models for their faith is considered. Traditionally, women had been blamed for the fall of humanity. It was believed that all women carried within themselves Eve,[1] and she was to bear the responsibility for the fall. A century earlier Tertullian had declared:

1. Clark, in *History, Theory, Text,* 177, states, "Nowhere is the universalizing tendency more obvious in patristic literature than in the amalgamation of all women with Eve."

And do you not know that you are (each) an Eve? The sentence of God on this sex of yours lives in this age: the guilt must of necessity live too. *You* are the devil's gateway: *you* are the unsealer of that (forbidden) tree: *you* are the first deserter of the divine law: *you* are she who persuaded him whom the devil was not valiant enough to attack. *You* destroyed so easily God's image, man. On account of *your* desert—that is, death—even the Son of God had to die.[2]

While the Cappadocians arrive at a more positive perspective, the optimism didn't last long. Soon after their passing Augustine stated, "What difference does it make whether it is in a wife or in a mother, provided that we nonetheless avoid Eve in any woman?"[3] It was believed that every woman seemed to reflect the image of Eve, and this image was ever viewed as corrupted. The restoration of Man was seen in Christ, but this left open the interpretation for the restoration of Woman. Therefore, by utilizing his mother and sister as the examples of restoration, Nazianzen was providing hope for all of humanity, male and female. These examples of restoration by Nazianzen infuse power into God's restorative reach and express the optimistic perspective that deification is possible for the entirety of humankind.

Marriage vs. virginity

The theological writings of the Cappadocians led one to believe that the best path to deification was by way of a life of asceticism dedicated to virginity. However, the curious placement of married women as examples of holy living and theosis in the Cappadocians' writings makes one suspect that their human experiences actually drove them beyond their theological writings. The use of two married women as examples of God's restorative power provides an interesting perspective on marriage. Marriage, in and of itself, was not seen as something evil, and one could be involved in deification, even if one were married. This was possible, in part, because of Nyssen's concept of virginity of the soul, with virginity understood as a metaphorical term.[4] This means that the quality of virginity was found within the process of deification or the level of participation in the divine nature of the individual. According to Jaeger: "The quality of virginity therefore is related to the process of the perfection (τελείωσις) of the true Christian who aims at

---

2. Tertullian, fourth part 4.2, *On the Apparel of Women* (*ANF* 4:25).

3. Augustine, *Works: Letters 211–270*, *Ep.* 243.10.

4. Jaeger, introduction to *Two Rediscovered Works*, 25.

attaining the divine good."[5] Therefore, marriage could become a reflection of the future eschatological hope of the relationship of God with human kind. Nyssen made it clear that virginity was not "confined to the body."[6] He stressed that it pertained "to all things" and extended "even to thought which is considered one of the achievements of the soul."[7] The soul adheres to its true bridegroom in a desire to become of one spirit with him.[8] Nazianzen also commented on this virginity which is beyond the flesh, "Let the mind also be virgin; let it not rove about; let it not wander; let it not carry in itself forms of evil things (for the form is a part of harlotry); let it not make idols in its soul of hateful things."[9] Therefore, according to Cameron, "*true* virginity can be claimed to be not the rejection of sexuality, but a state liberated from and above sexuality, a state *beyond gender*."[10] This state was capable for those who were single and married.

The Cappadocians understood that human interaction with God was required for the process of deification. For the likeness or image to be fully restored within the human, the human had to be an imitator of Christ. The human was involved in the process of deification by acts of virtue, and through these acts the human experienced ever-increasing participation in God. It is this synergistic relationship between the Triune God and people, which provided an optimistic eschatology for the Cappadocians. This concept of synergy was also to be seen within human relationships, very specifically in regard to the union of man and woman. The original intent of God in male-female relationships was to be a reflection of the relationship of Christ and the church. Thus, the illustration from marriage became powerful for understanding theosis. It was both the virgins and the married women who provided specific examples to the Cappadocians' understanding. The virgin who had united herself to Christ alone as his bride provided the penultimate example. However, at the same time, the married women provided a profoundly earthly example of the marriage which was to come between God and people. A truly Christian marriage was to become a foretaste of the relationship of humanity united together with God in theosis.

Just as the fallen virgin in Basil's *Letter* 46 has been generally overlooked in study, so too has Nazianzen's sister Gorgonia, about whom he wrote in *Oration* 8. We read about Gorgonia, as well his mother, Nonna, in

---

5. Ibid.

6. Nyssen, *DV* 15 (PG 46:384) (SC 119) (GNO VIII.I) (FC, 51).

7. Ibid.

8. Ibid.

9. Nazianzen, *Or.* 37.10 (PG 36:293) (SC 318) (*NPNF2* 7:341).

10. Cameron, "Sacred and Profane Love," 13.

this funeral oration. Historically, we recognize that *Oration* 8 on his sister Gorgonia is the first funeral oration written honoring the life of a woman. Burrus comments, "Gregory of Nazianzus' funeral oration for his sister Gorgonia seems to slip through the cracks of literary history, despite more than two decades of sustained interest in representations of women and rhetorics of gender in ancient Christian texts."[11] This document is unique as a panegyric dedicated in honor of Gorgonia. A decade later Nyssen would write *De Vita Macrinae*, but it is more hagiographic and does not belong to the same genre as does this panegyric. Burrus warns, "The persistent dubbing of Gregory of Nyssa's *Life of Macrina* as the first female hagiography effectively erases Nazianzen's fraternal tribute from the history of female lives."[12] The funeral orations of Gregory's two siblings predate *De Vita Macrinae* and therefore must be analyzed in light of their influence on Nazianzen's developing theological thought. Burris suggests that "female hagiography is more helpfully understood not as the legitimate Christian daughter of biography (or of any other genre) but rather as the collective effect of particular intertextual practices that transgress boundaries between genres promiscuously, producing a field of texts at once complexly overlapped and intricately differentiated."[13] It is in this complex overlap that we again discover intersections between Cappadocian theology and life experience.

The Cappadocian fathers had known similar life experiences when it came to significant women in their lives. It was these women who would become role models for their theological thought. Nazianzen became a great leader in the church of his day and is remembered in the Eastern Church as the "Theologian."[14] His path frequently crossed with Basil of Caesarea and his family. Nazianzen spent time with the entire family at Annesi, and the two families became intertwined. The nurture and care of Basil, Nyssen and Nazianzen by strong women in environments that allowed them to flourish to the greatest extent of their potential resulted in the three Cappadocian fathers who would forever be remembered as defenders of Nicene Orthodoxy.

11. Burrus, "Life after Death," 153.

12. Ibid., 154.

13. Ibid., 155.

14. McGuckin, *St. Gregory of Nazianzus*, xxii–xxiii. Here McGuckin comments on the Eastern Church's reference to Gregory as the Theologian, however, he finds that designation to be quite puzzling, since the majority of his works are not "dedicated to his theology proper."

Marriage as a sacrament

Nazianzen honors both Nonna and Gorgonia for their faithfulness in marriage in *Oration* 8. It is in this recognition of the married life, which may be viewed as an alternate path to theosis as compared to virginity, that Nazianzen establishes marriage itself as an analogy for the ultimate goal of theosis, or union with God. Within Orthodoxy the marriage ceremony is seen as a sacrament or a mystery. From a civil perspective, Christians followed Roman order, accepting marriage as "an agreement between two free parties."[15] However, for Christians, there was one major difference. When the consenting parties had both accepted baptism, it was not the ceremony but rather "*who* was accepting the marriage contract. If the parties were Christian, their marriage was a Christian marriage . . . for them, marriage was a sacrament, not simply a legal agreement."[16] It was not until later centuries that the Orthodox Church developed the sacrament of marriage, but it is this sacramental aspect of marriage which begins to take form in Nazianzen. Today the Orthodox marriage ceremony is broken into two segments, the first of which is the betrothal, or exchange of rings. The second portion is the crowning, which is "the sacramental action that makes the wedding truly Christian, truly a means of participating in the life of the heavenly Kingdom."[17] Marriage, according to Meyendorff, is "an entrance into the Kingdom of Christ . . . [where] human love will acquire a totally new dimension by being identified with the love of Christ for His Church."[18] Nazianzen, in his *Oration on Holy Baptism*, spoke to the catechumens, both married and unmarried, acknowledging that both states were acceptable in the Christian life.

> Are you not yet wedded to flesh? . . . You are pure even after marriage. I will take the risk of that. I will join you in wedlock. I will dress the bride. We do not dishonour marriage because we give a higher honour to virginity. . . . Only let marriage be pure and unmingled with filthy lusts.[19]

It is through baptism that one enters into the "realm of eternal life."[20] Therefore, when two individuals who have already entered that realm are

---

15. Meyendorff, *Marriage*, 16.
16. Ibid., 18.
17. Ford and Ford, *Marriage as a Path to Holiness*, xxi.
18. Meyendorff, *Marriage*, 34.
19. Nazianzen, *Or.* 40.18 (PG 36:381b–c) (SC 358) (*NPNF2* 7:256).
20. Meyendorff, *Marriage*, 19.

united together, it becomes a mystery (μυστήριον)[21] placed within the "eternal Kingdom."[22] "The husband becomes one single being, one single 'flesh' with his wife, just as the Son of God ceased to be only the Godself and became *also* man so that the community of His people may also become His Body."[23] It is in this marriage relationship that we see reflected the relationship between Christ and his bride. Nazianzen expresses this connection: "It is well for the wife to reverence Christ through her husband."[24] This theme of marriage is visible throughout the Scriptures where the kingdom of God is compared with a wedding feast, fulfilling "the Old Testament prophetic visions of a wedding between God and Israel, the elected people."[25] Therefore, marriage becomes an analogy for theosis, and Nazianzen is able to apply this to his understanding because of the marriages he has personally witnessed.

Nyssen also speaks out regarding the virtues of married life. While he was rather straightforward in believing that the life of virginity was certainly best, he could also see that there was joy in marriage.

> Truly, what is chiefly sought after in marriage is the joy of living with someone. Grant that this is so, and let the marriage be described as blessed in every respect: good family, sufficient wealth, harmony in age, the very flower of youth, much affection, and, what is divined in each by the other, that sweet rivalry in subduing one's own will in love.[26]

Nyssen has, at times, a rather negative perspective on marriage, but it appears to come more from personal experience. He personally suffered after the death of his young bride. It is this pain which seems to have had an impact on his opinions regarding virginity and marriage. He warns young people, "If only it were quite possible to examine things ahead of time, how frequent would be the race of deserters from marriage to virginity!"[27] These objections seem to stem more from experience than theological analysis. Both Nyssen and Nazianzen express an appreciation for virginity but also believe that theosis is possible for those married and unmarried alike. Nazianzen believes that all are called to a high standard. "Surely, it has been made clear that obedience to the Gospel is required of all of us, both mar-

---

21. Eph 5:32. This terminology for mystery means "sacrament."

22. Meyendorff, *Marriage*, 19.

23. Ibid.

24. Nazianzen *Or.* 37.7 (PG 36:289) (SC 318) (*NPNF2* 7:657).

25. Meyendorff, *Marriage*, 19.

26. Nyssen, *DV* 3 (PG 46:325) (SC 119) (GNO VIII.I) (FC, 13).

27. Ibid.

ried and celibate."[28] Nyssen also clarifies his stance: "Let no one think that, for these reasons, we are disregarding the institution of marriage. We are not ignorant of the fact that this also is not deprived of God's blessing."[29] Not only is marriage not deprived of God's blessing; marriage is a part of God's blessing.

In conversion one's capacity to reflect the divine nature is once again restored: the restoration of Eve

Adam and Eve, presented as the first humans, are a married couple. Before the fall of humanity, they are both presented as being created in the image of God. One could argue, therefore, that this first, prelapsarian marriage relationship reflected God's original intent for humanity. Nyssen argued that the differentiation of the sexes was not God's original intent in creation but that this became necessary because of God's foreknowledge of humanity's sin and the resultant need for procreation.[30] However, that does not preclude a relationship between Adam and Eve which existed before the fall. Nazianzen is the one who applies, with positivity, the language of Eve when describing his mother and his sister. For Nazianzen, Christ is the restored image for all of humankind. Now, he stretches beyond those bounds, again showing his optimistic hope for humanity by presenting two women as the hope of a restored Eve.

For this model of restoration Nazianzen presents both Gorgonia and Nonna as exceptional women. He writes of his mother, Nonna:

> One woman is famed for her domestic labours, another for her grace and chastity, another for her pious deeds and the pains she inflicts on her body, her tears, her prayers, and her charity; but Nonna is renowned for everything, and, if we may call this death, she died while praying.[31]

He remarks: "Our mother, from the beginning and by virtue of descent, consecrated to God and receiving piety as a necessary heritage not for herself alone, but also for her children."[32] She had come from a Christian heritage which Gregory referred to as a "golden chain."[33] She is remembered as

28. Basil, *On Renunciation of the World* (PG 31) (FC, 17).
29. Nyssen, *DV* 7 (PG 46:351) (SC 119) (GNO VIII.I) (FC, 31).
30. Nyssen, *DHO*.
31. Nazianzen, *Epigr.* 31 (*Anthologia Graeca* 8:10) (Paton, LCL).
32. Nazianzen, *Or.* 7.4 (PG 35:758) (SC 406) (FC, 7).
33. Nazianzen, *De vita sua* (PG 37:1029–166), trans. Meehan, 119.

a woman who was deeply devoted to her Christian faith. Schaff refers to her as "one of the noblest Christian women of antiquity, [who] exerted a deep and wholesome influence."[34]

Nazianzen presents Gorgonia as pure and so singularly focused that she "bloomed with virtue alone!"[35] Nazianzen's depiction of Gorgonia's life is similar to that of Nonna's, portraying her as perfection. However, if both Nonna and Gorgonia are to serve as models for restoration of the image as the new Eve, then this portrayal would be justified. These women, as the restored Eve, exemplify the power to overcome the gender and societal roles placed upon them yet living wholeheartedly dedicated to God.

Just as Christ is the second Adam, Nonna and Gorgonia are female figures in whom the image of Christ is restored, and through that restoration, they are able to overcome and set aright what had occurred because of Eve's behavior. "O bitter taste, and Eve, mother of our race and our sin, and deceptive serpent and death—all overcome by her self-mastery!"[36] This "self-discipline" is the praise of Gorgonia who practices a life of virtue, and when the practice of virtues are united with Christ, the result is synergistic. Therefore, Nazianzen can say that they have overcome the serpent and death by their self-discipline, for this is theosis. Nonna and Gorgonia have joined into the kenosis-theosis parabola by being united with Christ, "O emptying of Christ, and form of a servant, and suffering now honoured by this woman's mortification!"[37] The mortifications, or putting to death the things of the flesh, allow them to become for us the new Eve. According to Harrison, "Thus women are freed from Eve's destructive pattern by the Lord's redemptive work as well as by their own free choice."[38] This concept of restoration and perfect reflection of the image permeates Gorgonia's life story:

> There nobility consists in preserving his image and keeping one's likeness to the archetype; there reason and virtue and pure desire, and the gift of knowing whence and who we are and where we are heading, all bring this image to full reality, as they continue to form, on God's own pattern, genuine initiates in the sublime mysteries.[39]

34. Schaff, *History*, 910–11.

35. Nazianzen, *Or.* 8.14 (PG 35:806) (SC 406), trans. Daley, 70.

36. Ibid., 70–71.

37. Ibid., 71.

38. Harrison, *Male and Female*, 465.

39. Nazianzen, *Or.* 8.6 (PG 35:795) (SC 406), trans. Daley, 66.

Therefore, Nazianzen presented Gorgonia as one who understood the goal or *telos* of humanity and that is deification. It was within the process of deification that both Nonna and Gorgonia became, for Nazianzen, restored women and the new Eve. This speaks to the hope and potential for women who are in the process of deification.

Nyssen's concept of apokatastasis takes us beyond this human life in the final and ultimate restoration. Frances Young praises Nyssen's ability to recognize that in the apokatastasis humanity will return to its original androgynous nature. Therefore, it provides "justification for a discourse of gender consistency which points to gender transcendence; and gender transcendence permits the soul to be patterned on the model of Mary, both fecund and virgin."[40] The Cappadocian Marian texts are but a few, as compared to the number of texts dealing with the women in their families. The majority of the Marian texts are placed within the theological debates against Apollinarianism, and specifically deal with her role in the incarnation.[41] This does not negate the fact that the Cappadocians', and specifically Nyssen's, "discourse genuinely transcends gender, so that gender discourse is fluid and reversible, always pointing beyond itself."[42] The individual is always reaching higher to the eventual apokatastasis and the end of gender differentiation. Therefore, female role models are not just models for women, but for men and women alike.

Børtnes poses an important question, "How can embodied human beings be *eikons* of a godhead situated beyond all creation?"[43] In other words, how can Nazianzen utilize his mother and sister as *eikons* for restored female humanity? His rationale is found in the Cappadocians' understanding of image as a reflection of the original. Nazianzen utilizes himself as an *eikon*, the concept of which is transferable to the women.

> With these words he took a portion of the new-formed earth and established with his immortal hands my shape, bestowing upon it a share of his own life. He infused Spirit, which is a fragment of the Godhead without form. From dust and breath I was formed, a mortal man *eikon* of the immortal.[44]

40. Young, "Sexuality and Devotion."

41. Gambero, *Mary and the Fathers of the Church*, 142.

42. Young, "Sexuality and Devotion," 93.

43. Børtnes, "Rhetoric and Mental Images," 55.

44. Nazianzen, *Carm. 1.1.8.70–77*, prose trans. Sykes: St. Gregory of Nazianzus, *Poemata Arcana*, 37, modified and adjusted to the verses of the original by Børtnes, "Rhetoric and Mental Images," 53–54.

Nazianzen views himself as an *eikon* of the *eikon*, or the "mortal image of the immortal."[45] Nonna and Gorgonia have become the *eikon*s of the image of God in the female, since that *eikon* has been corrupted in Eve. While modern feminism seeks to find female role models and struggle with the male representation of a savior, it appears that Nazianzen had already bridged this gap in the fourth century. It is this bridge toward women which leads one to recognize the considerable influence of Nazianzen's women on his life, both personal and spiritual.

Prelapsarian marriage

In both Nonna and Gorgonia, we find examples of what may have been considered nontraditional marriage relationships. While Nazianzen had high regard and respect for virginity, one can see that he sees in his sister a model for one who was able to combine the best of both worlds.

Most people distinguish two patterns of living, marriage and celibacy, and consider the latter higher and more divine, but also more laborious and dangerous, and think the former less exalted but safer; she escaped the negative aspect of both states, and succeeded in garnering from both all that is best. She was able to bring both together in a single life—the loftiness of the one, the safety of the other—and to become chaste without becoming proud; she mingled the beauty of celibacy with marriage, and showed that neither of them binds us completely to God or to the world, or completely separates us from them, in such a way that one should be utterly shunned because of what it is, or the other unreservedly praised.[46]

We have seen previously that the Cappadocians considered virginity to be not only physical but also a state of mind or an attitude to which an individual might gravitate. "The mind, rather, must be the good supervisor of both marriage and virginity, and both must be arranged and moulded into virtue by the craft of reason."[47] Therefore, while a woman may be married, her focus or *telos* is on Christ, who is the ultimate head of her life. This is Nazianzen's representation of the new Eve. Fallen humanity had placed the wife in a subordinate position to the husband. Nazianzen's position is seen in contrast with understanding the headship of the husband as found in Eph 5:23, "For the husband is the head of the wife just as Christ is the head of the church, the body of which he is the Savior." The problem is the way in which humanity has distorted this headship, which has resulted in

45. Børtnes, "Rhetoric and Mental Images," 55.

46. Nazianzen, *Or.* 8.8 (PG 35:798) (SC 406), trans. Daley, 66–67.

47. Ibid., 67.

the husband becoming "a source of oppression and division."[48] Nazianzen represents this earthly headship as one which must come under the authority of the heavenly bridegroom within Christian marriages which reflect the restored image. Nyssen confirms this: "Thus, it is necessary for us, to move our bodies in accordance with the true Head towards every action and undertaking, wherever 'He that formed the eye' or 'He who shaped the ear'[49] leads. Moreover, since the Head looks 'to the things above,' it is entirely necessary for the members being in harmony with him to follow his lead and to be inclined to the things above."[50] Therefore, the picture is of a man and woman who are equal under Christ, but in marriage, the woman is under the man but does not have to go through the man to Christ.[51] Nazianzen utilizes the marriages of both Nonna and Gorgonia as examples of this type of understanding of headship.

The marriages of Nonna and Gorgonia did not fit the model of what has been defined as a Christian marriage. At the time of their marriages, neither of their husbands were baptized. Here we see Nonna juxtaposed against Eve. Eve, who was to have been a partner to her husband, a yoke-fellow, traded the relationship with her husband for "knowledge from the tree of life."[52] Nonna, however, instead of being the one to lead her husband to destruction, led him to salvation. When she married, her husband was not a Christian, but rather, from the sect of the hypsistarians,[53] who worshiped one being.[54] It was through her devotion to Christ and the virtue of prayer that he eventually converted to Christianity.[55] Gorgonia followed the example of her mother.

> For when she was joined to the flesh, she was not, by that same
> action, separated from the spirit; nor, because she looked on her
> husband as her head, did she disregard our chief head. Rather,
> after paying service for a little while to the world and to nature,
> as far as the law of flesh—or rather, as far as the one who gave

48. Ford and Ford, *Marriage as a Path to Holiness*, xxxi.

49. Ps 93:9.

50. Nyssen, *DP* (PG 46:275) (GNO III.I) (FC, 113).

51. Albrecht, *Das Leben der heiligen Makrina*, 219.

52. Nazianzen, *Or.* 18.8 (PG 35:993) (FC, 120).

53. Ibid., 18.5 (PG 35:989) (FC, 118).

54. Schaff, *History*, 910–11, see also Nazianzen, *Or.* 18.5, where Nazianzen gives greater detail in regard to the Hypsistarii and their worship.

55. Nazianzen, *Or.* 18.4 (PG 35:989) (FC, 117).

flesh its laws—demanded, she then consecrated herself entirely to God.[56]

Gorgonia was able to win over her husband and "gained for herself a virtuous fellow servant, rather than a virtual tyrant."[57]

As Nazianzen reflected on his parents' lives, he saw their relationship as genuinely Christian and as a model of prelapsarian marriage. Their relationship did not fit the bounds of what may have been considered normal by either society or the church. Nazianzen's understanding of the restoration of the image of God, which transcended gender, allowed for the type of partnered relationship he saw between his parents. "For the best in men and women was so united so that their marriage was more of a union of virtue than of bodies. Although they surpassed all others, they themselves were so evenly matched in virtue that they could not surpass each other."[58] For both Nonna and her husband, Gregory, the entire goal and focus of their lives was transformation into the image, and this *telos* usurped all else. Gregory and Nonna became a reflection of the restored marriage relationship.

> But she who was given by God to my father became not only his helper,—for this would be less wonderful,—but also a leader, personally guiding him by deed and word to what was most excellent. Although she deemed it best, in accordance with the law of marriage, to be overruled by her husband in other respects, she was not ashamed to show herself his master in piety . . . While beauty, natural as well as artificial, is wont to be a source of pride and glory to other women, she is one who has ever recognized only one beauty, that of the soul, and the preservation and, to the best of her power, the purification of the divine image in her soul.[59]

According to Harrison this example of Nonna "is particularly interesting because she is not represented as an obedient wife in contrast to insubordinate Eve."[60] Rather, she is portrayed as a wife who, in obedience to Christ, was willing, at times, to lead her husband. Nazianzen had said the same for Gorgonia.[61] As spouses, the couples were able to serve together as

56. Ibid., 8.8 (PG 35:798), trans. Daley, 67.

57. Ibid.

58. Ibid., 18.7 (PG 35:992) (FC, 120).

59. Ibid., 18.8 (PG 35:993) (FC, 121).

60. Harrison, *Male and Female*, 464.

61. Nazianzen, *Or.* 8.8 (PG 35:798).

equal partners, adjusting their roles in the circumstances of life, for whatever drew them on to deification was considered the highest authority.

Finally, it is in the presentation of Gorgonia as the new woman of Prov 31 that we find Nazianzen's completed picture of God's original intent for a woman in marriage. Gorgonia becomes a combination of the woman of Proverbs mixed with the New Testament picture found in Titus 2:4–5. According to Nazianzen, she outstrips the woman of Prov 31, for after he praises her in the areas described, he goes on to say, "To praise my sister for such activities, I would be praising the statue on the basis of its shadows, or the lion on the basis of its claws, and be missing the greater, more perfect things."[62] Gorgonia is depicted as loving and caring for her household as well as for her husband, but all of this built upon the foundation of Nazianzen's understanding of deification.[63] Her reach went far beyond her own home, and being recognized as a wise woman, she counselled even men. The men of the community "accepted her advice and exhortation as absolute law."[64] Nazianzen referred to her words as being "sagacious" (συνετώτερον).[65] She had become the ideal wife, and the new Eve, a woman who was just as comfortable in the home as she was being an equal partner with the men of her world, and all of this was possible by placing her life within the framework and understanding of theosis.

The practice of virtue

Not only does Gorgonia represent the perfect, prelapsarian wife, but Nazianzen also utilizes her as the role model for the practice of virtue for men and women. He speaks of her strength, "O woman's nature, defeating that of men in our common struggle for salvation, proving that female and male are differences of body, not of soul!"[66] Again, we see a reaffirmation of the

62. Ibid., 8.9 (PG 35:798), trans. Daley, 67.

63. Albrecht, *Das Leben der heiligen Makrina*, 220. See also Nazianzen *Or.* 8.11 (PG 35:801). Gorgonia presents herself to God "as a living temple." Albrecht says that Gorgonia is the ideal wife (Titus 2:4–5 and Prov 31) mixed with "Hellenistic moral philosophy." However, I would argue that what Albrecht is referring to as this philosophy, is actually the Cappadocians' Christianized view of deification. Also see *Or.* 8.23, trans. Daley, 75: "The light of the Trinity, which no longer eludes a mind bound and diffused by the senses but is contemplated as a whole by the whole mind, grasping us now and letting its radiance illumine our souls with the full light of the godhead. Now you enjoy all the things which, while yet on earth, you possessed only in distant distillations, through the clarity of your instinct for them."

64. Nazianzen, *Or.* 8.11 (PG 35:801), trans. Daley, 68–69.

65. Ibid.

66. Ibid., 8.14 (PG 35:806), trans. Daley, 70.

location of the image, not in the physical nature of male and female but rather imprinted on the soul of humanity. The hope of salvation was equal for men and for women; therefore, the Cappadocians could use female figures as illustrations for both genders.

A very important feature in deification for the Cappadocians was the role that the individual played in the process. This has become a rather controversial aspect of their theological position. As we have seen in the *Fallen Virgin*, God never turns his back on humanity. In essence, this represents the grace of God ever reaching out and searching for lost humanity. However, the question is raised as to the role of human response in this process, and this has led to a debate in the last half century regarding Gregory of Nyssa's understanding of grace and human will.[67] In Nyssen we find the synergy of God and people not only in the initial process of salvation or turning toward God but also in the process of deification. The goal, as far as God and people were concerned, was to become like God and to be a reflection of God on earth. However, this did not come about by the action of God alone, but rather by the interaction of God and the human. The responsibility of humanity was to imitate Christ and, in doing so, to become more like him. Therefore, the capacity to reflect the divine image is restored in salvation, but the quality of that reflection becomes dependent upon the effort which one puts into the process of deification. This is why the Cappadocians have, at times, been labelled semi-Pelagians.[68] One must bear in mind the Eastern understanding of grace, and ontology. The grace of God continuously reaches out to humanity in a desire to draw humans back into the original image. When the relationship between the human and God is restored, the grace of God continues to draw the human, in a proleptic manner, toward the image. Therefore, as the person practices virtues, there is a synergistic reaction between God and people. In essence, the human steps into the flow of God's grace and as he or she practices the virtues, he or she is being eternally drawn toward the *telos*, which is theosis. Knight tells us, "Cappadocian theology brings about an ontological revolution. It is the revolution which dissolves Hellenistic metaphysics and generates a genuine Christian understanding of reality . . . in which the fall is to be understood as subjection to slavery under nature and the depersonalization of humanity."[69] It is the

---

67. For an extensive discussion on this debate, see Ludlow, *Gregory of Nyssa*, locations 1515–63.

68. Jaeger, *Two Rediscovered Works*, 87–98, refers to this as being anachronistic, considering Pelagianism appeared at a later date. Meyendorff, *Christ in Eastern Christian Thought*, 124, argues that historically any attempt to place an Eastern understanding of grace into a Western or Protestant model is futile.

69. Knight, *Theology of John Zizioulas*, 88.

freedom which one experiences by having the image restored, which allows the human to become once again truly human. Human freedom allows us to be an imitator of Christ. Nyssen said, "For the aim of the life of virtue is to become like God; and this is the reason why the virtuous take great pains to cultivate purity of soul and freedom from the passions, so that the form, as it were, of transcendent Being might be revealed in them because of their more perfect life."[70]

The women continued to be a resource for the Cappadocians when it came to understanding the practice of virtues. Nazianzen presents Gorgonia's spiritual transformation as gradual. The process of deification included ever-increasing participation in God, which would include a gradual process throughout one's lifetime, leading to the final consummation of the relationship with the bridegroom. This meant that the reflection of the image in the life of the individuals would continue to grow and develop throughout their lifetimes, as they became more and more like God. Nazianzen tells us that Gorgonia practiced the virtues, which included a life of piety, in an effort to get to know God on a higher level.[71] She had been raised in a home where both of her parents were models of piety and "she was in no respect behind them in virtue."[72] She was a woman who had a full knowledge of "the things of God . . . both from the divine Scriptures, and from her own wisdom."[73]

Gorgonia's desire was that the image would be reflected in her life; therefore, one of the practices of virtue had to do with her outward appearance. She did not want anything about her outward appearance to be a distraction from the image. This meant that she did not dress or make herself up as some of the women of the day. Those who dressed with "blond braids" which were not modestly in "spirals of curls" and who wore "flowing, diaphanous robes" and adorned themselves with "the glitter of stones," Nazianzen equated with harlots.[74] When one looked upon a woman, one was to see the image of God and not the image of a harlot, for the image of God was, in Nazianzen's mind, true humanity and beauty. Nazianzen responded: "setting forth the divine form as an idol of shame by the honors he bestows, setting forth the divine form as an idol of lewdness for hungry eyes, so that spurious beauty might steal away the natural image meant for God, and for the age to come."[75] The beauty of the bride was to be saved for the

---

70. Nyssen, CC, Homily 9 (PG 44:960d–961c) (GNO VI), trans. Musurillo, 226.

71. Nazianzen, Or. 8.11 (PG 35:801).

72. Ibid., trans. Daley, 68.

73. Ibid.

74. Ibid., 8.10 (PG 35:800), trans. Daley, 68.

75. Ibid.

bridegroom; therefore the woman who was desiring theosis, was to adorn herself for God alone, and not for this world.

The life of virtue was one in which you were not to seek the luxuries of this world. Nyssen said, "*A paradise of pomegranates* to the souls of those who are attentive, teaches us that we ought never to grow soft in the indulgence and luxury of this life, but that we should choose the way of life that has become hardened by continence."[76] For the women related to the Cappadocians, this was a challenge, for they were all quite wealthy. Therefore, putting aside the life of luxury for a life of continence meant a radical change in their lifestyle. Nazianzen praised Gorgonia for not surrendering to luxury but instead practicing spiritual discipline, including a restrained appetite and long periods of fasting.[77] However, just as Nyssen had warned, she did not give herself over to extremes, and continued to allow herself the benefit of adequate and good sleep.[78] She showed discipline by reading and singing the Psalter, studying the Divine oracles, bending her knees as the tears flowed and as her prayers rose heavenward.[79]

Virtues—prayer

While Nazianzen gave his sister Gorgonia high praise in terms of her practice of virtue, he also recognized the example of his mother Nonna. The practices of virtue are the same for all, men, women, married and virgins, and according to Nazianzen, Nonna is the ornament of her sex and "not only simply ornaments, but also patterns of virtue."[80] While the practice of all virtues is important for spiritual development, it appears that prayer plays a unique role. Nonna seems to excel in the practice of prayer, and Nazianzen utilizes her as a pattern. Many of Nazianzen's numerous epigrams devoted to his mother "concentrate on the favored manner of her death, in mid-prayer, in church."[81] As one moves on to higher levels in deification one becomes more intense in the practice of virtues, and ever-increasing participation in God. Nazianzen utilized his mother's life of piety as an example. "Just as the sun strikes the earth most pleasantly with its morning rays and becomes hotter and more brilliant at midday, so she, who from the beginning showed

76. Nyssen, *CC*, Homily 9 (PG 44:969b–972a) (GNO VI), trans. Musurillo, 232.

77. Nazianzen, *Or.* 8.13 (PG 35:804).

78. Ibid. Some of the more severe ascetics had given themselves to either sleeping on a board, or spending the "night erect."

79. Nazianzen, *Or.* 8.13 (PG 35:804).

80. Ibid., 8.5 (PG 35:793), trans. Daley, 66.

81. Beagon, "Cappadocian Fathers," 171–72.

marked indications of piety, shone later with a brighter light."[82] That "fuller light" gave final expression through her death, where Nazianzen referred to her transformation as "God-like."[83] Nazianzen attributed this transformation in his mother to the long hours she had spent in prayer. He described her behavior: "'Thy prayers and the groans thou didst love, and sleepless nights, and the floor of the church bedewed with tears procured for thee, divine Nonna."[84] Nazianzen was able to utilize Nonna, revealing that the impetus to practice good deeds or virtue was not motivated by a desire to be a better person, but because of "love of God and Christ."[85] He stated that she had "received virtue as her patrimony."[86] Here again we see language which Nazianzen utilizes to illustrate the synergistic activity of God and humanity in the process of deification. Nonna's patrimony, or inheritance, from the Father was virtue. It was not something she simply willed or desired; rather, it was a gift from God. In return, the gift inspired her to a life of virtue in which she imitated Christ; therefore, she ascended to higher heights in her quest for the *telos*.

Nazianzen presented Nonna's prayer life as her crowning virtue, and as such gave illustrations of its efficacy. If one were to experience ever-increasing participation in God, then there were to be God-like results to prayer. Nyssen reminds that the grace of God seeks after those who are lost. Through her prayer life, Nonna's participation in God appeared to have included participation in this grace which seeks the lost. Beagon considers Nonna's greatest accomplishment the conversion of her husband.[87] She could not bear being unequally yoked, and therefore, according to Nazianzen:

> Therefore, she prostrated herself before God day and night and besought Him with many fastings and tears for the salvation of her husband, and zealously devoted herself to her husband, and strove to win him in various ways, by reproaches, admonitions, attentions, estrangements, and most of all by her own character and fervent piety, by means of which the soul is especially swayed and softened and willingly constrained to virtue. It was inevitable that the drop of water, constantly striking the rock,

---

82. Nazianzen, *Or.* 18.11 (PG 35:997) (FC, 124).

83. Nazianzen, *Epigr.* 36 (*Anthologia Graeca* 8:12) (Paton, LCL).

84. Ibid., 39 (*Anthologia Graeca* 8:12–13) (Paton, LCL).

85. Nazianzen, *Or.* 18.11 (PG 35:997) (FC, 124).

86. Ibid.

87. Beagon, "Cappadocian Fathers," 171–72.

should hollow it out and in time accomplish its purpose, as the sequel shows.[88]

After years of prayer and prodding, the elder Gregory finally was baptized and soon thereafter became the bishop of Nazianzus.[89]

Nonna's prayers were efficacious in the case of not only Nazianzen's father, but also in Nazianzen's own life and that of his siblings. He creates a comparison between God reaching out to lost humanity and a human, his mother, united with God in reaching the lost. Nonna was able to raise children who were committed to a life of virtue, and she became renowned for being the "mother of pious children."[90] Earlier in life Nonna suffered from infertility, and Nazianzen credited his very existence to his mother's prayer life. Nazianzen equated Nonna with Hannah, who bore a son, but gave him away "to be a holy servant in the temple."[91] The results of her prayers were twofold: bringing about his birth but also drawing him into his life calling.[92]

The inheritance for Nazianzen included a life of ministry. Nonna had, in prayer, dedicated her son to God's service. Nazianzen again presents his mother as participating in God's grace, drawing him back toward the intended purpose in his life, which was ministry. However, as a young man he was not interested in a life of virtue or ministry. He literally ran away from home and his mother. Nazianzen utilized this situation to demonstrate Nonna's ever-increasing participation in an infinite God, who is not bound by time and space. While on a journey at sea he faced a terrible storm and possible shipwreck and promised God that he would serve him, if only he would survive.[93] Nazianzen credited Nonna's prayers with bringing him to this moment of crisis in his life and it was in the midst of the "violent storm"[94] that Nonna's prayers were answered. Physical death was not to be feared, but rather spiritual death, and this was his "greater fear"[95] for he had never been baptized.

> My shipmates, in spite of their common danger, joined in my cries as not even many relatives would have done, being kindly strangers who had learned sympathy from their perils. Thus did

---

88. Nazianzen, Or. 18.11 (PG 35:997) (FC, 124).

89. Nazianzen, Epigr. 27 (Anthologia Graeca 8:9) (LCL, 412–13).

90. Ibid., 38 (Anthologia Graeca 8:12) (LCL, 418–19).

91. Ibid., 26 (Anthologia Graeca 8:9) (LCL, 412–13). Ibid., 79, 80 (Anthologia Graeca 8:20–21) (LCL, 434–35).

92. Nazianzen, De vita sua (PG 37:1029–66), trans. Meehan, 437–50.

93. Ibid., trans. Meehan, 195–202.

94. Nazianzen, Or. 18.31 (PG 35:1024) (FC, 140).

95. Ibid.

I suffer, and my parents suffered with me, sharing my danger which became known to them in a dream. And they brought help from the land, calming the waves by prayer, as afterward we learned upon reckoning the time when I returned home. . . . Another one of my fellow voyagers . . . thought he saw my mother walk upon the sea and seize the ship and with no great effort draw it to land. And this vision was believed. As a result of that peril, we ourselves became an offering. We promised ourselves to God if we were saved, and, on being saved, we gave ourselves to Him.[96]

No longer does Nazianzen simply hint at Nonna's uniting with Christ, but rather in this illustration, Nonna takes the place of Christ in a story from the New Testament. Through her participation in God, through Christ, it is Nonna who is seen walking on the water coming to save her son and all of those on the ship. As Nonna represents Christ reaching out to lost humanity, those on the ship are saved both physically and spiritually.

Nonna practiced other virtues besides prayer, and Nazianzen continued to utilize his mother and sister as role models for the life of piety. Just as Christ had served the poor, one imitating Christ was to serve the poor. Nazianzen presented his mother, who had been wealthy, as stripping herself of wealth "for God and the poor."[97] He also valued the virtue of hospitality and his sister Gorgonia was an example of one who would open her home and minister to others, being sympathetic to the poor and liberal to those in want.[98] Nazianzen encouraged the practice of reverence in the presence of God through the example of his mother. "She honoured the sanctuary by her silence, that she never turned her back upon the holy table, not spat upon the hallowed pavement, that she never grasped the hand nor kissed the lips of any pagan woman, however honourable in other respects and however closely related."[99] It is in this final statement that one may find the perfect facade of Nonna crumbling, or perhaps a bit of her true humanity being revealed. Nonna would have considered her in-laws as heathen. Raymond Van Dam comments, "This attempt to transform Nonna's obstinate piety into a virtue was perhaps a veiled admission that she had been unwilling to demonstrate a proper deference to her new mother-in-law and her other in-laws."[100] Little more is said on the subject, and we are left to wrestle with

---

96. Ibid. (FC, 141).
97. Ibid., 18.8 (PG 35:993) (FC, 121).
98. Ibid., 8.12 (PG 35:801).
99. Ibid., 18.10 (PG 35:996) (FC, 122).
100. Van Dam, *Families and Friends*, 88.

whether this was an act of piety or rather a moment in which Nazianzen allows us to see the real Nonna and not just the *deified* version.

While Nazianzen extolled many of Nonna's virtues, we return to the greatest virtue for which Nonna was known, and that was prayer. "Another of the saints might vie with the other good works of Nonna; let it be allowed to one to vie with the extent of her prayers."[101] Nonna left the world behind and flew to her beloved Christ, where her passion for prayer and intercession continued and she took on a new role, "and now from heaven she prays aloud for mortals."[102] She is now standing in the presence of her Bridegroom and "prays in the home of the blest."[103]

Conclusions

Nazianzen broke barriers when he utilized these married women as illustrations of theosis. The kenosis of Christ, his assumption of human nature, made it possible for humanity to be restored to its original nature. Nonna and Gorgonia became the avenue by which Gregory could portray the restored human nature. Specifically, he equated them with Eve and placed them in the role of the new Eve, providing an example for women in marriage and life in general. While they were living examples for the women of his time, he saw them as crossing the gender gap, at times rising above the stereotype of their gender, and becoming perfected templates for men and women alike. They were examples because they practiced a life of virtue. In conversion, their capacity to reflect the divine nature had been restored, but the intensity of the image grew when seen through the lens of a life of virtue. Transformation occurred in the lives of both of these women as they imitated Christ.

This transformation led humanity to the final goal—to be united with Christ. In the funeral oration for Gorgonia, she became a representative for all of humanity, male and female, celibate and married. Somehow Nazianzen wrapped all of these figures into his sister, so in her story, all of humanity can find themselves in the process of theosis. Gorgonia, while living here on this earth, was already a "partaker in the mysteries of life eternal."[104] She gave everything that she had in service to God, and when she died, she left nothing here on this earth because "she dedicated all on high."[105]

101. Nazianzen, *Epigr.* 56 (*Anthologia Graeca* 8:16) (LCL, 426–27).

102. Ibid., 35 (*Anthologia Graeca* 8:11–12) (LCL, 416–17).

103. Ibid., 66 (*Anthologia Graeca* 8:18) (LCL, 428–29).

104. Ibid., 101 (*Anthologia Graeca* 8:25) (LCL, 444–45).

105. Ibid., 102 (*Anthologia Graeca* 8:25) (LCL, 444–45).

Nonna too passed from this earth, and Nazianzen presented a portrait of her transformation. After her death, he wrote more than fifty epigrams in honor of his mother. In *Epigram* 26 Nazianzen expresses his grief at the loss of his mother: "How are Nonna's goodly knees relaxed, how are her lips closed, why sheds she not fountains from her eyes?"[106] The virtue of prayer had become the normal state for Nonna in a life of wholehearted devotion to the Lord and daily sacrifice.[107] The result of this activity was the *telos* for all of humanity, theosis. In her final moments, Nonna had taken "to her bosom the great Christ,"[108] having "laid aside there her body."[109] This is Nazianzen's description of the union which awaited those who had lived a life of virtue and had always longed for the "heavenly life."[110] Her life of virtue led to purity and she became "one of the guardians of her sex." In her death she was not only united with Christ, but she shared in the "glory of the pious women, Susanna, Mary and the two Annas."[111]

These two women exemplified theosis for Nazianzen, specifically in his understanding of restoration and transformation through virtue. The goal for humanity was to be lifted to higher levels, which included incessant transformation and ever-increasing participation in God, with the resultant apokatastasis, or restoration of all things. The best path for this was to become a bride of Christ. Nonna and Gorgonia are presented as married women who transcended the barrier of marriage and were able to, in the end, become brides of Christ.

---

106. Ibid., 26 (*Anthologia Graeca* 8:9) (LCL, 412–13).

107. Ibid., 51 (*Anthologia Graeca* 8:15) (LCL, 422–23).

108. Ibid., 27 (*Anthologia Graeca* 8:9) (LCL, 412–13). See also *Epigr.* 29, where he states, "but Nonna the bearer of Christ."

109. Ibid., 27 (*Anthologia Graeca* 8:9) (LCL, 412–13).

110. Ibid., 32 (*Anthologia Graeca* 8:11) (LCL, 414–15).

111. Ibid., 28 (*Anthologia Graeca* 8:10) (LCL, 412–13). Here he is referring to Hannah the mother of Samuel, Anna from Luke 2:36, Mary the mother of Jesus, and Susanna, one of the wealthy women who sponsored Jesus in Luke 8:2.

CHAPTER 7

Macrina, the Perfect Virgin Bride

WHILE GORGONIA AND NONNA became, for the Cappadocians, and specifically Nazianzen, examples of married women becoming brides of Christ, it is Nyssen who describes the greatest bride, his virgin sister Macrina. In an endeavor to make this mystical union with Christ comprehensible and possibly palatable, Gregory utilizes his sister Macrina as his model. While in *De Vita Macrinae* the entire kenosis-theosis parabola exists, it is in Nyssen's portrayals of the more mature years of her life that we find represented the stages five and six, the final two stages of theosis: (5) The Christian life becomes one of "incessant transformation into the likeness of God as man stretches out with the divine infinity,"[1] and (6) Throughout this journey there is an "ever-greater participation in God."[2] These become the climax of the spiritual journey for those who are being *deified*. Because of the Cappadocians' emphasis on purity of heart through asceticism, it is in Nyssen's hagiographic document *De Vita Macrinae* that we discover their perfected blueprint of the life of theosis. Macrina's life will be explored in terms of the kenosis-theosis parabola and the importance of her journey through incessant transformation to becoming the bride of Christ. Her life as a virgin becomes representative for men and women, all of whom may become brides through acts of virtue, resulting in participation in God. Finally, the life of the virgin and bride in Nyssen's *Commentary on the Song of Songs* will be explored as the *telos* for Christian life. While the purity of Macrina, the virgin, makes her the unsullied example of the virgin bride of Christ, the positive influence of the marriages which the Cappadocians had witnessed first-hand caused them to appreciate the imagery found in Song of Songs. While at first glance, the book may be of a controversial nature because of the descriptions of human sexual desire, it becomes for the Cappadocians the ideal image of the final stages of deification. Humanity is

1. Nyssen, *DVMo*, trans. Malherbe and Ferguson, 12.
2. Ibid.

to participate wholly and intimately in God, and Nyssen's sister Macrina, as the bride of Christ, illustrates that final purpose.

Song of Songs

Macrina provided for Nyssen an example of what it meant for one to become involved in incessant transformation and ever-increasing participation in God with the goal of becoming the bride of Christ. It is this bridal imagery which brings us to the apex of the goal. While there is ever-increasing participation in Christ, which is seen in Macrina's earthly life, her life becomes one of continuous preparation for the final consummation as she becomes a bride of Christ. For Nyssen, this is the pinnacle of the Christian life. Not only does he utilize Macrina for this model, but his *Commentary on the Song of Songs* becomes a rather explicit representation of this life of holiness which becomes overwhelmed with desire for the holy lover. Love for the bridegroom becomes the central feature for one pursuing theosis, and the Cappadocians, and specifically Nyssen, see the placement of the Song of Songs as crucial to understanding the spiritual life as one of ascent, and the final unity with Christ. The Cappadocians' heritage, which was received from Origen, provided them with an ability to recognize the allegorical nature of the Scriptures. At the council of Jamnia, Rabbi Aqiba stated, "The whole world is not worth the day on which the Song of Songs was given to Israel, for all the Scriptures are holy, but the Song of Songs is the Holy of Holies."[3] It is this response which allows us to see the Song of Songs in "metaphorical language [which] could be taken to refer to something other than its surface-meaning."[4] For Nyssen the metaphorical or allegorical reading of Song of Songs defines his understanding of the final stages of deification. It is in this marriage that one becomes involved in incessant transformation and ever-increasing participation in God, through Christ, the bridegroom. All three of the Fathers had experienced excellent examples of earthly marriage in the homes in which they were raised. Marriage, for them was a relationship in which two individuals were bound together deeply by love, and the resulting relationship was one in which each individual became more than he or she could have been without the other. Therefore, it is not uncharacteristic for them to view marriage to Christ as the ultimate goal of theosis.

Origen deeply influenced the Cappadocians and wrote a commentary on the Song of Songs. Nyssen would have been familiar with this work.

3. Pope, *Song of Songs*, 19.
4. Young, "Sexuality and Devotion," 84.

Origen's commentary is "among the most influential works in the formation of patristic and Byzantine spirituality."[5] This commentary became a "central text in Christian asceticism,"[6] doing so "precisely because it lent itself so well to a series of allegorical interpretations whereby it could be made to refer to the Christian soul and its relation with God."[7] He writes that this book is "a marriage-song, which Solomon wrote in the form of a drama and sang under the figure of the bride, about to wed and burning with heavenly love towards her bridegroom, who is the Word of God. And deeply indeed did she love him, whether we take her as the soul made in his image, or as the church."[8] Origen warns that this book is not for those who have just begun their spiritual journey but rather for those who have come to a place of maturity. Just as young children do not experience romantic love, so also the young and immature in their faith would not be able to comprehend the mysteries of this book.[9] For Origen it was the soul of the individual, which is neither male nor female, which would be instilled with "the love of things divine and heavenly."[10] He goes on to explain that God uses for his purposes "the figure of the Bride and Bridegroom, and teaches us that communion with God must be attained by paths of charity and love."[11]

Men and women as brides

Nyssen built on Origen's understanding, and the result was that by using the metaphor of the bride and the bridegroom, all of humanity would take on femaleness, specifically, relating to the bride. Therefore, utilizing Macrina as a model was a theological message not just to women but to all men and women hoping to be united with Christ in the *eschaton*. As a result, all of humanity could view themselves as brides. Harrison comments on Nyssen's *Seventh Homily on the Song of Songs*, believing that for Nyssen "the names 'mother' and 'father' have the same meaning because there is neither male

5. Cameron, "Sacred and Profane Love," 11. See on this Harrison, "Allegory and Eroticism." Gregory *allegorized* the expression of conjugal love which he found in the Song of Songs, because it was "pastorally inapplicable in its literal sense." But the desire felt by the ascetic is real; see 123 on the concept of desire in Gregory of Nyssa's interpretation of the Song of Songs, and 124: the "essential work of the ascetic" is the redirection of energy away from bodily pleasure and toward God.

6. Cameron, "Sacred and Profane Love," 11.

7. Ibid.

8. Origen, *Homily on the Song of Songs*, trans. Lawson, 21.

9. Ibid., 22.

10. Ibid., 41.

11. Ibid.

nor female in the divine nature. Citing Gen 1:27 and Gal 3:28, he adds that in the *eschaton*, when all are one in Christ, the gender distinction will be absent in the human nature as well."[12] Nyssen goes as far as to say, "So too Paul is a bride, who imitated the virtues of his Bridegroom and took as a model for his life that eternal Beauty; he compounded his spikenard from the fruits *of the spirit*, from *charity, joy, peace*, and all others,[13] saying he was *the good odour of Christ*."[14] The goal for all of humanity was to become a bride.

Often it has been argued that the Song of Songs is an allegorical picture representing Christ and the church, who becomes his bride. If this is so, then how can one individual, Macrina, be a model? Francis Young views Origen's understanding of the soul on two levels, one being the "wisdom and understanding that comes through Christ. This is granted to the Church and also to the individual believer, the latter both receiving from the Church and in a sense representing the Church."[15] Therefore, this imagery is in relation to the human soul and to the church, as a whole. According to Young, Nyssen "is often characterized as a mystic, and his exegesis of the Song tends to focus principally on the individual soul, though the ecclesial dimension found in Origen's work is so subtly interwoven one should really speak of deeper integration: the story of 'everyman' is the story of the human race, and the spiritual journey of the believer is that of the Church."[16] Therefore, the love story contained in the Song of Songs is for all of Christianity, both singularly and collectively. It is this *Commentary* which draws us to Macrina, the virgin sister of Basil and Nyssen, who ultimately becomes the bride of Christ.[17]

---

12. Harrison, "Gender, Generation, and Virginity," 40. See GNO 6.212–13.

13. Gal 5:22.

14. Nyssen, *CC*, Homily 3 (PG 44:824a–825c) (GNO VI), trans. Musurillo, 165. 2 Cor 2:15.

15. Young, "Sexuality and Devotion," 87.

16. Ibid., 91.

17. The commentary is actually dedicated to Olympias, who was recognized as "one of the most outstanding women of the age" (Daniélou , *From Glory to Glory*, 8.) See also Kelly, *Golden Mouth*, 265–68. She is a widow in Constantinople who goes on to serve the church there alongside John Chrysostom. Nyssen could have become acquainted with her while in Constantinople for the council meeting in 381. He would have been twenty-five years her senior, with her only twenty-one years of age of at the time of the council. Therefore, while the document is dedicated to her, Macrina, whose entire life he had experienced and who had already died would have provided the model of the bride, this being written in 389.

Macrina

Of all the women located within the scope of this study, Macrina the Younger is perhaps the most widely known. Within the last half century, she has been examined and her story brought to light because of the documents written by her brother, Gregory. Obviously, Gregory had a purpose in mind when writing *De Vita Macrinae*, which is hagiographic in nature. The second document, *On the Soul and the Resurrection*, provides us with additional information regarding Macrina, the teacher, as the result of a philosophical discussion. Because of these documents, wholly dedicated to her, she has received more attention than the other women, whom we have found to be more hidden in other writings.

Gregory provides introductory material in *De Vita Macrinae* which becomes foundational to our understanding of Macrina and the role which she is intended to play, whether in real life, or within his text. As with all of our women, it is not the intent of this study to determine what might be considered real verses hagiographic. Instead, each woman can be seen to represent a portion of the Cappadocians' theological development and formation. Macrina, therefore, is presented as the model of theosis in the form of a woman whose entire life is spent in preparation for the moment when she will become the bride of Christ. Gregory reveals this to us from the moment that the curtain is drawn on her life. Just moments before she is to give birth, Macrina's mother, Emmelia, is visited by what appears to be an angel who announces what the very nature of this child will be, revealed in the secret name that she is to be given, the name Thecla.

Thecla

Before the arrival of Macrina, third- and fourth-century Cappadocia already had a female virgin who had become a legend and a hero. It was not Mary the Mother of God but rather a woman by the name of Thecla.[18] A shrine had developed in the area of Seleucia, where thousands of pilgrims a year traveled to worship God.[19] This shrine had developed around the site where it is believed that Thecla had concluded her years of ministry and asceticism as a virgin. While contemporary historians may argue the existence of a woman named Thecla, the reality is that by the fourth-century Thecla had become a

---

18. Cameron, "Virginity as Metaphor," 193. Mary, the mother of Jesus, does not gain much traction as a figure until the theological arguments in which she becomes the *Theotokis*, or the "Bearer of God."

19. Davis, *Cult of St. Thecla*, location 397.

legend, enough so that the name had become popular in usage.[20] Therefore, when Emmelia was told that her daughter was to bear this secret name, there were implications involved, for Emmelia would have been raised with these legendary stories.[21] Macrina was not to be called by the name Thecla; however, the use of the secret name was utilized by Nyssen to introduce Macrina and what kind of woman she would become. According to Beagon, "That Macrina should bear this secret name [Thecla] is one indication that Gregory's account is much more than just a biography of his sister."[22] She was to follow "in the tradition of the great virgin saint."[23] This virgin saint had, through her life and legend, become a whole new role model for young Christian women. As a result, Nyssen was establishing Macrina as the new Thecla, building upon the legend of the past and providing a new model for virginity, a life of asceticism and complete devotion to God, leading to transformation and ultimately union with God as his bride.

The Christian life becomes one of incessant transformation into the likeness of God as people stretch out with the divine infinity

As humanity experienced participation with the divine infinity through deification there would be continual transformation in the life of the individual. The result was transformation into the very likeness of God. Interestingly, while Nyssen's language includes that of apokatastasis, while the flesh may experience restoration, the process of deification continues throughout eternity, for humanity is united with an infinite God. The parabola has no end, and the spiritual life never reaches a conclusion. The marriage of the bride to the groom is simply the beginning of a new phase in the relationship which continues to grow and expand throughout eternity. It is into this parabola that we may place Nyssen's Macrina, and she becomes his theological statement on this final phase of life.

Nyssen's purpose in writing *De Vita Macrinae* was to honor his sister but also to represent Macrina as the living model of theosis or deification. He explains his purpose: "Such a life should not be lost sight of in time

---

20. Nazianzen, *Ep.* 56 (PG 37:110–12). See also Nazianzen's *Ep.* 36, *To Thekla*, written in 389, and *Ep.* 37, *Also to Her*. See also *Святитель Григорий Богослов Творения: Том второй*, 453–54. These are other Theclas who were contemporaries of Nazianzen. Also Pederson, *Lost Apostle*, 61, in reference to the practice of naming daughters Thecla.

21. Nyssen, *DVM* (PG 46:960) (SC 178) (GNO VIII.I).

22. Beagon, "Cappadocian Fathers," 168.

23. Smith, "Just and Reasonable Grief," 65.

and, that having raised herself to the highest peak of human virtue through philosophy, she should not be passed over in silence and her life rendered ineffective."[24] There is no attempt in this writing to dissect who the *real* Macrina may have been, or what may be more of a creation of this *hagiography*, for in Nyssen, the purpose is for Macrina's life to illustrate his theology. He presents her entire life as the embodiment of what it meant to be transformed into the image and *likeness* of God. Gregory is cautious in his writing style, wanting to present Macrina as a *spiritual* model and as such he seems to exercise restraint, not quoting a single pagan author.[25] Elm contends, "Macrina's life is conceived as a homogeneous unity reflecting the heroine's continuous progress from the earliest childhood towards her perfection. In Macrina's case, perfection carried a very specific sense: her destiny, the ideal towards which she progressed, was that of a saint."[26] Elm recognizes the holiness of Macrina's life with the goal of sainthood. However, this is not as complete an understanding of the journey as when it is placed within the process of deification. The ideal presented here is truly an expression of the Cappadocians' understanding of theosis, and Macrina's life simply becomes the incarnational model of the kenosis-theosis parabola.

Nyssen, while presenting the human side of the young Macrina, also revealed a girl who was extraordinary from a very young age. She had "responded brilliantly"[27] when given instruction and became "extraordinarily skilled in the working of wool."[28] Evidently, she was also extremely attractive, something that even her brother acknowledged. "The young girl's beauty did not escape notice, although it had been concealed. Nor did there seem to be anything in all the country comparable to her beauty and her loveliness."[29] Because of her beauty, there seemed to be no end of suitors seeking her affection, and finally her father decided it best to arrange a marriage to a "young man in the family known for his moderation, who had recently finished school."[30] Sadly, the young man died before they could be married.

24. Nyssen, *DVM* (PG 46:960) (SC 178) (GNO VIII.I) (FC, 163).

25. Frank, "Macrina's Scar," 521. The significance here is that Gregory himself would have studied the pagan authors and often his writing reflects the use of language and/or rhetoric from the secular age in which he lived and studied. Here, he attempts to present Macrina as pure and untouched by these outside sources.

26. Elm, *"Virgins of God,"* 39.

27. Nyssen, *DVM* (PG 46:962) (SC 178) (GNO VIII.I) (FC, 165).

28. Ibid.

29. Ibid.

30. Ibid. (PG 46:964) (SC 178) (GNO VIII.I) (FC, 166).

The death of this young man became a turning point in Macrina's life. Macrina, still a teen, determined that she would not marry. "She called her father's decision a marriage on the grounds that what had been decided had actually taken place and she determined to spend the rest of her life by herself."[31] The terminology here is very specific, laying the foundation for the type of life which Macrina intended to live and that was "by herself" (ἐφ᾽ἑαητῆς). It is in the use of this phrase that we catch Nyssen's purpose in this document, for this is the language of Plato in reference to one leading the *philosophical* life. Here, again, Nyssen utilizes Macrina as a guide for the life of deification, for his use of language, Christianized through Origen and Nyssen, now represents the desire for a life of virginity. This life, "by herself," is a life of virginity, but it also becomes a life of preparation for another marriage. Macrina's life is presented as one of preparation.[32] She follows the example of Christ, pouring herself out to him in a lifelong commitment of humble service while being transformed into his image here on earth.

Within the family home Macrina gave herself to those around her, including the servants. Elm comments, "Macrina took a conscious step to humble herself considerably before those who were in a position to observe her, and perhaps most of all in her estimation by herself. By baking her mother's bread she engaged in work strictly reserved for slaves."[33] It was a number of years before Macrina and her mother along with their servants, were able to move to Annesi and begin the life together that Macrina had envisioned. When they began that life, Macrina made no distinction between herself and those who had been her servants. "By undertaking a service task Macrina consciously overstepped the rigid boundaries set by her rank and social class, and introduced a new dimension into her life."[34] This attitude of a servant, however, did not mean oppression or repression. Rather, every point of service became a moment of transformation, one in which to share and touch Christ, her future bridegroom.

It is in the imagery of a marital relationship that we can reflect on Macrina's behavior. It was as she grew into this image of Christ that she practiced, in the physical dimension, service to her future Bridegroom. In a very sensual way, as this relationship between Macrina and Christ developed, there were moments of touch. Nyssen describes this interaction with the Word as a kiss. "A kiss is an operation of the sense of touch: in a kiss two pairs of lips touch. There is, however, a spiritual faculty of touch,

31. Ibid.

32. Nyssen, CC, Homily 1 (PG 44:764d–765c) (GNO VI), trans. Musurillo, 153.

33. Elm, "Virgins of God," 46.

34. Ibid.

which comes in contact with the Word, and this is actuated by the spiritual and immaterial sense of touch, as it is said: *Our hands have handled the word of life.*"[35] Macrina's activities were lived out of her passion for the one with whom she was falling in love. As the relationship developed, the two became closer with more frequent moments of touches, or kisses, resulting in Macrina's incessant transformation into the image of her bridegroom.

Throughout this journey there is an "ever-greater participation in God": acts of virtue as participation

Every Cappadocian mother expressed her imitation of Christ through virtue. Acts of virtue were the process in which a human could participate in God. The grace of God drew the individual toward the *telos*, but the acts practiced along the way revealed God's creative abilities as the virtues were unique to the talents, abilities, and social position of each individual. God's original intent for humanity was full participation in God. Through the practice of virtues one could again be restored to that original state which God had intended for true humanity.

In Macrina's case there were particular virtues which made her remarkable; the most unique was her ability to teach. It is in this role as a teacher she took on a virtue traditionally thought as reserved for men. It is in Nyssen's presentation of Macrina's development as a teacher that he again reveals the eschatological hope found in their theology of deification and the fact that social barriers were already being destroyed within the kingdom of God. Macrina had intuitive skills which helped her recognize needs within the household and for her to have an impact on her younger siblings. She had good relationships with her brothers and in most cases, was seen as a peer, and often as their leader. The youngest in the family was a boy named Peter, who was born about the same time as their father's death. Emmelia, their mother, was overcome with the responsibilities of their vast estates as well as the care of the household. Macrina, seeing the need, took Peter, and raised him, leading "him to all the higher education. . . . She became all things to the boy; father, teacher, attendant, mother, the counsellor of every good, . . . [and] he was raised to the high goal of philosophy."[36] Gregory himself mentioned that she had been his "teacher in all things."[37] On her deathbed, Macrina continued in the role of teacher to her siblings,

---

35. Nyssen, *CC*, Homily 1 (PG 44:780c–781c) (GNO VI), trans. Musurillo, 156. 1 John 1:1.

36. Nyssen, *DVM* (PG 46:972) (SC 178) (GNO VIII.I) (FC, 171–72).

37. Ibid. (PG 46:977) (SC 178) (GNO VIII.I) (FC, 176).

sharing with Gregory the passion of her life, which was to move toward higher philosophy.[38] This teaching at the very end of her life may have been the spark which led Gregory to create his philosophical work, *On the Soul and the Resurrection*, utilizing the voice of Macrina.

It is also in this teaching role that we see Macrina portrayed as the one who shines above the rest for she is the "fairest among women."[39] Here, again, Nyssen is lifting her up as a model for the transcendence of earthly stereotypes. "You alone are made in the likeness of that nature which surpasses all understanding; you alone are a similitude of eternal beauty, a receptacle of happiness, an image of the true Light; and if you look up to Him, you will become what He is, imitating Him Who shines within you, Whose glory is reflected in your purity."[40] Her skill in teaching and leadership in the home was a practice of virtue which led her to higher levels of participation in God. When a person, male or female participates in God the virtues which they practice are characteristics of God himself. Therefore, Macrina is not just an example of a woman who can, through participation with Christ, transcend the barriers of the day and be a sign of eschatological hope, but the skills revealed in her are an actual reflection of the grace of God and his desire to teach and nurture each and every individual.

Virtue as a transitional phase

What we find in the practice of the virtue becomes twofold as one continues to progress in deification. That is, the practice of virtue helps to form one into the image of Christ, but at the same time, the characteristics of Christ become reflected in the life of the individual as the individual is continually transformed into the image. Therefore, what we may first see as the practice of virtue, or imitation of Christ, does lead to ever-increasing participation in Christ, and as a result, Christ himself is revealed in the virtues. Nyssen says, "Through these and such things, we also will be a rock, imitating, as far as is possible in our changing nature, the unchanging and permanent nature of the Master."[41] The virtues reveal the very nature of Christ.

At Annesi, Macrina led the entire community in the practice of virtue with one visitor referring to their community as "the monastery of virtue."[42]

38. Ibid. (PG 46:976) (SC 178) (GNO VIII.I) (FC, 175).

39. Song 1:7.

40. Nyssen, CC, Homily 2 (PG 44:804a–808b) (GNO VI), trans. Musurillo, 162.

41. Nyssen, DP (GNO III.I) (FC, 108).

42. Nyssen, DVM (PG 46:996) (SC 178) (GNO VIII.I) (FC, 188).

This included "discovering goods leading them to greater purity."[43] These goods led them not to a life of solitude but to a life that constantly reached out beyond the walls of their community. It was in this behavior that we see the transformational phase, or the line which cannot be drawn between the practice of virtues, or imitation of Christ, and the actual reflection of Christ in them. Basil had declared that the ascetics were to be the likeness of the image to the world around them, and Macrina modeled this practice, becoming the very reflection of the Image. Through the practice of virtue "we become an image of the image, having achieved the beauty of the Prototype through activity as a kind of imitation, as did Paul, who became an 'imitator of Christ,'[44] through his life of virtue."[45] Nyssen said that "by coming closer to the inaccessible Beauty you have yourself become beautiful, and like a mirror, as it were, you have taken on my appearance,"[46] meaning the beautiful appearance of the bridegroom. "Hence the Word says to her: You have become fair because you have come near to my light, and by this closeness to me you have attracted this participation in beauty."[47] In this transformation, attention is no longer paid to Macrina's outward beauty; attention is paid to the beauty found within her as she reflected Christ and participated in him. Nyssen presents her here as the model for understanding this transitional aspect of deification. She is being transformed into the very image of Christ through participation in Christ.

Miracles

Macrina is an example of one being *deified* by being transformed into the image, but Nyssen also begins to attribute to Macrina Christ-like abilities and this is found specifically in the area of miracles. The grandchildren of Macrina the Elder were no strangers to miracles, considering their grandmother had been a disciple of Gregory Thaumaturgus, *the Wonderworker*. Gregory of Nyssa wrote *The Life of Gregory the Wonderworker*, in which he included many of the miracle stories of Gregory, undoubtedly those he had learned as a child. For Nyssen, miracles became a sign of one's participation in God and therefore spoke to the virtue of the individual and the nature of Christ. As Macrina continued to be transformed in her walk with God, her life began to resemble what Jesus had promised in John 14:12, "Very truly,

43. Ibid. (PG 46:972) (SC 178) (GNO VIII.I) (FC, 171).

44. 1 Cor 4:16.

45. Nyssen, *DP* (GNO III.I) (FC, 111).

46. Nyssen, *CC*, Homily 4 (PG 44:832–33c) (GNO VI), trans. Musurillo, 171.

47. Ibid.

I tell you, the one who believes in me will also do the works that I do and, in fact, will do greater works than these, because I am going to the Father." This seemed to indicate that because of the presence of the Holy Spirit in the lives of those who would come after Christ and their resultant participation in God, they would be able to perform miracles.

Macrina was the bride with her eyes fixed on the bridegroom. The bridegroom became the ever present goal before her eyes; therefore, "*Thy eyes, He says, are as those of doves*."[48] Nyssen speculates that "when the pupils of one's eyes are clear you can see in them the faces of those who look into them."[49] "Thus the beauty of the bride's eyes is praised because of the image of the Dove which appears in her pupils. For we receive within ourselves the likeness of whatever we look upon."[50] For Nyssen, the dove represents the presence of the Holy Spirit. Therefore, the longer one gazes at the bridegroom, the very presence of the Holy Spirit is reflected in the eyes and behavior of the individual. "This is the reason why the Bridegroom praises the soul that has been freed of all carnal passion by saying that the image of the Dove is in its eyes; for this means that the impression of the spiritual life shines within the clarity of the soul."[51] Macrina the bride was filled with the Holy Spirit as she gazed upon her beloved. The result was a power which helped her to live a life of virtue which included the ability to perform miracles.

> When therefore it [the Word] draws human nature to participate in its perfection, because of the divine transcendence it must always be superior to our nature in the same degree. The soul grows by its constant participation in that which transcends it; and yet the perfection in which the soul shares remains ever the same, and is always discovered by the soul to be transcendent to the same degree.
>
> We see the Word, then, leading the bride up a rising staircase, as it were, up to the heights by the ascent of perfection. . . .
>
> In bidding the bride to become beautiful even though she is beautiful, He reminds us of the words of the Apostle who bids *the same image* to be *transformed from glory to glory*.[52]

---

48. Song 1:14.

49. Nyssen, CC, Homily 4 (PG 44:833c–836c) (GNO VI), trans. Musurillo, 171–72.

50. Ibid., 172.

51. Ibid.

52. Ibid., Homily 5 (PG 44:873c–876c) (GNO VI), trans. Musurillo, 190–91. 2 Cor 3:18.

Macrina was empowered to live a life of virtue, but as she moved to higher heights, from *glory to glory*, she was able to perform miracles.

Gregory indicates that numerous miracles were associated with Macrina and her ministry throughout her years at Annesi. He briefly mentions the time of famine "when grain was given out in proportion to the need, the amount did not seem to grow smaller, but remained the same as it was before it was given to those asking for it."[53] There were other stories such as "the healing of disease, the casting out of devils, [and] true prophecies of future events."[54] There is a sense that the miracles became commonplace and there was no need to record them in detail just as John the Evangelist noted that Jesus' miracles were so numerous and commonplace that they too could not all be recorded.[55]

Macrina's soul continued to rise as she lived her life of virtue, specifically "proceeding, as the Prophet says, *from virtue to virtue*,"[56] or as Paul would say, "*glory to glory*."[57] This life of virtue became visible to all those around her, and very specifically when she was involved in miracles of healing. Within these miracles, Macrina stepped into fellowship with her bridegroom and he used her to share grace with those needing relief.[58] Gregory had said, "the distribution of graces is in proportion to one's faith, meagre for those of little faith, great for those who have within themselves great room for faith."[59] Macrina's faith grew in proportion to her relationship with Christ and the resultant miracles as she participated in him. What becomes visible is this intermingling of one with the other. It has not yet reached the culmination but is a foretaste of what is to come.

Numerous miracles were associated with the life of Macrina, yet when preparing her body for burial, Lampadium, her assistant, insisted that Gregory did not "pass over the greatest of the miracles of the saint."[60] This final miracle leads us to an understanding of this transition in relationship in terms of one practicing virtues and one who takes on the very nature of Christ. Nyssen was unaware that Macrina herself had been healed. There

53. Nyssen, *DVM* (PG 46:997) (SC 178) (GNO VIII.I) (FC, 190).

54. Ibid.

55. "But there are also many other things that Jesus did; if every one of them were written down, I suppose that the world itself could not contain the books that would be written" (John 21:25 NRSV).

56. Nyssen, *CC*, Homily 5 (PG 44:888c–893c) (GNO VI), trans. Musurillo, 200. Ps 83:38.

57. 2 Cor 3:18.

58. Nyssen, *DP* (GNO III.I) (FC, 107).

59. Nyssen, *DVM* (PG 46:999) (SC 178) (GNO VIII.I) (FC, 191).

60. Ibid. (PG 46:992) (SC 178) (GNO VIII.I) (FC, 185).

on Macrina's chest just below the neck was a thin "almost imperceptible scar."[61] Gregory described it as a "mark made by a small needle."[62] Lampadium explained that Macrina had been ill with a terrible sore on her chest. Her mother had begged her to get medical help, but Macrina did not want to bare her body to a doctor and, instead "went in the sanctuary and all night supplicated the God of healing, pouring out a stream from her eyes upon the ground, and she used the mud from her tears as a remedy for the disease."[63] Later, her mother again pleaded with her to go to the doctor, and instead, Macrina asked her mother to make the sign of the cross over the sore on her chest. When her mother did so, the sore was gone and all that remained was the tiny scar.

Lampadium assumed the scar served as a reminder to Macrina to be thankful to God for the healing, but could it be that there was more to this incident? Did the scar actually become a physical representation of Macrina's participation in Christ and in his suffering? Georgia Frank argues that Gregory inserted a scar into a story which required none, and by doing so, "Gregory can insert Macrina into a long tradition of the saintly wounded. The scar's location on the breast recalls Christ's chest wound. Moreover, the scar's permanence also marks Macrina's continuing progress toward a resurrection body."[64] It is as if she stepped into the role of the martyrs who had gone before and were dearly venerated that she indicating that she had moved on to a higher level in the life of philosophy. Augustine would later comment:

> But the love we bear to the blessed martyrs causes us, I know not how, to desire to see in the heavenly kingdom the marks of the wounds which they received for the name of Christ, and possibly we shall see them. For this will not be a deformity, but a mark of honor, and will add lustre to their appearance, and a spiritual, if not a bodily beauty.[65]

Macrina's scar was a physical reminder of her relationship with Christ. The miracle which was accomplished in her own flesh was simply an outward sign of the growing relationship between Macrina and her groom. Not only could this scar have connected her with the martyrs, but it could also have represented something much deeper to Nyssen.

61. Ibid.
62. Ibid.
63. Ibid.
64. Frank, "Macrina's Scar," 514.
65. Augustine, *De Civitate Dei* (CCSL, 47–48); English trans. Bettenson, *City of God*, locations 15954–56.

It is by placing Macrina in the place of the bride in the Song of Songs that her participation in Christ takes on new meaning. Gone is the desire to simply be an imitator of Christ by the practice of virtues; love for the bridegroom now becomes the passion that drives one's life. In Nyssen's *De Vita Macrinae*, the scar left on her body after her miraculous healing may very well have represented her participation with Christ; however, in light of the *Commentary* and her place as a bride, the scar takes on new meaning.

> The bride says: *Because I am wounded with love*. Here she explains the dart that has gone right through her heart, and the bowman is love. From the scriptures we learn that *God is love*,[66] and also that he sends forth his only begotten Son as his *chosen arrow*[67] to the elect, dipping the triple point at its tip in the Spirit of life. . . . As the soul is raised up by these divine elevations, she sees within herself the sweet dart of love that has wounded her, and she glories in the wound: *I am wounded with love*. Indeed it is a good wound and the sweet pain by which life penetrates the soul; for by the tearing of the arrow she opens, as it were, a door, an entrance into herself. For no sooner does she receive the dart of love than the image of archery is transformed into a scene of nuptial joy.[68]

It is quite possible that Nyssen transforms the scar on his sister's chest from a symbol of martyrdom into this wound of love. In this way participation with God is seen as a relationship defined by love. The greater the participation in God, the greater the amount of God's love which can pour into the wound of the one who has been opened by the tearing of the arrow. Nyssen identifies God's very nature as love, and this love is then reflected in the image of the one who is fully focused on the beloved. "She communicates to her Beloved the dispositions of her heart. For she has received within her God's special dart, she has been wounded in the heart by the point of faith; she has been mortally wounded by the arrow of love. And *God is love*."[69] Lampadium had referred to this as the greatest miracle, which indeed it became when viewed as the miracle which drove the bride to the marriage bed. Nyssen explains further:

> By a delicious wound she receives His special dart in her heart; and then she herself becomes the arrow in the hand of

---

66. 1 John 4:8.

67. Isa 49:2.

68. Nyssen, *CC*, Homily 4 (PG 44:852a–853a) (GNO VI), trans. Musurillo, 178–79.

69. Ibid., Homily 12 (PG 44:1029a–1037c) (GNO VI), trans. Musurillo, 271.

the Bowman, who with his right hand draws the arrow near to himself, and with his left directs its head towards the heavenly goal.[70]

By being filled with the love of the bowman, her head is now turned heavenward, and the focus of all her attention becomes the bridegroom. No longer is transformation the goal; he is the goal.[71]

Premonition of physical deification

Nyssen presents us with a glimpse of his understanding of deification and the final apokatastasis in *De Vita Macrinae* that goes beyond the spiritual. He reveals a picture of the physical transformation which may also occur in theosis, even while one is here on earth. It is in this one small incident that Gregory reveals several different aspects of his understanding of the concept of ever-increasing participation in an infinite God. These include the physical nature of apokatastasis, an early understanding of apophaticism which leads one to the infinite nature of God, and eternal transformation.

Gregory had spent a great amount of his ministry fighting ecclesial battles and was exiled repeatedly.[72] The result was that a period of eight years passed without his returning to Annesi and visiting Macrina. He resolved to see her, but while on his journey, he had a vision, or rather a premonition, regarding the condition of his sister. "That same night, the vision occurred three times. I was not able to interpret its meaning clearly, but I foresaw some grief for my soul and I was waiting for the outcome to clarify the dream."[73] In the vision he was carrying the relics of martyrs. As he opened his hand and looked at the relics, "a light seemed to come from them, as happens when the sun is reflected on a bright mirror or that the eye is dazzled by the brilliance of the beam."[74] While Gregory said that he wasn't sure of the meaning of the vision, one might consider that this was a visual representation of Gregory's understanding of deification and the path that his sister would soon be taking. In the process of deification or theosis, as the individual becomes more like God, the individual becomes holy, taking on Christ's holiness. This was believed to be the case in both the spiritual and the physical sense. This resulted in the attraction and collection of holy

70. Ibid., Homily 6 (PG 44:888c–893c) (GNO VI), trans. Musurillo, 198.

71. This is where Elm falls short in stating that the goal is sainthood. Rather, the goal becomes Christ himself, the object of one's love as the Bride.

72. Nyssen, *DVM* (PG 46:976) (SC 178) (GNO VIII.I) (FC, 174).

73. Ibid.

74. Ibid.

relics. Why not collect relics of those who have become the most like God and keep them in your vicinity? In essence, the presence of God was then closer to you as well; hence, the collection of relics was important to the church and individuals. Emmelia, the mother of Nyssen and Macrina, had collected the relics of seven martyrs and placed them in a tomb on the very property of Annesi.

Soon, Macrina would be passing from this life onto the next, and in that process she would move onto even higher heights of participation in God. One might think that Nyssen sees in death the apokatastasis, but because of God's infinite nature, the participation in God never ends but goes on throughout eternity. The apokatastasis simply returns humanity fully to the starting point which God had originally intended.

Arriving at this point, the bride is then instructed that, far from attaining perfection, she has not even begun to approach it. Now, she says, that I have been deemed worthy of the nuptial rites, I rest as it were upon the *bed* of all that I have hitherto understood. But I am suddenly introduced into the realm of the invisible, surrounded by the divine darkness, searching for him who is hidden in the *dark cloud*.[75]

What becomes interesting in Nyssen's understanding is that all things are not completed in this apokatastasis, or restoration; instead, because of God's infinite nature, this becomes the beginning. It is only here that we begin to discover the reality of the nature of God or the fact that the full nature of God will always be unknowable to the human. Nyssen begins to reveal this concept of apophaticism: the more we get to know God, the more we recognize what we cannot comprehend about God. So, as the bride participates in the bridegroom, there is a realization that she will never be able to fully know him. "Then it was that I felt that love for him whom I desired—though the Beloved himself resists the grasp of our thoughts."[76] As long as Macrina remained in her earthly body she would experience the already, and not yet, of participation in the bridegroom. "*I called him, but he answered not.*[77] For then I recognized that *of the magnificence of the glory of His holiness* there is no end."[78] Therefore, the life of holiness or theosis has no end. The more one knows God, the more one realizes that they do not know God, for he is infinite.

---

75. Nyssen, *CC*, Homily 5 (PG 44:888c–893c) (GNO VI), trans. Musurillo, 201.

76. Ibid.

77. Song 3:1.

78. Nyssen, *CC*, Homily 5 (PG 44:888c–893c) (GNO VI), trans. Musurillo, 202. Ps 144:5, 30.

Again, we return to Nyssen, who was gazing on the relics which he saw in his hand. The light which shone from the relics may well have represented what later became referred to as the "energies of God." That is, we as humans cannot actually become the *ousia* of God, but we may be partakers of the energy of God's divine nature. Later Eastern theologians such as Palamas would continue to develop this line of thought. While writing *De Vita Macrinae*, Gregory was also arguing for Nicene Orthodoxy, and in the creed itself, Christ is referred to as the light. Could this light shining from the relics represent the *koinonia* fellowship of those who have become partakers of the divine nature? If so, then it is a prophetic vision of Macrina's future. Macrina, the one who has been faithful, consistently attaining to the higher levels in the life of philosophy, will soon move on to yet another level, the eventual apokatastasis. According to Ramelli, Nyssen's purpose in writing of Macrina's life is that in Macrina and her virgins we might see a life that they are anticipating "the blessed condition of the resurrection and, even more, the eventual *apokatastasis*."[79] However, in this vision of Nyssen, we find much more than the apokatastasis and realize that the goal goes beyond. Restoration simply becomes the starting point to heights which are beyond humanity's comprehension.

The prophetic vision of Gregory is fulfilled when he arrives at Annesi. Here, Macrina becomes the culmination of his theological principles concerning the final moments of deification. She is the faithful servant and the beautifully adorned bride awaiting the final union with her bridegroom. Macrina is presented as a woman prepared for death, no longer attached to the things of this world, for "she kept her mind free in the contemplation of higher things and unimpeded by the disease."[80] Macrina had spent her entire life loving Christ, and on her deathbed those present seemed to sense, "the divine and pure love of the unseen Bridegroom which she had secretly nourished in the depths of her soul. . . . Truly, her race towards the Beloved and nothing of the pleasure of life diverted her attention."[81] Nyssen imagined that the angels surrounded the bridegroom and that the bride's transformation brought her closer to the form of the angels.[82] Nyssen describes this moment as one in which she becomes "a kind of living mirror possessing free will: When I face my Beloved with my entire surface, and all the beauty of his form is reflected within me."[83] She can say wholeheartedly, "*I to my*

---

79. Ramelli, "Theosebia," 100. See also Ramelli, *Christian Doctrine of "Apokatastasis."*
80. Nyssen, *DVM* (PG 46:977) (SC 178) (GNO VIII.I) (FC, 176).
81. Ibid. (PG 46:983) (SC 178) (GNO VIII.I) (FC, 179).
82. Nyssen, *CC*, Homily 8 (PG 44:945d–949b) (GNO VI), trans. Musurillo, 217.
83. Ibid., Homily 15 (PG 44:1093c–1096d) (GNO VI), trans. Musurillo, 282.

beloved, and my beloved to me."[84] Macrina has offered herself to her beloved "and now receives from him his own Beauty within herself."[85] The result is what Nyssen describes as "true holiness, purity, incorruptibility, light, truth, and all the rest, and these pasture my soul not in the dry undershrubs or in the pastures, but *in the brightness of the saints.*"[86]

For her funeral Macrina was adorned as a bride for her bridegroom.[87] She has been transformed into beauty by her desire for the bridegroom. This beauty is seen by Nyssen in not only a spiritual but also a physical sense. In his *Commentary on the Canticle* Gregory writes:

> Now, however, they do not consider any of her previous attributes; but qualifying her with the highest perfection, they marvel not only at the height she has reached but also the depths from which she has risen. . . . She has risen so high out of her devotion and her continence that she causes even the friends of the Bridegroom to marvel. . . . After their praise of the bride's beauty, the Bridegroom's friends who prepare the holy bridal chamber and are the escorts for the virginal bride, point out to her the beauty of the royal bed, for they wish to arouse in her a more intense desire for that spotless and divine marriage with Him.[88]

Nyssen depicts Macrina as the beautiful bride awaiting the consummation of the relationship with the bridegroom in which the two become one. At that moment, she is united both spiritually and physically with Christ. This is the point at which it becomes difficult to comprehend Nyssen's understanding fully, and that may be why he chooses the direction of apophaticism and illustration. Macrina's story becomes the perfect vehicle through which he may present his theology in narrative form, for to comprehend these concepts through words alone may have been too difficult to grasp. However, this was an attempt at describing Nyssen's anthropology and resultant understanding of deification.

Nyssen goes to great length to describe the scene which occurred immediately after Macrina's death. He helped to prepare her body for burial but believed that she was far too beautiful for the virgins at Annesi to behold, for she had become, after all, the bride of Christ. Thinking that the

---

84. Song 6:20.

85. Nyssen, *CC*, Homily 15 (PG 44:1093c–1096d) (GNO VI), trans. Musurillo, 284.

86. Ibid. (PG 44:1093c–1096d) (GNO VI), trans. Musurillo, 283. Ps 109:3.

87. He was traveling with his own funeral shroud and because she had none, dressed her in his own gown.

88. Nyssen, *CC*, Homily 5 (PG 44:896b–897d) (GNO VI), trans. Musurillo, 203–6.

beauty of the bride should be saved for the groom alone, he covered her body with a mantle. Here Gregory represents the physical theosis which has occurred. The mantle was unable to cover or extinguish what he had seen in his vision, a foreshadowing of what she was to become, for "even in the dark, the body glowed, the divine power adding such grace to her body that, as in the vision of my dream, rays seemed to be shining forth from her loveliness."[89] Nyssen was determined to show that she had become holy by uniting with Christ and had been transformed into Christ's image. Her body now shone with the radiance of his glory, as she continued to progress "from glory to glory." For Nyssen, she had become what God had initially intended for humanity: the "*image and likeness* of eternal life . . . truly and exceedingly good, radiant with the luminous form of life."[90] In Macrina's death, the physical restoration of her body may have been completed, but it simply became a preparation of more that was to come.

> That in our constant participation in the blessed nature of the Good, the graces that we receive at every point are indeed great, but the path that lies beyond our immediate grasp is infinite. This will constantly happen to those who thus share in the divine Goodness, and they will always enjoy a greater and greater participation in grace throughout all eternity.[91]

On earth, we are left with bones, the relics, which reflect the very glory of God, depicting his presence. For this reason, it becomes important to keep the remains of those who have lived a life of theosis in close proximity. In the case of Macrina her remains were taken to the tomb of the Holy Martyrs where the other relics had already been brought, to sanctify the very ground of Annesi where the spiritual life of the ascetics in the line of Basilian monasticism would continue.

Macrina had few earthly possessions, but after her death it was discovered that around her neck was a very simple necklace on which was an "iron cross and a ring of the same material."[92] When examined, there was a cross carved into the seal of the ring, but on the inside was a hollowed out portion in which there was a "piece of the wood of life."[93] It is possible that this had originally been the ring of betrothal from her young suitor, but throughout life's journey, it had become the symbol of her betrothal to the one represented by the cross. She had quite literally given her life to become the bride

89. Nyssen, *DVM* (PG 46:992) (SC 178) (GNO VIII.I) (FC, 186).

90. Nyssen, *CC*, Homily 12 (PG 44:1016c–1024b) (GNO VI), trans. Musurillo, 257.

91. Ibid., Homily 8 (PG 44:940c–941c) (GNO VI), trans. Musurillo, 212.

92. Nyssen, *DVM* (PG 46:989) (SC 178) (GNO VIII.I) (FC, 184).

93. Ibid. (PG 46:989) (SC 178) (GNO VIII.I) (FC, 185).

of Christ. Gregory portrays her in her final moments of life as one whose entire focus of life was being drawn by the lover. "Indeed, as she neared her end and saw the beauty of the Bridegroom more clearly, she rushed with greater impulse towards the One she desired, no longer speaking to those of us who were present, but to that very One toward whom she looked with steadfast eyes."[94] It was the crowning moment of her deification. She had reached the goal and been united with Christ, where she would remain for all of eternity with ever-increasing participation in his infinity.

Conclusions

In the opening chapters of the Scriptures, we find the creation story and within it God's hope for humanity. There we find Adam and Eve in a pre-fallen state. Their marriage is one of mutuality, in which one helps the other reach his or her highest potential. They are facing God their creator, and they reflect the image of God. As they walk the garden from day to day, they are invited to participate in fellowship with God in the Trinity. They are drawn toward the Creator and are being transformed into God's image. Their earthly marriage is a reflection of the holy love which is found in the Trinity. When they sin, they turn their backs on God, and the reflection is lost. Not only is the reflection lost, but the relationship with God is lost. The marital relationship between Adam and Eve is also corrupted. No longer are they partners together facing God, but rather the woman is placed in a subordinate position to the man. The Cappadocians' theology of theosis was built around this relational theme found in the Trinity and in God's intended hope of marriage. That is why Nyssen brings the hope of humanity back to a wedding. In the very center of the Scriptures, we find the Song of Songs. Could it possibly be a reminder that God is calling creation back into a faithful relationship, one of holy love and of greater passion and depth than humanity could possibly begin to imagine? All of the hope of humanity is bound up in the restoration of the relationships that have been broken. Macrina's life is one in which we are ushered through the journey of kenosis-theosis, and her story becomes one of eternal optimism that the relationship between God and humanity can be restored to God's original intent and purpose. It also becomes the picture of God's desire for humanity to understand the beauty which may be found in a marriage based on God's principles and foundations. When one becomes consumed with passion for the object of one's love, the expression comes from the very soul of the one whom God created. God created humans to be passionate,

94. Ibid. (PG 46:983) (SC 178) (GNO VIII.I) (FC, 179).

loving individuals being driven by an intense love for God and others. This understanding is what drove all of the Cappadocians, both the men and the women. Their desire and passion became Jesus Christ and him alone. How better to express this than to present a clean and unsullied bride in the form of Macrina? She becomes the culmination of all things and the hope of all things. So, as the Scriptures begin with a marriage and are filled with the reminder of marital passion in the Song, so Revelation ends with the Spirit and the Bride who stand over the earth and say, "Come." Nyssen witnesses the life of his sister and sees in her the hope for all, the perfect virgin bride.

CHAPTER 8

Practical Implications for Life and Ministry: Macrina the Elder, Emmelia, and Theosebia

MACRINA THE YOUNGER WAS the idealized image of perfection in seeking theosis. However, the life Macrina lived was not necessarily practical for all. We have seen how the *Fallen Virgin* struggled to live up to the persona embodied in her older sister. The life of the ascetic behind the walls of the monastery was not necessarily the calling for all women. What we discover within the families of the Cappadocians are other women who found their way to God and theosis within their particular contexts and callings. The greatest achievement of these women was to become living examples of their theological understanding of theosis. As we have demonstrated, at each level of the theological framework of the kenosis-theosis parabola, one could find the influence of a female relative. This influence went beyond the development of their theological concepts and infused very practical aspects of their work and ministry. As a result of this study, we have not only discovered that the women of the Cappadocians became examples of their theology but also found additional implications that relate directly to the life of holiness for women. In this final section, we will explore the practical implications which grow out of their theological framework. These include a kingdom perspective on gender and class equality, women in ministry, and, finally, marriage and parenting.

Gender and class equality

Many factors influenced the Cappadocians' perspective on gender equality. The influence of Origen cannot be denied with its resultant allegorical reading of Scripture. The influence of the women combined with their understanding of the nature of God resulted in a developed understanding of the image which is best recognized as gender neutral. According to Beagon, the "stress in their thinking is upon the equality of men and women rather than the subordination of the female to the male."[1] This was necessary for conformity with the totality of their experiences and observations. Therefore, we find in the story of their lives and in the self-revelations of their writings a glimpse of God's view and understanding of women within the kingdom. This is a view developed within the context of profound female influence and in tandem with the theological underpinnings found in Gal 3:28, "There is no longer Jew or Greek, there is no longer slave or free, there is no longer male and female; for all of you are one in Christ Jesus" (NRSV). The Cappadocians, and especially Nyssen, had located the image of God in the human before gender differentiation; and therefore, their understanding of apokatastasis led them to the conclusion that all humans were of equal value in the sight of God. According to Ramelli, "The ideal, to be pursued already in this life, is that of the *telos*, the *apokatastasis*, in which gender differences will vanish and evil and its consequences will no longer exist."[2]

The Cappadocians' overall attitude toward women was not typical of their period.[3] The historian Raymond Van Dam records that the men of Caesarea gathered for regular council meetings and left written records, or canons, from these proceedings which give us insight into the general consensus regarding the women of their community.

> Despite the lack of any precise context, these canons nicely exemplify the essential characteristics of so much of the surviving information about women in ancient society: men talking about women, men worrying about and feeling threatened by women's behavior, men trying to control women's behavior. In these canons, as in many other writings, discussions about gender and sex became displays of power, as men imposed regulations and as they wrote the texts that codified those regulations and explained the rationales behind them.[4]

1. Beagon, "Cappadocian Fathers," 166.

2. Ramelli, "Theosebia," 101.

3. For the epic discussion on this topic, see Harrison, "Male and Female."

4. Van Dam, *Families and Friends*, 83. He notes, "The canons of this council survive only in an Armenian translation; for a Latin translation, see Lebon (1938) 106–10,

In striking contrast, within the writings of the Cappadocians, we find a different attitude toward women. Much of their discussion regarding the equality of women was written in regard to the image of God, which has been previously discussed. However, it is interesting to note several other arguments for equality, including one in Nazianzen's *Oration* 37 where he makes it clear that he believes men and women are to be treated as equals. Nyssen tackles the fall of humanity, a familiar topic in his day, and stresses that he does not see the female as having greater responsibility for the fall.[5] This is significant because other authors within the period of the early church were much more critical of Eve's role in the fall of humanity and therefore placed this guilt on all women. Tertullian stated, "You (woman) destroyed so easily God's image, man."[6] In this regard, he not only placed the guilt with Eve but also directly stated that the image is male. Augustine finds the image located in the role of the woman rather than in her nature.[7]

> The woman together with her husband is the image of God, so that the whole substance is one image. But when she is assigned as a helpmate, a function that pertains to her alone, then she is not the image of God, but as far as the man is concerned, he is by himself alone the image of God, just as fully and completely as when he and the woman are joined together into one.[8]

In contrast to this opinion, Nazianzen gives voice to the concerns of women. He recognized the inequality which resulted from the patriarchal power structures which created the laws, complaining, "I do not accept this legislation; I do not approve this custom. They who made the Law were men, and therefore their legislation is hard on women."[9] He was arguing from the premise of male-female equality, and therefore he demanded "equal standards of fidelity."[10]

Basil also commented regarding the equal status of women. He wrote three canonical letters, *Epistle* 188.9 and *Epistle* 199.18 and 21, which relate to women. Here Basil seems to struggle with the inequality that he finds in the treatment of women, specifically in the case of infidelity. Unlike Nazianzen, he is not clear in his response and appears somewhat reluctant in

---

with Barnes (1981) 65, dating the council to the summer or autumn of 314, and Parvis (2001), discussing the authenticity of these canons."

5. Nazianzen, *Or.* 37.7 (PG 36:289) (SC 318) (*NPNF2* 7:340).

6. Tertullian, *De Cultu Feminarum*, 1.1 (*ANF* 4:6).

7. Miles, *Practicing Christianity*, 38–39.

8. Augustine, *On the Trinity* 12.7 (FC).

9. Nazianzen *Or.* 37.6 (PG 36:289) (SC 318) (*NPNF2* 7:339).

10. Beagon, "Cappadocian Fathers," 178n31.

the argument, concluding *Canon* 21 by stating, "The reasoning is not easy, but the custom has so obtained."[11] However, while Basil seemed to reluctantly support the customs of the day in regard to punishment, he seemed to present a more egalitarian view when it came to the spiritual life. We know that he was most profoundly influenced by the Macrinas in his life, both grandmother and older sister. These two were both women of virtue and strength and provided the model for his understanding of the spiritual woman. Therefore, one is not easily surprised by the following passage written by Basil regarding the martyr Julitta:

> But she did not run so eagerly to any of the delights of this life as she came to those flames. In face and in habit and in the words that she uttered and in the glow of her radiance she manifested her exceeding joy of soul, exhorting the women standing by not to slacken in their labours on behalf of piety, nor to allege the weakness of nature as an excuse, "for we are from the same compound," she said, "as men. We are made *according to the image of God* just as they are. The female is made by the Creator equally capable of virtue as the male. Indeed are we not cognate with men in all things? For it was not *flesh* alone that was taken for the fashioning of woman, but *bone from bones* (Gen 2.5). Hence firmness and vigour and endurance are as equally due from us as from men to the Master." When she had said these things, she was taken to the fire, which enveloped the body of the holy woman like some luminous inner chamber, and sent her soul to the heavenly country, even to the portion that befitted her.[12]

Basil portrayed women not as being weaker but rather equal to men in the image, virtue, firmness, vigour and endurance. Ultimately, this image of a strong woman who is an equal to man is seen throughout the personal experiences of all three of the Cappadocians and is highlighted by their writings.

The attitude of equality spread beyond the sexes toward the issue of slavery, and class equality. In a very practical sense, they acted out their theology in their daily relationships. When Macrina and Emmelia, along with Peter, moved to the family estate at Annesi, they took all of their servants with them and then lived as equals with them within the new community. There was no longer any slave nor free in the household of these Cappadocians. This was true not only in the household at Annesi but also in the life of the brother, Naucratius. He and his servant treated those around

11. Basil, *Ep.* 199.21 (PG 32:722) (Deferrari, LCL).

12. Basil, *Homily on the Martyr Julitta* (PG 31:237–62; specifically PG 31:241ab), trans. Silvas. A special thanks to Anna Silvas for personally providing me with this recent translation.

them as equals. Known as a great hunter, Naucratius and his servant shared the bounty of their hunting expeditions with those within their fellowship. It appears that Nyssen's rejection of slavery more than likely ran parallel with his "rejection of discrimination against women."[13] The eschatological view presented in theology was being realized within their sphere of social influence.

Women and ministry

The Cappadocians' understanding of theosis also led to practical implications in terms of the role of women in ministry. Because of their egalitarian perspective in regard to women, their acceptance of women in expanded roles of ministry should not be surprising. All three of the men served the church of their day in official functions. While Basil of Caesarea, Gregory of Nyssa, and Gregory of Nazianzus all served as bishops within ecclesial life in the fourth century, the ever-present influence of the women in their lives, combined with their understanding of deification, provided them with a flexible framework which provided space for women in the church. This flexible framework had allowed Nyssen to reject slavery and to make a direct connection between slavery and the "discrimination against women in church ministries."[14] Nyssen's theological thought and development directly affected his practical ministry.

The connection between Nyssen's attitude toward slaves and women in ministry may be found in his use of vocabulary. He utilizes the word ὁμότιμος when describing the relationship between Macrina and the members of her household who had previously been slaves. They had become her peers, or equals. Nyssen was not alone in the use of this term. This same word was used by Basil to declare the equal dignity of a man and woman and by Nazianzen when discussing the role of Theosebia and Nyssen in service to the church.[15] Schüssler Fiorenza suggested that Nyssen had inherited his perspective from Origen, whom we have seen, understood that the *telos* was the final apokatastasis, where there truly would no longer be any slave nor free, Jew nor Greek, male and female. Therefore, the presence of women within the life of the church became an "eschatological symbol" of hope for all of humanity.[16]

---

13. Ramelli, "Theosebia," 101.

14. Ibid.

15. Ibid.

16. Schüssler Fiorenza, *Sharing Her Word*, 76–87, 112, and *Rhetoric and Ethics*, 7.

According to Beagon, the Cappadocian Fathers had a progressive view of male-female equality which allowed them to assign a vital role to women in the "development of ecclesiastical structures in Cappadocia at the time and also in the theological debates then raging."[17] Two perspectives that of service through asceticism, and another by way of official service in the church, may be identified within the Cappadocians regarding the role of women in ministry. Nyssen presents a perspective, inspired by Origen, which appreciates the ministry of ascetics as spiritual leaders over and above official positions of ministry within the life of the church. Origen's allegorical interpretation went beyond the bounds of Scripture enveloping and informing his perspective on the practical ministries of the church, including the ordination of ministers, the practice of liturgy and the sacraments.[18] Therefore, Origen found ordained ministry not only on earth but also in heaven. This ordination stretches beyond the bounds of the official church. There are those who serve on earth who will not be worthy of serving in heaven, and likewise, there are those who have not been allowed to serve on earth who will serve in heaven.[19] It is in this that we find the eschatological hope of the church and the role which women in ministry play for the Cappadocians. Whether they are allowed to serve in official capacities in the earthly church or not, this will not prohibit them from service in heaven. Therefore, while Macrina did not serve in an official function as a presbyter in the church here on earth, Nyssen valued her ministry and saw her as a presbyter in heaven where gender barriers would be destroyed.[20] Later, we will see that Nazianzen's emphasis differed, focusing on the official structures of the church. Therefore, his perspective placed value on those women who were already presenting that eschatological hope while in service to the church here on earth.

Double monasticism and female leadership

It is within the family monastery at Annesi that we find much of Basil's and Nyssen's development regarding the role of women and, specifically, ascetics within the church and the community at large. What grew out of Annesi was a new form of asceticism, greatly influenced by the presence of women and, very specifically, by the strong female leader, Macrina. The

17. Beagon, "Cappadocian Fathers," 166.

18. Ramelli, "Theosebia," 101.

19. Origen, *Comm. Matt* 11 16.20–23 (PG 13:936).

20. Ramelli, "Theosebia," 101.

result was something which has become known as "double monasticism."[21] It was this specific monastic lifestyle which created space for the women who were being called to the spiritual life and to leadership. It was not a mixed monastery, but rather a "single monastic unit of men and women,"[22] where Macrina served as the overall leader, or head of all of those present. While this type of monasticism is usually referred to as Basilian, Verna Harrison and others would suggest that it was Macrina who was the founder,[23] organizing this community of men and women under her spiritual leadership.[24] It was simply Basil who authored the structures which had already been established and existed at Annesi. The Seventh Ecumenical Council approved these structures, which came to be known as the *Rule of Basil*, in 787. This type of monasticism continued to be practiced until the fall of Constantinople in 1453.[25]

Rousseau argues against this understanding of the situation and claims that what we find at Annesi is household asceticism, rather than an official convent.[26] Therefore, he questions the validity of Macrina's leadership role. Household asceticism had been developing since the persecutions had subsided. Rousseau is hesitant to declare the community at Annesi as a monastery. He is critical of those who interpret *De Vita Macrinae* as illustrating an established work.[27] The truth is probably somewhere between the two, recognizing that it was a work in progress and it is undeniable that it had begun as a household. After the death of the father, Macrina and her mother, Emmelia, along with the entire household, moved to Annesi. Early on, Peter lived under the same roof with Macrina and Emmelia.[28] It was only in later years that Peter moved into a separate building to provide oversight for the men in the community. Through the years the household underwent a type of metamorphosis, from a household to a monastery. What had begun as a home of wealth became a humble household where goods were shared equally and where masters placed themselves at the same status as those who had previously been their servants. The household fell into a routine of spiritual worship and practice of virtue. Over time, others

---

21. For a lengthy discussion of this type of monasticism and its relationship to Annesi, see Stramara, "Double Monasticism."

22. Ibid., 272.

23. Harrison, "Male and Female," 445. See also Elm, *"Virgins of God,"* 104.

24. Stramara, "Double Monasticism," 276.

25. Ibid., 270.

26. Rousseau, "Pious Household," 186.

27. Ibid.

28. Nyssen, *DVM* (PG 42:976) (SC 178) (GNO VIII.I) (FC, 172).

joined the community, and as a result it grew, developed and by necessity became more formalized.[29] It is Basil's penning of the *Rules*, not Nyssen's *De Vita Macrinae*, which transformed the setting from a household to a monastery. It was a community in which both men and women lived together in celibacy, practicing the virtues through a life of asceticism, all the while pursuing deification. The head of the entire community was Macrina, who served as spiritual leader and teacher for both male and female.

The pursuit of deification represented the eschatological hope for all believers. Therefore, for the Cappadocians, the presence of women in the life of the church provided humanity with the hope of the kingdom of God which was already here on this earth, however, was not yet completely experienced. As long as they lived in the flesh of their bodies, they would not realize the ultimate apokatastasis, which could only come after death. However, the women serving within the Christian community had already stepped outside the social confines of their day, and even with the limitations placed upon them, they were able to participate in the kingdom of God. Therefore, Origen understood that while earthly structures might try to prohibit women from priestly functions, in the apokatastasis this would no longer be a barrier. When women began to serve the church, the world could see the merging of heaven on earth with a glimpse of the hope which was to be found in the life to come. The Cappadocian women became models for an inaugurated eschatology, their lives a theological message with which it was difficult to argue.

Both Basil and Nyssen, strongly influenced by Origen, valued the spiritual role played by women within the Christian community without need for an official voice within the life of the church. Basil hints at the role of female leadership in his *Rules* for the monastic life. Basil seems cautious when it comes to disturbing the mores of his day and while intimating there may be female leadership of the double monastery, he does not make this clear. One assumes this is because Macrina has been his model for leadership from what he has observed at Annesi. He is unable to deny the role she had played yet seems reticent to make this official for future circumstances. Both Nyssen and Basil would have seen Macrina as the exception rather than the norm for women. Annesi had certainly developed into a form of double monasticism as Peter became the leader of the men. Still, Macrina was not allowed to have an official voice within the church institutions but rather filled the role of spiritual leader and guide. She is notably revered by church leadership; for there is evidence they celebrated her funeral. While Basil appears sympathetic to her role as leader, in subsequent years the

29. Elm, *"Virgins of God,"* 91.

leadership of those who practice Basilian monasticism is predominantly male. Historically, this does not invalidate the influential role of the spiritual leader within the life of the church. Later it would be said that when one was seeking guidance in prayer, one turned toward Athos and not Constantinople, implying that official church leadership did not necessarily connote spiritual leadership. Macrina filled this void between the official life of the church and the spiritual, becoming the model of the spiritual life and, as we have seen, the pure bride of Christ. For Basil and Nyssen these are of greater value than any official position within the church hierarchy. Ludlow would argue that value placed on, and study of, the spiritual influence of women has only occurred because women were not given space within official structures.[30] However, when the Cappadocians are examined *in toto* one discovers a broader view that encompasses more than the spiritual life, but also, one of leadership and official ministry within the life of the church.

The Cappadocians' silence on certain formal matters of women in ministry may have been the best way to approach the subject in their day. The very existence of the women within the life of the church spoke volumes regarding their theology. All three of the Cappadocian Fathers had experienced the influence of deeply spiritual, talented and capable women in their lives. The influence of the Cappadocian women began long before the Fathers were conceived and continued throughout their lives, helping them to form their orthodoxy and orthopraxy, making it difficult to determine whether it is their theology which has informed their practice, or their practice that has informed their theology. Ramelli argues that it is precisely the theological perspective of the Cappadocians that informs their social realities.[31] The social reality was that during the theological struggles of the day, a vacuum was created in the life of the church, one that had to be filled by women. It appears that whenever human structures were measured against the goal of deification, the work of deification became the higher authority, and this theological perspective created space for women to break the bounds of official church structure.

Theosebia

Theosebia, an obscure figure barely mentioned in the writings of the Cappadocians, provides the bridge between the spiritual and official ministry of women. We will explore how she became a woman who stood in the gap; however, first, she must be recovered from history. Iconography often tells a

30. Ludlow, *Gregory of Nyssa*, locations 2504–7.
31. Ramelli, "Theosebia," 102.

story which may be hidden or unclear in writings. A recent acquisition of an icon of "The Holy Family" revealed not Mary, Joseph and the baby Jesus, but rather an icon of the Holy Family of St. Basil.[32] At the top stands Emmelia, the Mother of all Saints, followed by her holy children, including Macrina and another named daughter, Theosebia. On the level below the daughters are Naucratius, Peter, Basil the father, Basil the Great, and Gregory of Nyssa. However, it was the curious location of Theosebia, as a daughter, which raised the question of her identity. Early scholarship recognized Theosebia as the wife of Gregory of Nyssa. Cecilia Robinson in 1898, studying the historic ministry of deaconesses, stated that although there are some who dispute the fact, "the evidence in favour of it is strong" that Theosebia is Nyssen's wife.[33] Agnes Dunbar, writing in 1905, clearly identified Theosebia as the wife of St. Gregory of Nyssa.[34] Others, such as J. Emile Pfister, have simply noted that Emmelia gave birth to five daughters, "Macrina, the virgin and also the eldest child, and the four others who married."[35] This would certainly not locate Theosebia as either Nyssen's wife, or as one of the virgins. It was Nazianzen who mentioned this woman not once, but twice. In *Epigram* 164 he stated, "And you, Theosebia, child of noble Emmelia, and in truth the companion of great Gregory, lie here in sacred earth, you who were the support of devout women and departed this life at a seasonable age."[36] In *Letter* 197, Nazianzen wrote the following words to Nyssen on the death of Theosebia:

> But what must we feel in presence of a long prevailing law of God which has now taken my Theosebia (for I call her mine because she lived a godly life; for spiritual kindred is better than bodily), Theosebia, the glory of the church, the adornment of Christ, the helper of our generation, the hope of woman; Theosebia, the most beautiful and glorious among all the beauty of the Brethren; Theosebia, truly sacred, truly consort of a priest, and of equal honour and worthy of the Great Sacraments? Theosebia, whom all future time shall receive, resting on immortal pillars, that is, on the souls of all who have known her now, and of all who shall be hereafter. And do not wonder that I often invoke her name. For I rejoice even in the remembrance of the blessed one. Let this, a great deal in few words, be her epitaph

32. This orthodox icon was purchased in Athens in January 2011. It is titled, "The holy οἰκογένεια." It is created by Kanems NNP.

33. Robinson, *Ministry of Deaconess*, 41.

34. Dunbar, *Dictionary of Saintly Women*, vol. 2.

35. Pfister, "Biographical Note," 113.

36. Nazianzen, *Epigr.* 164 (*Anthologia Graeca* 8:164), trans. Silvas, 82.

from me, and my word of condolence for you, though you your-self are quite able to console others in this way through your *philosophy* in all things.[37]

To further confuse the matter, the editors of the *Nicene and Post-Nicene Fathers* state, "Some writers have imagined that she was the wife of Gregory Nazianzen himself, but there is no evidence to show that he was ever married."[38] In the introduction to Nazianzen's epigrams in the Loeb edition, the editor writes, "Gregory's [Nazianzen's] wife was Basil's sister" and he references *Epigram* 164.[39] More thorough readings of these texts, however, lead us to a different conclusion and the contention that she is the younger sister of Macrina, Basil, and Nyssen. Nazianzen would have known her for many years during his times of visitation at the family estate at Anessi, and it would not be too far-fetched to imagine that he had grown fond of this young lady who had given her life in service to the Lord. There-fore, he could have felt that she was also his.

After the death of Emmelia, Nazianzen wrote *Epigram* 161 in which he stated of Emmelia, "She alone among mortals had both good children and many children. Three of her sons were illustrious priests, and one daughter the companion of a priest, and the rest were like an army of saints."[40] The timing and language of this *Epigram* are significant. Silvas argues that *Epigram* 161 was "probably written after Peter, the youngest born, had become Bishop of Sebasteia, soon after the Council of Constantinople in 381."[41] This would have been after the death of Macrina, for Peter is recorded as ministering together with her at the time of her death, but it would also account for the reference of three sons as being priests. The language is also significant as earlier in the *Epigram* Nazianzen refers to Emmelia's children as being "both sons and daughters married and unmarried" (υἱέας ἠδέ θύγατρας ὁμόζυγας ἀζυγέας τε), but the word translated companion σύζηγος is different. It is in the translation of the word σύζυγος, which can mean *companion, consort* or even *yolk-fellow*, which creates the confusion regarding Theosebia. The word, in its feminine form, may be used to mean "spouse," but at the same time "it also encompasses those who share inti-mately in the same work—even to rivals in gladiatorial contests."[42] The same term, in its masculine form, is used by Paul in Phil 4:3 where it is translated

---

37. Nazianzen, *Ep.* 197 (PG 37:321) (GCS 53) (*NPNF2* 7:462).

38. Ibid.

39. Nazianzen, *Epigr.* 164 (*Anthologia Graeca* 8:471) (Paton, LCL).

40. Ibid., 161 (*Anthologia Graeca* 8:39), trans. Silvas, 81.

41. Silvas, *Macrina the Younger*, 81.

42. Ibid., 7.

yolk-fellow by the NIV and *loyal companion* in the NRSV. The confusion in the case of Theosebia is because she is female; therefore, the female form of the word is used, leading one to think she may be a spouse, when in reality she more than likely was simply the companion, or partner with Nyssen in his ministry.

Daniélou argues that there are two distinct Theosebias to whom Nazianzen refers, stating the name Theosebia was simply a very popular female name of the day.[43] This would suggest that one Theosebia is the sister of Nyssen; and the other his wife. Elm also leaves the door open to this possibility. "If so, Emmelia had a daughter named Theosebia married to a priest named Gregory, and a son called Gregory who became a priest and was married to yet another Theosebia."[44] However, the timeline for this simply does not work, considering the fact that Nyssen seems to speak passionately and with much grief and detail about the death of a young wife (presumably his) during childbirth in *De Virginitate*, written around 372.[45] It would be difficult to imagine that Nyssen were not referring to his own wife in this regard because in the very same document he refers to the fact that he can never be a virgin. However, if this were the case and she had died prior to 372, why would Nazianzen write a condolence after 381? In both of Nazianzen's documents he mentions that Theosebia has died at a seasonable age, probably subsequent to 381. If Nyssen's wife died at a young age during childbirth, how could she have lived to a seasonable age? Silvas argues, "That the one author, Nazianzen, should write of two Theosebias, both of whom are 'yolk fellows' of an eminent priest Gregory is to beg too much of coincidence."[46]

It would appear that Theosebia, sister to Nyssen, became his companion after she had devoted herself to a life of virginity and after he had suffered the death of his wife.[47] She had a very close relationship with Nyssen, to the extent that she lived with him in his home and served together with him in his ministry, which would have been appropriate, given their relationship as brother and sister. *Canon* III of the Council of Nicaea declared, "The great Synod has stringently forbidden any bishop, presbyter, deacon, or any one of the clergy whatever, to have a *subintroducta* dwelling with him, except only a mother, or sister, or aunt, or such persons only as are

---

43. Daniélou, "Le Mariage de Grégoire de Nysse."

44. Elm, *"Virgins of God,"* 157.

45. Nyssen, *DV* (PG 46:329c–d) (SC 119) (GNO VIII.I) (FC, 15–16).

46. Silvas, *Macrina the Younger*, 7.

47. Ramelli, "Theosebia," 89, makes this same argument.

beyond all suspicion."[48] This pattern of ministry was already well established in the family where Macrina and Peter were serving together in the family monastery. Therefore, it would not have been uncommon for this pattern to be repeated in the life and ministry of Gregory and Theosebia. Not only did Theosebia serve together with Nyssen, but the Benedictine editors have traditionally regarded Theosebia as "a Deaconess of the church of Nyssa."[49] Ramelli agrees that Theosebia is not only the sister of Gregory of Nyssa but also a presbyter. She further explores the idea that Theosebia became a leader in the church at Nyssa and "probably substituted for her brother during his exile and supported him against 'Arianism.'"[50]

Nazianzen, in *Epigram* 161, lists the ministry of Theosebia immediately following that of the three brothers who were priests. Considering the fact that it is the name Macrina which has become widely known through the centuries, one might be curious as to the placement of Theosebia in this list. What exists is the possibility that later in life the official ministry of Theosebia surpassed the spiritual ministry of Macrina. While Macrina served as the abbess of the community at Annesi, Theosebia stepped out into official life and served the church of her day. Nazianzen asks this question, "Theosebia, truly sacred, truly consort of a priest, and of equal honour and worthy of the Great Sacraments?"[51] The important word here is ὁμότιμος. Note again the use of this word to describe the relationships found in the home of Macrina. Theosebia is a peer or colleague who is at the same level as the ιερεύς or priest. Ramelli believes that this language ensures that she was most "certainly ordained, and probably a presbyter."[52] The final portion of this sentence by Nazianzen "worthy of the Great Sacraments" (καί τῶν μεγάλον μυστερίον ἀξίαν), solidifies the argument for her official role as a presbyter. The implication here is that she served the Sacraments together with her brother Gregory. Ramelli believes that this certainly was the case and that "her offices included the celebration of the Mass, perhaps leading the performance of the Divine Office, and surely the spiritual, and maybe also material, support of pious women, the 'choir of virgins' in Nyssa and probably also Christian women in Nyssa."[53] The "choir of virgins" most

---

48. *First Council of Nicaea*, trans. Percival (*NPNF2* 12).

49. *NPNF2* 7:879.

50. Ramelli, "Theosebia," 79.

51. Nazianzen, *Ep.* 197 (PG 37:321) (GCS 53) (*NPNF2* 7:462).

52. Ramelli, "Theosebia," 99.

53. Ibid.

certainly existed and is referenced in Nyssen's *Letter 3* to *Ablabius*, to whom he writes on his return from exile:[54]

> But after we had persuaded them with difficulty to allow us to get down, and to let our mules pass, we were crushed on every side by folks crowding round, insomuch that their excessive kindness all but made us faint. And when we were near the inside of the portico, we see a stream of fire flowing into the church; for the choir of virgins, carrying their wax torches in their hands, were just marching in file along the entrance of the church, kindling the whole into splendour with their blaze. And when I was within and had rejoiced and wept with my people— for I experienced both emotions from witnessing both in the multitude . . . .[55]

Gregory's exile had been the result of his theological battles against the Arians. It is believed that Gregory was exiled and absent from Nyssa for at least two years. Theosebia, having been raised under the influence of her grandmother Macrina, would have learned the importance of maintaining the faith during times of persecution. Not only did she learn perseverance, but considering the home in which she was raised, she would have understood the doctrinal debates of her day.[56] This would have been a rather delicate accomplishment, for Gregory had been banished from his post by the emperor, and more than likely the opposition would have had influence in the local community. The fact that Gregory was greeted with such exuberance on his return becomes a testimony to the work of his sister Theosebia. It reflects the fact that she maintained a united congregation, in support of their bishop and also in support of Nicene Orthodoxy.

Ramelli refers to Theosebia as a presbyter, but tradition has recognized her as a deaconess of Nyssa, the most formal title or function given to many of the Cappadocian women.[57] At the time in which she served, the church

---

54. Silvas, *Gregory of Nyssa*, 140. She states, "The exceptional exuberance both of joy and of tears demonstrated here seems to reflect the longest and most painful absence of his exile from 376 to 378." Nyssen himself makes reference in *DVM* (PG 46:976) (SC 178) (GNO VIII.I) (FC, 174) to his exiles, "since I was exiled time and again by the leaders of heresy."

55. Nyssen, *Ep. 3 to Ablabius*, trans. Silvas, in *Gregory of Nyssa*, 140.

56. See Elm, *"Virgins of God,"* 42. A discussion of the likely education which occurred in the home. In referring to the girls: "Their syllabus was virtually identical to that of the boys."

57. Ramelli, "Theosebia," 83. "The Cappadocians read what Origen wrote in his commentary on Romans and elsewhere about the ordination and ministry of women in the church. Moreover, they read these passages not in a fourth-or fifth-century Latin compendious translation such as that of Rufinus, but in the original third-century

allowed for the ordination of women to the position of deaconess. The following is an excerpt from a *Letter of Atto, Bishop of Vercelli, to Ambrose the Priest* referring to what had occurred in the fourth through sixth centuries:[58]

> We believe female deacons truly to have been ministers of such things. For we say that a minister is a deacon (*diaconum*), from which we perceive female deacon (*deaconam*) to have been derived. Finally, we read in the fifteenth canon of the Council of Chalcedon that a female deacon is not to be ordained before her fortieth year—and this was the highest gravity. We believe women were enjoined to the Office of baptizing so that the bodies of other women might be handled by them without any deeply felt sense of shame . . . just as those who were called female presbyters (*presbyterae*) assumed the Office of preaching, leading and teaching, so female deacons had taken up the Office of ministry and of baptizing a custom that no longer is expedient.[59]

While all three of the Cappadocian Fathers were deeply theological, they were also practical. Practical experience had taught them that the women to whom they were related were perfectly capable of sustaining the faith in the midst of crisis. Whether they were surviving persecution, famine, sickness or the unbelief of a spouse, these women did not waver in their faith, or in their practice. Again picking up on the perspective of Atto:

> Because your prudence has moved you to inquire how we should understand "female priest" (*presbyteram*) or "female deacon" (*diaconam*) in the canons: it seems to me that in the primitive church, according to the word of the Lord, "the harvest was great and laborers few"; religious women (*religiosae mulieres*) used to be ordained as caretakers (*cultrices ordinabantur*) in the holy church, as Blessed Paul shows in the *Letter* to the Romans, when he says, "I commend to you my sister Phoebe, who is in the ministry of the church in Cenchrea." Here it is understood that not only men but also women presided over the churches (*sed etiam feminae praeerat ecclesiis*) because of their

---

Greek text. It was natural for them to apply Origen's reflection on the ecclesiastical ministries of women to their own ecclesiastical reality, that of the Cappadocia of the late fourth century, where several ordained women besides Theosebia herself were well known. But while those other women seem to have been deacons, Theosebia was more likely a presbyter."

58. Madigan and Osiek, *Ordained Women*, location 4611.

59. Ibid., 4636. See also Tanner, *Decrees of the Ecumenical Councils*. "15 No woman under forty years of age is to be ordained a deacon, and then only after close scrutiny. If after receiving ordination and spending some time in the ministry she despises God's grace and gets married, such a person is to be anathematized along with her spouse."

great usefulness. For women, long accustomed to the rites of the pagans and instructed also in philosophical teachings, were, for these reasons converted more easily and taught more liberally in the worship of religion.[60]

For practical purposes, the Cappadocians did not speak too loudly on the official service of women in the church. As Gillian Cloke rightly points out, "One cleric's meat for debate was another cleric's poison, and women were praised or denounced for comparable actions simply depending on which writer addressed them; even the same woman could be called by the same cleric at different times 'the most noble of the women of Rome' and 'the new Thecla' . . . and 'she whose black name bears witness to the darkness of her treachery.'"[61] During the fourth century, the church was faced with the reality of a mass influx of people as Christianity continued to gain a foothold as the religion of the empire. The fields were certainly ripe unto harvest, and the women were needed as labourers, especially since more women were being converted than men. The battle of the day was theological and not practical, and that was the battle which the Fathers chose to fight. Basil stated, "Women too join the campaign at Christ's side, being enrolled in the campaign owing to the manliness of their souls and not rejected for the weakness of the body."[62] In the practical sense, they knew they needed and could depend upon the partnership of the women in the ministry. As in the case of Theosebia, she kept the ministry active and even thriving during the absence of her brother Gregory.

The Cappadocians respected numerous practices of virtue and paths toward deification, and while it may seem at first glance they valued the life of asceticism over that of official service in the church, they also respected official service and recognized this as a path for deification. Nyssen refers to Basil's position as bishop of Caesarea, explaining that he "led his brother to the holy vocation of the priesthood, and consecrated him in the mystical services himself. And through this also, their life progressed to a loftier and higher degree, seeing that their *philosophy* was enhanced by the consecration."[63] Why would this consecration not be available to women as well if the goal were deification? Macrina also had a high respect for those of official ministry. Nyssen recalled that when he came to visit her on her

60. Madigan and Osiek, *Ordained Women*, location 4624.

61. Cloke, *This Female Man of God*, 10. Cloke is quoting Jerome, *Ep.* 133.3 (CSEL 56:246). Jerome is speaking of Melania the Elder, implicating her for her Origenism.

62. Basil, *Institutio Praevia Ascetica* (PG 31:624d–625a), trans. Beagon, "Cappadocian Fathers," 173.

63. Nyssen, *DVM* (PG 46:973) (SC 178) (GNO VIII.I) (FC, 173).

deathbed she "fixed her hands on the floor and, stretching as far forward as she could, she paid me the honour of a bow."[64] After Macrina's death, Lampadium, the deaconess at Annesi, commented that Macrina had always honored Gregory's priesthood.[65] There is no official record of Theosebia's ministry, but it would have been politically incorrect in their day to have too openly affirmed her function as a priest within the community at Nyssa. However, by examining the contextual evidence, it becomes apparent that she served in priestly function and maintained the work of the church in the absence of her brother.

The practical nature of the experience with Theosebia leads one to question whether the church is only open to the flexible interpretations of deification when it is practical. It appears that in times of crisis the church is willing to embrace the eschatological hope found in the Cappadocians and the view that women are needed to serve within the kingdom. However, when the persecutions end, the church steps back into the status quo and more rigid theological interpretations.

Historically, the Cappadocians have provided us with two avenues for women to fulfil their calling to ministry. When official structures remain closed, women fulfil their calling and desire through spiritual service. Macrina becomes the example of this type of service, and she is highly valued by both Basil and Nyssen. However, if official service is acceptable from a traditional perspective and is valued as a virtue, should that avenue not also be open to women? Nazianzen seems to agree with this perspective. While he appreciates the work of Macrina, he "places more emphasis on officially ordained ministry."[66] By the time Nazianzen wrote about Theosebia, he had served as bishop at Constantinople and presided over the council meeting of 381. He had become a large figure in the official church and would have had more opportunity to appreciate the more visible ministry within the church at Nyssa completed by Theosebia, rather than Macrina's work, which was completed in seclusion at Annesi. Therefore, within the Cappadocians we find affirmation for women pursuing deification through two different avenues of service to the church. There is a place for women pursuing the spiritual life and serving as spiritual guides and leaders and (if our interpretation is correct) for those who become priests and deacons with the authority to participate in the sacraments. All of these women, serving in differing roles in the life of the church, represent a particular reflection of the image and represent the eschatological hope found in Christ. The

64. Ibid. (PG 46:976) (SC 178) (GNO VIII.I) (FC, 175).

65. Ibid. (PG 46:989) (SC 178) (GNO VIII.I) (FC, 184).

66. Ramelli, "Theosebia," 100.

Cappadocians' perspective has been lost for centuries, but the implications found within their understanding of deification may be vital to the life and future of the church.

Marriage and the family

The central feature of life for the Cappadocians was a desire for a lifestyle of philosophy which led to deification. This desire for deification permeated every aspect of their lives and led them to the conclusion that a life without the distractions of marriage was the best path to reach to higher levels in pursuit of God. The result was a transformation in Christian households, from a traditional model to that of a monastery. While this was highly praised at the time, it was done without consideration for the long-term implications of removing the center of holiness from the home and local church and placing it in the monastery.[67] Long before these particular Cappadocians entered the landscape, the faithfulness of their ancestors was creating the environment that would nurture and mold their spiritual journey. The spiritual ancestry of the family of Basil could be traced back through a godly mother who had faithfully survived being orphaned and grandparents who had outlived the persecutions as disciples of Thaumaturgus, who himself had been a student of Origen. These great theologians did not suddenly develop as young adults, but rather, they were cultivated. How else is it possible that Emmelia is remembered as the mother of saints, having six of her children honored by the church? Therefore, the shift to monasticism, while providing an excellent environment for the development of the spiritual life, did not exert influence on young people until they were in their early teens. This may have resulted in less spiritual training occurring in the home. This study would imply that it was the nurture in a holy home by godly women which brought about the development of theological giants known as the Cappadocian Fathers. Their mother, Emmelia, and grandmother, Macrina the Elder, raised Basil and Nyssen, while Nazianzen's mother, Nonna, reared him. These women recognized that the development of a nurturing household of holiness was to be their practice of virtue as they themselves pursued deification.

Macrina the Elder, Emmelia and Nonna are all remembered as being holy women who lived lives of virtue, and yet they were all married. Interestingly, while the Cappadocians certainly seemed to favour the life of celibacy, they did speak about marriage. Nyssen regularly encouraged his followers to live in moderation. He had personally seen the ravages of

---

67. Brown, *Body and Society*, 262.

exuberance on the part of his brother in regard to fasting, which had created chronic health problems. It is within this framework of moderation that Nyssen contended that marriage was acceptable. "And we, on our part, know this about marriage, that the zeal and the desire for divine things come first, but that one should not scorn the moderate and measured use of the duty of marriage."[68] He continued on, "That if it is possible, one should neither remain aloof from the more divine desires, nor should one reject the idea of marriage. It is not reasonable to disregard the economy of nature or to slander what is honourable as disgusting."[69] In other words, he did not see that marriage was, in and of itself, a bad thing. Both Nyssen and Nazianzen realized, rather obviously, that there could be no virgins if it were not for married women.[70] If persons were married, they were not to shirk their earthly responsibilities in favour of heavenly relationships. Rather, married women were encouraged to see their marriage as a practice of virtue and, therefore, to put effort into this earthly and physical relationship, viewing it as spiritual. So as not to be rejected, the bride was to make an effort to "have a fine appearance, fitting adornment and sufficient wealth."[71] She was also to take care that she would not "be a burden because of [her] way of life or [her] family background."[72] The model for this life was Gorgonia, who had exceeded the woman of Proverbs 31.

The care and nurture of the holy home included the rearing of children and Nyssen believed that the role of married women was to raise children. "The divine injunctions have often revealed to us that childbearing and the begetting of children are a good thing, and they have indicated the kind of procreation sought after among God's saints."[73] Nyssen and Nazianzen, while extolling the virtues of virginity, realized that procreation was necessary to the Christian faith. How can there be virgins if there are no mothers! Therefore, in his *Panegyric* to his sister, Nazianzen stressed the virtue of motherhood which he saw in her.

> She turned the fruit of her body—I mean her children and grandchildren—into the fruit of the Spirit, consecrating her whole family and household, not just a single soul to God, and giving marriage a good reputation, both through what was

68. Nyssen, *DV* 8 (PG 46:353) (SC 119) (GNO VIII.I) (FC, 33).

69. Ibid.

70. Nazianzen, *Or.* 37.10 (PG 36:293) (SC 318) (*NPNF2* 7:341); Nyssen, *DV* 8 (PG 46:353) (SC 119) (GNO VIII.I) (FC, 33).

71. Nyssen, *DV* 20 (PG 46:397) (SC 119) (GNO VIII.I) (FC, 63).

72. Ibid.

73. Ibid., 19 (PG 46:396) (SC 119) (GNO VIII.I) (FC, 61).

pleasing to God in marriage itself and through the good fruit that it produced. She presented herself, as long as she lived, as a model of every good virtue to her descendants.[74]

They were not only to bear children but also to raise them well. This meant

mothers were to become models for their children in the life of philosophy. Gregory knew this from personal experience and noted, "The guidance of deeds is more effective than instructions in words."[75] The women exemplified *theosis* for they had lived it out in the home, and these men, simply had to apply their theological understandings to the models of holiness by whom they had been raised in order to understand God's desire for humanity.

Nyssen commented, "Grace begins at home."[76] The grace of God reaches out to humanity, allowing humanity to participate in the virtues resulting in a synergistic relationship with God. In the home Nyssen began to encounter this grace in a practical way. It was in the practical aspects of human life—daily living, education, both spiritual and secular, and relationships that he was drawn toward the life of philosophy which would mould the individual and prepare them for the higher calling. The childhood home was a "workshop of the virtues in which such a life is purified to the highest point."[77] The practice of virtues in the Christian home included the activities of daily life, education and relationships, and these produced an environment of experiential grace.

Not all Christian households were virtuous, for not all households saw deification as the goal for all of those within her walls. The home, a workshop of virtues, was "not respected because of its earthly possessions, but because of the abundance of its heavenly treasures."[78] This included all aspects of daily life and one's attitude toward earthly possessions. The Cappadocians experienced their own home of virtue in which one was encouraged to give up his earthly possessions in favour of the greater good. However, they were able to compare and contrast this with what was found within their own community. Van Dam compares Cappadocia with Texas, where one finds wealthy ranchers, with their large herds of horses enjoying

---

74. Nazianzen, *Or.* 8.8 (PG 35:798), trans. Daley, 67.
75. Nyssen, *DV* 23 (PG 46:405) (SC 119) (GNO VIII.I) (FC, 68).
76. Ibid.
77. Ibid.
78. Ibid., 20 (PG 46:397) (SC 119) (GNO VIII.I) (FC, 63).

a wealthy lifestyle.[79] The Cappadocians did not mince words when it came to the behaviors of these wealthy rancher women, whom they did not see as virtuous. More than likely it was before the famine of 369 that Basil delivered an address entitled *To the Rich*, in which he criticized those who had become preoccupied with the things of the world:

> You gorgeously array your walls, but do not clothe your fellow human being; you adorn horses, but turn away from the shameful plight of your brother or sister; you allow grain to rot in your barns, but do not feed those who are starving; you hide gold in the earth but ignore the oppressed! And if your wife happens to be a money-loving person, then the disease is doubled in its effects. She stirs up the love of luxury and inflames the craving for pleasure, spurring on fruitless pursuits. Such women contrive to procure precious stones and metals of all kinds. . . . They do not give anyone a second to breathe with their incessant demands![80]

Basil's frustration with a community that would not embrace a life of virtue was apparent. He was especially critical of the women whom he saw as influential in setting the tone in the home.

In contrast, devout Christian families who early embraced baptism became households in which, according to Silvas:

> The Graeco-Roman civic *politeia* mingled with and gradually yielded to more explicitly Christian virtues. The cultural shift is seen especially in the fostering at home of the Scriptures and church traditions, in the practice of hospitality, personal frugality and a Gospel charity in which the ruling idea is no longer philanthropy with a view to winning civic kudos, but self-effacing succour of the poor in imitation of Christ.[81]

A new Christian culture was being developed and defined by these families, one that lived juxtaposed to civil society. This was often seen in aristocratic families, like that of Basil and Nyssen, where the entire household gave themselves over to a life of piety, as the woman of the house took the lead.[82] It was these households that became "the seed-beds of a latent Christian radicalism,"[83] giving rise to martyrs, confessors, virgins and

---

79. Van Dam, *Kingdom of Snow*, 23.

80. Basil, *Homily 7, To the Rich* 4.47.

81. Silvas, *Macrina the Younger*, 3.

82. Ibid., 4.

83. Ibid.

priests.[84] This new type of home and heritage is what the Cappadocians experienced and recognized as a virtue.

Because of the value placed on the life of theosis, the spiritual nurture of the children was of foremost importance in the homes of the Cappadocians. This was certainly true in the home which Emmelia provided for her children. Most literature lists five of Emmelia's children as saints, not including Theosebia whose identity has been considered uncertain. However, if one includes Theosebia, then six of her children were recognized as saints, which is remarkable.

Nonna, too, was a mother who invested heavily in her children and was determined to pass along the faith that she had inherited. Gorgonia, her daughter, was the first born, and she later gave birth to her two sons, Gregory Nazianzen and Caesarius. The "golden chain" of her faith, "she cast about her children, displaying in female form the spirit of a man,"[85] for Nonna's greatest desire for her children was that they "should be known as Christ's and be called His" and that they would practice virtue and have "kinship with the Chief Good."[86] Her home was one in which the children were raised with an eye for heaven and in which "the seeds of piety"[87] had been sown. All three of Nonna's children, Gorgonia, Gregory and Caesarius, were later regarded as saints in the church. Their mother had led them into lives molded by holiness.[88]

The passion for motherhood was great among these women, who took women of Scriptures as their models for holiness. While women were generally not afforded a secular education, all of these Cappadocian mothers had been educated in the Scriptures. Unlike the family of Basil, it appears that Nazianzen's parents, Gregory and Nonna, may have struggled with infertility and did not have children until they were older than the norm.[89] Nazianzen frequently refers to them as Abraham and Sarah and to himself as Isaac.[90] There are other times when he refers to Nonna's prayers for a child as those of Hannah who prayed for Samuel.[91] Placing themselves within a

---

84. Ibid.

85. Nazianzen, *De vita sua* (PG 37:1029–166), trans. Meehan, 119–20.

86. Nazianzen, *Or.* 7.4 (PG 35:758) (SC 406) (FC, 4).

87. Ibid., 8.6 (PG 35:795), trans. Daley, 66.

88. Nazianzen, *De vita sua* (PG 37:1029–166), trans. Meehan, 451–53.

89. For an extensive discussion on the age of Nonna and Gregory, see Van Dam, *Families and Friends*, 88.

90. Nazianzen, *Or.* 8.4 (PG 35:795).

91. Nazianzen, *De vita sua* (PG 37:1029–166), trans. Meehan, 69–82.

biblical setting, the Cappadocian mothers were able to develop a scriptural framework for motherhood and also for the order of the home.

Emmelia, the Mother of Saints—spiritual education

Emmelia, the mother of Basil and Gregory, is honored for her virtue of parenting. No other woman since her time has had six children officially recognized as saints. In a contemporary icon of Emmelia, one finds her holding a plaque which is inscribed: "Behold I and the children which God hath given me."[92] She is honored by the Orthodox Church with the following Troparion, which gives a brief but concise record of her life and influence:

> That which was created in the image of God
>
> Was preserved in you, O Mother;
>
> For taking up the cross, you followed after Christ.
>
> By your deeds you have taught us to reject the flesh, for it passes away,
>
> But to care for the soul as a thing immortal.
>
> Therefore, O venerable Emmelia, your soul rejoices with the angels.[93]

Nazianzen, as a result of his close relationship to Basil, spent much time with the family of Emmelia. He could not help but speak words of praise regarding her: "Who has not known Emmelia, whose name was a presage of what she became or whose life exemplified her name. She truly bore the name of Emmelia, which means harmony, for, to speak briefly, she was regarded among women as he was among men."[94] However, upon reflection, Nazianzen noted that Emmelia would be remembered because of the exemplary children which she raised.[95] All nine of the surviving children had been taught the life of virtue, which would lead to deification, and this became the *telos* for all of life.

One of the central features of this new type of nurturing Christian home was an emphasis on spiritual education from a very early age. Emmelia provides for us an excellent example of a mother whose focus was primarily on the spiritual. Emmelia had a great deal of influence on her children, and she seemed to be able to nurture each one in a unique and individualistic

92. "Come and See Icons," http://www.christopherklitou.com/icon_1_jan_emmelia.htm.

93. See "Troparion to St. Emilia," available online at www.monachos.net/conversation/topic/4414-being-stalked-by-st-emilyemilia.

94. Nazianzen, *Or.* 43.10 (PG 36:505) (SC 384) (FC, 30).

95. Ibid., 43.9 (PG 36:494) (SC 384).

manner. She was deeply concerned with their education and saw to it that each received instruction, "but not in the secular curriculum."[96] Her desire was to point her children in the way of virtue and purity; therefore the Scriptures became their textbook. "Whatever of inspired Scripture was adaptable to the early years, this was the child's subject matter, especially the Wisdom of Solomon and beyond this whatever leads us to a moral life."[97] Basil said of himself: "I was reared from the very beginning by Christian parents. From them I learned even in babyhood the Holy Scriptures which led me to a knowledge of the truth."[98] Nazianzen's eulogy for Basil again reveals the significance of the hand of a parent in the development of such a great individual as Basil. He comments, "It was neither fitting that he be born of other parents, nor that they be called the parents of any other than him. Accordingly, this was happily realized."[99] Emmelia knew how to shape and develop Basil until his brother commented of him, "His life and the outstanding activities through which he became famous everywhere under the sun and eclipsed in reputation all those conspicuous in virtue, would make a long treatise and take much time."[100] Emmelia's concern, however, was that her children be virtuous rather than famous. In this she was successful.

Macrina the Elder—theological roots

The spiritual education of the children included theological training. Within the household of Basil and Nyssen, it was their grandmother Macrina who provided theological cohesion. She was not cast aside in the care of the children, but instead became one of the forces that shaped the environment providing for their development. It was the grandmother's experiences, long before the children were born, which laid the foundation for the household. Having been raised as a Christian in the town of Neocaesarea, she was most certainly a disciple of Thamaturgus. Later in life, Basil, in a letter to the church in Neocaesarea, referred to the faith and influence of his grandmother: "who molded and formed us while still young in the doctrines of piety."[101]

---

96. Nyssen, *DVM* (PG 46:964) (SC 178) (GNO VIII.I) (FC, 165).

97. Ibid.

98. Basil, *Preface on the Judgment of God*, in Wagner, *Basil of Caesarea: Ascetical Works* (FC, 37).

99. Nazianzen, *Or.* 43.10 (PG 36:505) (SC 384) (FC, 30).

100. Nyssen, *DVM* (PG 46:965) (SC 178) (GNO VIII.I) (FC, 168).

101. Basil, *Ep.* 204 (PG 32:745) (Deferrari, LCL).

Macrina the Elder was a woman who valued a life of piety and understood the concepts regarding a life of *philosophy* which Origen had so convincingly preached. This became part of the very fiber of her being, as her life and experiences worked to transform her into the very likeness of the Image. Believing in the work of God upon the heart and life of an individual, she worked diligently to help raise her children and grandchildren so that they too would not only seek the face of God but also become defenders of the very faith for which she and her husband had personally suffered.

It was in the Neocaesarean region of Pontus where the elder Macrina and her husband, along with a handful of fellow Christians, took refuge during the time of the persecutions. Macrina and her husband came from ample means, accustomed to the aristocratic lifestyle. Obviously, Macrina developed stamina as she and her husband endured seven years in the wilderness.[102] In later years, her grandson Gregory recalled that his grandparents "had been deprived of their possessions because of the confession of Christ."[103] Her husband's name is not recorded, and it is assumed that he must have died at a relatively young age, leaving her a widow.[104] Those who survived the persecutions, including the grandmother Macrina, were considered heroes of the faith.[105] What began with grandmother Macrina, and became instilled in future generations, was a wholehearted dedication to a Christian lifestyle of piety which was defined by doctrine. Therefore, as the opportunity presented itself, Macrina the Elder educated her grandchildren in the doctrines of Thaumaturgus. Thaumaturgus' five years under the tutelage of Origen was transformational as "Gregory's soul was knit to Cappadocian Fathers had for Origen can be seen as a result of the passions which were passed on to them through their education and training in the home by their grandmother. The importance of this doctrinal training becomes relevant during the decades long debates regarding Nicene orthodoxy in which her grandsons, Basil and Gregory, became important players. In Basil's *Letter* 223 written to Eustathius of Sebaste, he emphasizes the impact of the doctrine learned in the home.

> The teaching about God which I had received as a boy from my blessed mother and my grandmother Macrina, I have ever held with increased conviction. On my coming to ripe years of reason I did not shift my opinions from one to another, but carried

---

102. Nazianzen, *Or.* 43.9 (PG 36:494) (SC 384).

103. Nyssen, *DVM* (PG 46:977) (SC 178) (GNO VIII.I) (FC, 177).

104. It is presumed that his name may have been Gregory, for whom Nyssen would have been named, with Basil having been given the name of his father Basil the Elder.

105. Nazianzen, *Or.* 43.5 (PG 36:499) (SC 384) (*NPNF2* 7:397).

out the principles delivered to me by my parents. Just as the
seed when it grows is first tiny and then gets bigger but always
preserves its identity, not changed in kind though gradually perfected in growth, so I reckon the same doctrine to have grown in
my case through gradually advancing stages. What I hold now
has not replaced what I held at the beginning.[106]

Silvas states that Basil's grandmother "represented a doctrine of God
that avoided the extremes of Sabellianism (which began by stressing the
oneness in the Trinity) and even of moderate Arianism (which began by
stressing the threeness)."[107] Basil had mentioned that his grandmother had
taught him the words of Thaumaturgus. Silvas argues that "there is little
doubt that Gregory [Nyssen] takes advantage of Basil's remarks about the
doctrinal tradition inherited through their grandmother."[108] In Nyssen's
De Vita Gregorii Thaumaturgi he "utilizes the same term, τὰ ῥήματα, to
describe the statement of Trinitarian faith."[109] One must then consider the
influence of Macrina the Elder in the formation of the short creed which
Nyssen attributes to Thaumaturgus.[110] This creed was one which existed in
the church of Neocaesarea, and was purported to have been signed by the
hand of Thaumaturgus himself. While there are those who argue whether
the creed is authentic,[111] what we do know is that the grandchildren of Macrina had been taught, and more than likely had memorized, the sayings of
Thaumaturgus. It is this teaching which Nyssen utilized while defending his
understanding of the Trinity. Therefore, whether we wish to argue whether
the entire creed came from Thaumaturgus, or was, as Basil mentioned, a
seed which had grown, we do know that Nyssen gained his initial Trinitarian doctrine, the seed, while being taught by his grandmother.

Because of the writings which have been left to us, we know that the
brothers were well trained in doctrine; however, we can assume that their
sisters, who were given the same home instruction, also understood the
theological and doctrinal issues of the day. It should be of no surprise that
the congregation of Nyssa did not fall into Arian hands during the time
of Gregory's exile, for it remained under the firm leadership of Theosebia.
Nyssen also felt comfortable utilizing the voice of his sister Macrina while

106. Basil of Caesarea, *Ep.* 223.3 (PG 32) (*NPNF2* 8:599–601).

107. Silvas, *Macrina the Younger*, 14.

108. Ibid.

109. Ibid.

110. Nyssen, *Life of Gregory the Wonderworker* (PG 46:912–13). The critical text
prepared by Heil, in *Gregorii Nysseni Sermones*, pars II, 3–57.

111. See Van Dam, "Hagiography and History," 282.

arguing theological positions in *On the Soul and the Resurrection*, and referred to her as the Teacher. Being the eldest child of the family, Macrina would have been the one to have had the privilege of spending the most time with the great woman for whom she was named. Therefore, the honor of the title of *Teacher* on sister Macrina may well have been a reflection on the role and influence of Grandmother Macrina.

But while this doctrinal training was invaluable to the young Cappadocians, so was the practice of the Christian life of piety. It was in Thaumaturgus that a lifestyle of holiness was developed, a lifestyle which was to be a pattern reflective of the incarnation of the heavenly life. What occurred in the spiritual life was to have an exterior pattern. There could be no separation between the inner spiritual life and the life lived by the individual.

Secular education

The virtuous Christian home was to include an education in Scripture and theology. However, these mothers, Emmelia and Nonna, also invested heavily in the secular education of their children. Basil was sent to the very best schools of the day, beginning in Caesarea and culminating with his days in Athens. While Nyssen did not follow him all the way to Athens, he, too, was well schooled in Caesarea in the study of rhetoric. Nonna had invested in a private tutor, Carterius, to develop her children to their highest educational potential.[112] Nazianzen recalls, "We were also thoroughly trained in the studies available in this city."[113] Caesarius, Nazianzen's younger brother, "excelled the majority in quickness and range of talent."[114] Caesarius became a highly educated physician and teacher of geometry and astrology. Gregory studied rhetoric in Palestine, while his brother went on to further education in Alexandria.[115] Caesarius' brilliance and lofty education elevated him to a number of positions of authority within the empire.[116] Julian, with whom Basil and Nazianzen had been acquainted while studying Athens, became emperor. After becoming emperor, Julian renounced Christianity and is remembered as Julian the Apostate. Nevertheless, he offered the position of First Physician of the Empire to Caesarius, Nazianzen's younger brother, who accepted.[117] During Caesarius' time of service to the emperor, Julian

---

112. Meehan, *Three Poems*, 5. Nazianzen, *Epigr.* 142 (Paton, LCL).

113. Nazianzen, *Or.* 7.6 (PG 35:761) (SC 406) (FC, 4).

114. Ibid.

115. Ibid.

116. Ibid., 7.7 (PG 35:761) (SC 406), and *Or.* 7.9 (PG 35:766) (SC 406).

117. Ibid., 7.10 (PG 35:766) (SC 406).

challenged him to a debate over the topic of Christianity. Nazianzen saw the irony in this challenge. Julian may have been emperor, but Caesarius had been raised in the home of Nonna! "Alas for this madness and folly if he hoped to take Caesarius, a man such as he was, my brother and the son of these parents, for his prey!"[118] Caesarius won the debate in favour of Christianity, and Nazianzen noted, "For victory is with Christ, who overcame the world."[119] For Nazianzen, the holy home in which they were raised provided an education above and beyond that which was provided for the emperor himself.

Transformation of the household

Emmelia's life was a journey of transformation, becoming an example to her children of the life of virtue and deification. The very household at Annesi became a proleptic vision of the eschatological hope to be found in theosis. After the death of Naucratius, Emmelia and Macrina adopted a lifestyle which was designed with one purpose in mind, to bring them closer to God. Nyssen found their lifestyle so lofty that it transcended description.[120] Gregory, seeing these changes, witnessed to them as ever increasing participation with God. "Just as by death souls are freed from the body and released from the cares of this life, so their life was separated from these things, divorced from all mortal vanity and attuned to an imitation of the existence of the angels."[121] He went on to explain that "although living in the flesh because of their affinity to the bodiless powers, they were not weighted down by the allurements of the body, but, borne upwards in midair, they participated in the life of the celestial powers."[122] The result was a transformation of their very character as they became clearer reflections of the image.

For women like Emmelia, parenthood was a virtue and a way in which she could be united with God. The lifelong devotion to her children could be seen at Emmelia's moment of death at "a rich old age" as she went to God while in the arms of both Peter and Macrina.[123] On her deathbed she blessed each one of her children, "suitably remembering each of the absent ones so that none would be without a blessing, and through prayer entrusting

---

118. Ibid., 7.11 (PG 35:768) (SC 406) (FC, 10).

119. Ibid., 7.13 (PG 35:769) (SC 406) (FC, 10).

120. Nyssen, *DVM* (PG 46:969) (SC 178) (GNO VIII.I) (FC, 170).

121. Ibid. (PG 46:972) (SC 178) (GNO VIII.I) (FC, 170–71).

122. Ibid. (PG 46:972) (SC 178) (GNO VIII.I) (FC, 171).

123. Ibid. (PG 46:972) (SC 178) (GNO VIII.I) (FC, 172).

especially to God the two who were with her."[124] Nyssen records her final words, spoken as she reached out to touch both Macrina and Peter, "To you, O Lord, I offer the first and tenth fruit of my pains. The first fruit, my eldest daughter here, and this my tenth, my last-born son. Both have been dedicated to you by law and are your votive offerings. May sanctification, (ἀγιασμός) therefore, come to this first and tenth."[125] This sanctification was a mother's desire for theosis in the life of all of her children. The children themselves realized that they had been raised in an unusual household and by parents completely dedicated to God. Macrina thanked God on her deathbed for her parents' lives which had been "enhanced by divine favor."[126] Emmelia's children literally became an army of Saints which influenced not only the Christian world of their day, but by participating in an infinite God, they continue to lead us in the direction of theosis today. Emmelia's ever-increasing participation in God continues to this moment as the effects of her obedience continue throughout eternity, and in this, she has and will continue to experience theosis.

Conclusions

Theosis was not simply an intellectual pursuit for the Cappadocians, but rather a lifestyle that affected every facet of their daily lives. Therefore the implications for a life focused on deification went beyond the spiritual real and informed the daily lives of them all, including the women related to them. The concepts seemed to grow and develop as the Cappadocian Fathers themselves grew and developed in regard to theosis. Nyssen and Macrina's attitude toward slavery developed in their adult lives when they chose to live a lifestyle that put them on equal status with those around them. Basil adopted a life of asceticism as he believed this would help him in the process of theosis. Basil was not alone in this practice of asceticism, but as he saw it worked it out at Annesi, he penned the rules which would guide future orders of ascetics. As Christianity continued to expand throughout the fourth century the Cappadocians saw practical applications for their understanding of theosis which included the use of women in ministry settings. The sisters Macrina and Theosebia did not fulfil traditional roles within the family, nor within the life of the church. The goal of theosis led to them to new heights which stretched beyond the bounds of culture.

124. Ibid.
125. Ibid.
126. Ibid. (PG 46:980) (SC 178) (GNO VIII.I) (FC, 177).

The greatest criticism of the Cappadocians is that their theological writings did not place enough emphasis on the value of theosis in marriage and the home. On a personal level, they greatly admired the homes in which they were raised. However, their continual emphasis on asceticism and the life of celibacy created a shift in Christianity, which would have dire consequences. Van Dam commented, "In the end, the Cappadocian Fathers choose not to continue their families' lineages. For all their prominence as founders of or participants in ascetic communities, by not having children they had failed to sustain their own families. Their decisions not to marry or not to have children doomed their families to social extinction."[127] Their theological trajectories actually destroyed the development of very environments in which someone like them could be raised and nurtured. While later ascetics and virgins were able to influence the world by their work and ministry, one wonders what spiritual centers were lost with the focus on monasticism and celibacy.

---

127. Van Dam, *Families and Friends*, 86.

CHAPTER 9

The Mothers Exemplify
Deification

WE HAVE EXAMINED THE theology of deification as it was understood by the Cappadocian Fathers, while recognizing that their development of theology did not occur in a vacuum. Significantly, they each wrote about the women who were involved in their lives. The stories of these women have been included and as a result, our understanding of theosis or deification has become more robust. The lives of their female relatives were the source of the concrete experience of personal relationships and manner of life which shaped the Cappadocians' theology of theosis, making it more than mere theory. The Cappadocian women exemplified theosis at all levels.

The Cappadocian Fathers took the time to include their female relatives in their writings, and we have been asking the question, "why?" We have been searching for the plot, and specifically, what we were to learn from their stories. The question of objectivity continues to rise; and the reality is that one cannot be completely objective in the evaluation of these stories, for they are hagiographic in nature and beg to be read within their context. Gabrielle Spiegel encourages a reading which registers the *social logic*, and that has emerged as we have read these documents from a *theological perspective*.[1] For the Cappadocians, the human experience that is portrayed within the lives of the women provides the flesh stretched over their theological skeleton of theosis. They are the living examples of their theological perspectives. They provide the illustrations for individuals in all manner of life, male and female, for living a life completely devoted to God.

The three Cappadocian Fathers fought the major theological battles of their day and after great personal sacrifice came out the victors, and yet, theological victory was not the goal, but rather, the goal was God himself. Their lifestyle was just as important to them as their theology, for their

1. Clark, "Lady Vanishes," 23.

theology was a lived-out theology which had been instilled in all of them from their very childhood. The ultimate goal of theosis meant that the Cappadocians could interpret their theology within several different contexts. When Nyssen gave his discourse *De Virginitate*, he suggested that everyone desiring to live a life of virtue must find a "fitting guide for such a life," one who "by the grace of God" can "point the way to the safeguarding of a life of virtue."[2] He reminded his readers that there are saints who have been placed before us who were on their way to God and these lives serve as guiding lights.[3] Those worth emulating were not young people, new in their faith, but rather those who were adorned with heads of gray hair.[4] For these great men, it was the community of women who nurtured them, taught them, cajoled them, led them and loved them that became their *fitting guides* and taught them what it really meant to have the image restored, become united with Christ and, ultimately, to become his bride. Basil had said, "You are children of confessors and children of martyrs, who strove unto blood against sin. Let each of you use his own kin as example of constancy on behalf of piety."[5] These women became for the Cappadocian Fathers the flame on a lit candle. This was a light which the women shared with all of those around them so that they too could become light but without diminishing the original light, their light becoming "equally present in those lighted from it."[6] In this way they have distributed the dignity of this life "to those who come near . . . for the prophetic word is true that one associating with the holy and the innocent and the elect will take on their characteristics."[7] Basil the Great, his brother Gregory of Nyssa and his friend Gregory Nazianzen all took upon themselves characteristics of the holy women who had helped to shape their lives. The very holiness of these women became a part of their nature and infused them to the very core with a desire for God and Christlikeness. This drive toward Christlikeness, or transformation into the image of God, changed them on a personal level, not by their own ability, but by the grace of God combined with the life of virtue. Nyssen explained, "Being like the divine is not our function, nor is

---

2. Nyssen, *DV* (PG 46:320) (SC 119) (GNO VIII.I) (FC, 7). Interestingly later in *DV* 6 he uses Elias and John the Baptist as role models, which seems a bit curious. It seems that he may have discovered that the bent toward female models of virginity was dominant and therefore needed to include male models. Overall, however, he returns to female role models for the bride of Christ and virginity.

3. Nyssen, *DV* 12 (PG 46:369) (SC 119) (GNO VIII.I) (FC, 42).

4. Ibid., 23 (PG 46:405) (SC 119) (GNO VIII.I) (FC, 70).

5. Basil, *Ep.* 240 (Deferrari, LCL).

6. Nyssen, *DV* 23 (PG 46:405) (SC 119) (GNO VIII.I) (FC, 72).

7. Ibid. Ps 17:26–27.

it the product of human ability, but it is part of the generosity of God who freely, at the birth of the first man, gave our nature a likeness to Himself."[8] The women paved the way, living lives of virtue which became road maps for men and women alike, leading all to the very likeness of Christ.

This study has included placing the lives of the women on a road map, that of the kenosis-theosis parabola. While it may not have been the intent of the Cappadocians to place them within the parabola, the goal and theology of theosis so permeated their lives that this pattern emerged. Along the way the life of a woman emerged which became illustrative of their theology. The emotion expressed in regard to the Fallen Virgin brought about a clearer understanding of the restoration of the image. Nonna and Gorgonia became for all of humanity the new Eve and presented a clearer picture of God's original intent for a marriage of partners which reflected the perichoretic relationship found in the Trinity. Macrina, pure and undefiled, living a life of virginity completely focused on Christ became his bride. The emphasis on theosis and women like Macrina the Elder and Emmelia also provided additional implications in understanding the purpose of holiness in the home. Sadly they may not have fully understood these implications at the time. And finally, the focus on deification allowed the Cappadocians to develop thoughts on slavery and gender equality, and women in ministry which are appreciated to this day.

Theosebia's presence and ministry in Nyssa asks us to examine the present and future role of women in ministry. For both the Orthodox and Roman Catholic Churches, tradition is the authority. If, traditionally, women such as Theosebia were ordained into official roles of ministry in the early church, why should women not be ordained today? This brings into question whether the goal of the church today continues to be deification. The Cappadocians' theology appears open to various applications if one remains within the framework of deification. As with the case of Nonna and Gregory, the roles of husband and wife become malleable when the goal is theosis.

It is nearly impossible to dissect the intertwined relationships and influences of the Cappadocian Mothers on the Fathers. In many ways, they are all one and the same. Their theological thoughts belong to one another, and each helped to form the other along the way. Overall, the theology of deification in the Cappadocians combined with the influence of the women in their lives led them to the development of an optimistic eschatology for men and women alike. The Cappadocian Fathers chose to write about these women, and it must be recognized that this had a purpose, and the reasons

8. Nyssen, *DV* 12 (PG 46:369) (SC 119) (GNO VIII.I) (FC, 44).

are not simple. Averil Cameron in referring to Nyssen and Nazianzen states, "For just as real women were denied an answer to the rhetoric of their portrayal, so a male author ostensibly writing about women was writing about authority and control, and about the resolution of irreconcilable polarities."[9] She believes that the Fathers were very conscious of the broader issues at hand and completely conscious of the effect the women had on them. The Fathers had to write about these women within the confines of the rhetoric of their day. While we have not endeavored to prove the literal truth of all of their writings, it is obvious that the women in many ways informed their theology.[10] The difficulty is in determining which came first, the theology, or the practice. Ramelli argued that the Cappadocians' "theological perspectives informed social realities."[11] Elm believes the exact opposite stating, "I am not arguing that shifts in theology cause shifts in practice."[12] I concur with Ramelli that the Cappadocians' theological perspectives did inform their realities, and this is why so many of their perspectives were progressive for their day. At the same time, their social realities and relationships informed their theology. The homes in which they were raised provided a theological foundation on which the rest of their thought was developed. The women provided the living examples of their theological thought. Given the raw actuality of their experience there were those whom they simply could not discount, like Macrina and Theosebia who had become significant in the life of the church.

At the close of the fourth century, the Cappadocians were dying off, and the voice of Augustine was rising up from the new center of power in the Latin West. He did not embrace the same perspectives as the Cappadocians in regard to women, and the result on the life of women both within and without the church was profound. Lost was the hope found in the Cappadocians, and the church has yet to recover. By returning to the Cappadocians and their women, we have are optimistic. As we have seen, their perspective for both married women and virgins appears to be quite positive. There is the hope of salvation, for the grace of God reaches out to all who are lost. There is the hope of restoration in the image of God for all of humanity, for the image is neither male nor female. Therefore, the women can be, and do serve as models of theosis for both women and men. A woman has a renewed hope of restoration so as to be as the original Eve. There is the hope of a marriage within the original state which God intended. There

9. Cameron, "Virginity as Metaphor," 200.

10. Ibid.

11. Ramelli, "Theosebia," 80.

12. Elm, *Virgins of God*, 382.

is the hope for women in ministry and leadership, and ultimately, there is the future hope of being united with Christ.

As Kruger so poignantly said about the sacramental nature of Macrina's life, we may now say about all of these women's lives. The Cappadocians have gifted us with their women, and all of them, not just Macrina, are a sacrament. As the host of Eucharist remains ever available, needing only to be consecrated for us in order to be properly received by us, so too they are *for us* and *by us*.[13] These lives, so long hidden within history, are now placed on the table inviting us to join with them as "participants of the divine nature."[14]

13. Kruger, "Writing and the Liturgy," 510.

14. 2 Pet 1:4 NRSV.

Bibliography

Primary Sources

Acts of Paul and Thecla. English and Greek translation by Jeremy W. Barrier in *The Acts of Paul and Thecla: A Critical Introduction and Commentary*. Wissenschafliche Untersuchungen zum Neuen Testament 2. Tübingen: Mohr, 2009.

Acts of Paul and Thecla: The Life of the Holy Martyr Thecla of Iconium, Equal to the Apostles. English translation by Jeremiah Jones. http://www.fordham.edu/halsall/basis/thecla.html.

Athanasius. *The Incarnation of the Word*. Patrologia Graeca 25:192. *Athanase d'Alexandrie: Sur l'Incarnation du verbe*, edited and translated by C. Kannengiesser. Sources chrétiennes 199. Paris: Éditions du Cerf, 1973. English and Greek translations in *On the Incarnation: St. Athanasius*, edited by John Behr. Popular Patristics Series 44a. Crestwood, NY: St. Vladimir's Seminary Press, 2012. English translation in vol. 4 of *Nicene and Post-Nicene Fathers*, ser. 2, edited by Philip Schaff.

Augustine. *Epistles 211–270*. Patrologia Latina 33:958–1994. English translation in *The Works of Saint Augustine: Letters 211–270*. Hyde Park, NY: New City, 2005.

———. *De Civitate Dei*. Corpus Christianorum Series Latina 47–48. English translation by Henry Bettenson in *City of God*. London: Penguin, 1972.

Basil of Caesarea. *Ascetica*. Patrologia Graeca 31:619–1305. Latin translation by Rufinus in *Basili regula a Rufino latine versa*, edited by Klaus Zelzer. Corpus Scriptorum Ecclesiasticorum Latinorum 86. Viena: Hoelder-Pichter-Tempsky, 1986. English translation by W. K. Lowther Clarke in *The Ascetic Works of Saint Basil*. London: SPCK, 1925. English translation by M. Monica Wagner in *Basil of Caesarea: Ascetical Works*. Fathers of the Church 9. Repr., Washington, DC: Fathers of the Church, 1999.

———. *De spiritu sancto*. Patrologia Graeca 32:67–218. *Basile de Césarée, Sur le Saint-Espirit*, edited and translated by Benoît Pruche. 2nd ed. Sources chrétiennes 17 bis. Paris: Éditions du Cerf, 1968. English translation by Blonfield Jackson in *St. Basil the Great on the Holy Spirit*, revised by David Anderson. Crestwood, NY: St. Vladimir's Seminary Press, 1980.

———. *Epistulae*. Patrologia Graeca 32:219–1112. *Saint Basile, Lettres*, edited and translated by Yves Courtonne. 3 vols. Collection Guillaume Budé. Paris: Les Belles Lettres, 1957, 1961, 1966. English translation by Roy J. Deferrari in *Saint Basil, The Letters*. 4 vols. Loeb Classical Library. Cambridge: Harvard University

Press, 1950–53. English translation by Agnes Clare Way in *Saint Basil, Letters,*
translated. 2 vols. Fathers of the Church 13 & 28. Repr., Washington, DC: Fathers
of the Church, 1969. And vol. 8 of *The Nicene and Post-Nicene Fathers,* ser. 2,
edited by Philip Schaff. Repr., Albany, OR: Ages Electronic Library, 1997.

———. *Hexameron 1–9.* Patrologia Graeca 29:4–208. *Basile de Césarée, Homélies sur
l'Hexaéméron,* edited and translated by Stanislas Giet. 2nd ed. Sources chrétiennes
26 bis. Paris: Éditions du Cerf, 1968. English translation by Agnes Clare Way
in *Saint Basil, Exegetic Homilies,* 3–150. Fathers of the Church 46. Washington,
DC: Catholic University of America Press, 1963.

———. *Hexameron 10–11. Basile de Césarée, Homélies sur l'Hexaéméron (Homélies X et
XI de l'Hexaéméron),* edited and translated by Alexis Smets and Michel van Esbroek.
Sources chrétiennes 160. Paris: Éditions du Cerf, 1970. Russian translation in
Святитель Василий Великий. *Творения. Том Первый. Догматико полемические
творения экзегетические сочинения беседы.* В Полное собрание творений
святых отцов церкви и церковных писателей в русском переводе. Сибирская
Благозвонница: Москва, 2008. «Беседы о сотворении человека» 18.

———. *Homilia(e).* Patrologia Graeca 29:209–494; 31:163–618, 1429–514. English
translation of homilies on the Psalms by Agnes Clare Way, *Basil of Caesarea,
Exegetical Homilies.* Fathers of the Church 56. Washington, DC: Catholic
University of America Press, 1963. English translation of "I Will Pull Down
My Barns" by M. F. Toal in *The Sunday Sermons of the Great Fathers,* 3:327. San
Francisco: Ignatius, 2000.

Egeria. *The Pilgrimage of Etheria.* Edited and translated by M. L. McClure and C. L.
Feltoe. London: Society for Promoting Christian Knowledge, 1919.

Gregory Nazianzen. *De vita sua = Carmina de seipso* 11. Patrologia Graeca 37:1029–
166. Edited by Christoph Jungck, with German translation, intro and commentary.
Heidelberg: Winter, 1974. English translation by Denis Molaise Meehan in *St.
Gregory of Nazianzus, Three Poems.* Fathers of the Church 75. Repr., Washington,
DC: Fathers of the Church, 2001.

———. *Epigrammata 1–94.* Patrologia Graeca 38:81–130. English and Greek Epigrams
in *The Greek Anthology,* edited and translated by W. Paton, vol. 2, bk. 7, *Sepulchral
Epigrams;* book 8, *The Epigrams of St. Gregory the Theologian.* Loeb Classical
Library. Cambridge: Harvard University Press, 1917.

———. *Epigram 161, On Emmelia, the Mother of St. Basil.* Anthologia Graeca 8:39.
English translation by Anna Silvas in *Macrina the Younger, Philosopher of God.*
Turnhout: Brepols, 2008. Russian translation in Святеитель Грегорий Богослов.
Епиграмма 54, "Емилии, матери св. Василия Велоково" *Польное Собрание
Творений Святиых Отцов Церкви и Церковных Писателей в Русском
Переводе* Том Второй (Сибирская Благозонница, Москва, 2007), 379. In
Russian, Epigrams 161 and 162 are combined into one, listed as Epigram 54.

———. *Epigram 162, On the Same Emmelia.* Anthologia Graeca 8:39. English
translation by Anna Silvas in *Macrina the Younger, Philosopher of God.* Turnhout:
Brepols, 2008. Russian translation in Святеитель Грегорий Богослов. Епиграмма
54, "Емилии, матери св. Василия Велоково" *Польное Собрание Творений
Святиых Отцов Церкви и Церковных Писателей в Русском Переводе* Том
Второй (Сибирская Благозонница, Москва, 2007), 379. In Russian, Epigrams
161 and 162 are combined into one, listed as Epigram 54.

————. *Epigram 164, For Theosebia*. Anthologia Graeca 8:40. English translation by Anna Silvas in *Macrina the Younger, Philosopher of God*. Turnhout: Brepols, 2008.

————. *Epistulae*. Patrologia Graeca 37. *Saint Grégoire de Nazianze, Lettres*, edited and translated by Paul Gallay. 2 vols. Collection Guillaume Budé. Paris: Les Belles Lettres, 1964, 1967. See also *Gregor von Nazianz, Briefe*, edited by Paul Gallay. Griechischen Christlichen Schriftsteller 53. Berlin: Akademie-Verlag, 1969. English translations in vol. 7 of *Nicene and Post-Nicene Fathers*, ser. 2, edited by Philip Schaff. Repr., Albany, OR: Ages Electronic Library, 1997. Russian translation Святитель Григорий Богослов Архиепископ Константинопольский, *Письмо 56 & 57. Творения, в двух томах*. Сибирская Благозвонница, Москва, 2007. English translation of *Epistle 76* by Brian E. Daley in *Gregory of Nazianzus: The Early Church Fathers*. London: Routledge, 2006. *Epistle 101* also found in Sources chrétiennes 208. Russian translation of *Epistle 230* in *Полное Собрание Творений Святых Отцов Церкви и Церковных Писателей в Русском переводе: Святитель Григорий Богослов Творения: Том второй*. Сибирская Благозвонница, Москва 2006.

————. *Oration 1–2*. Patrologia Graeca 35:398–513. *Grégoire de Nazianze: Discours 1–3*, edited and translated by Jean Bernardi. Sources chrétiennes 247. Paris: Éditions du Cerf, 1978. English translation in vol. 7 of *The Nicene and Post-Nicene Fathers*, ser. 2, edited by Philip Schaff. Repr., Albany, OR: Ages Electronic Library, 1997.

————. *Oration 7, Panegyeric on His Brother Caesarius*. Patrologia Graeca 35:755–87. *Grégoire de Nazianze: Discours 6–12*, edited and translated by Marie-Ange Calvet-Sebasti. Sources chrétiennes 406. Paris: Éditions du Cerf, 1995. English translation by Leo P. McCauley et al. in *Funeral Orations by St. Gregory Nazianzen and St. Ambrose*. Fathers of the Church 22. New York: Fathers of the Church, 1953. See also vol. 7 of *The Nicene and Post-Nicene Fathers*, ser. 2, edited by Philip Schaff. Repr., Albany, OR: Ages Electronic Library, 1997.

————. *Oration 8, Funeral Oration on His Sister Gorgonia*. Patrologia Graeca 35:789–817. *Grégoire de Nazianze: Discours 6–12*, edited and translated by Marie-Ange Calvet-Sebasti. Sources chrétiennes 406. Paris: Éditions du Cerf, 1995. English translation by Brian E. Daley in *Gregory of Nazianzus: The Early Church Fathers*. London: Routledge, 2006. English translation by Leo P. McCauley et al. in *Funeral Orations by St. Gregory Nazianzen and St. Ambrose*. Fathers of the Church 22. New York: Fathers of the Church, 1953. And vol. 7 of *The Nicene and Post-Nicene Fathers*, ser. 2, edited by Philip Schaff. Repr., Albany, OR: Ages Electronic Library, 1997.

————. *Oration 18, On the Death of His Father*. Patrologia Graeca 35:985–1044. English translation by Leo P. McCauley et al. in *Funeral Orations by St. Gregory Nazianzen and St. Ambrose*. Fathers of the Church 22. New York: Fathers of the Church, 1953. English translation by Brian E. Daley in *Gregory of Nazianzus: The Early Church Fathers*. London: Routledge, 2006. See also vol. 7 of *The Nicene and Post-Nicene Fathers*, ser. 2, edited by Philip Schaff. Repr., Albany, OR: Ages Electronic Library, 1997.

————. *Oration 21, On Athanasius of Alexandria*. Patrologia Graeca 35:1081. *Grégoire de Nazianze: Discours 20–23*, edited and translated by Justin Mossay. Sources chrétiennes 270. Paris: Éditions du Cerf, 1980. English translation in vol. 7 of *The*

Nicene and Post-Nicene Fathers, ser. 2, edited by Philip Schaff. Repr., Albany, OR: Ages Electronic Library, 1997.

————. *Orations 27–31*. Patrologia Graeca 36:40. *Grégoire de Nazianze: Discours 27–31*, edited and translated by Paul Gallay and Maurice Jourjon. Sources chrétiennes 250. Paris: Éditions du Cerf, 1978. English translation by Frederick Williams (27) and Lionel Wickham (28–31) in *On God and Christ*; *St. Gregory of Nazianzus, The Five Theological Orations and Two Letters to Cledonius*. Popular Patristic Series. Crestwood, NY: St. Vladimir's Seminary Press, 2002.

————. *Oration 37, On the Words of the Gospel Matthew 19:1*. Patrologia Graeca 36:282. *Grégoire de Nazianze: Discours 32–37*, edited and translated by Claudio Moreschini. Sources chrétiennes 318. Paris: Éditions du Cerf, 1985. English translation in vol. 7 of *The Nicene and Post-Nicene Fathers*, ser. 2, edited by Philip Schaff. Repr., Albany, OR: Ages Electronic Library, 1997.

————. *Oration 38, On the Theophany*. Patrologia Graeca 36:324. *Grégoire de Nazianze: Discours 38–41*, edited and translated by Claudio Moreschini. Sources chrétiennes 358. Paris: Éditions du Cerf, 1990. English translation by Brian E. Daley in *Gregory of Nazianzus: The Early Church Fathers*. London: Routledge, 2006. See also vol. 7 of *The Nicene and Post-Nicene Fathers*, ser. 2, edited by Philip Schaff. Repr., Albany, OR: Ages Electronic Library, 1997.

————. *Oration 40, On Holy Baptism*. Patrologia Graeca 36:381. *Grégoire de Nazianze: Discours 38–41*, edited and translated by Claudio Moreschini. Sources chrétiennes 358. Paris: Éditions du Cerf, 1990. English translation in vol. 7 of *The Nicene and Post-Nicene Fathers*, ser. 2, edited by Philip Schaff. Repr., Albany, OR: Ages Electronic Library, 1997.

————. *Oration 43, The Panegyric on Saint Basil*. Patrologia Graeca 36:493–605. *Grégoire de Nazianze: Discours 42–43*, edited and translated by Jean Bernardi. Sources chrétiennes 384. Paris: Éditions du Cerf, 1992. English translation by Leo P. McCauley et al. in *Funeral Orations by St. Gregory Nazianzen and St. Ambrose*. Fathers of the Church 22. New York: Fathers of the Church, 1953. See also vol. 7 of *The Nicene and Post-Nicene Fathers*, ser. 2, edited by Philip Schaff. Repr., Albany, OR: Ages Electronic Library, 1997.

————. *Testimony to Olympia*. Patrologia Graeca 37:1542. *Ad Olympiade*, edited by Lucia Bacci. Pisa: Edizioni ETS, 1996. Russian translation Полное Собрание Творений Святых Отцов Церкви и Церковных Писателей в Русском переводе: Святитель Григорий Богослов Творения: Том второй. Сибирская Благозвонница, Москва 2006.

Gregory of Nyssa. *Contra Eunomium 2, 3*. Patrologia Graeca 42:464, 572. *Gregorii Nysseni opera*, edited by Werner Jaeger, vols. 1 and 2. Leiden: Brill, 1960. English translation in vol. 5 of *The Nicene and Post-Nicene Fathers*, ser. 2, edited by Philip Schaff. Repr., Albany, OR: Ages Electronic Library, 1997.

————. *De Anima et Resurrectione* [On the soul and the resurrection]. Patrologia Graeca 46:11–160. *S. Gregorii eposcopi Nysseni De Anima et resurrectione cum sorore sua Macrina dialogus*, edited by J. G. Krabinger. Leipzig, 1837. English translation by Catharine P. Roth in *On the Soul and the Resurrection*. Crestwood, NY: St. Vladimir's Seminary Press, 1993. English translation by Virginia Callahan in *St. Gregory Ascetical Works*. Fathers of the Church 58. Repr., Washington, DC: Fathers of the Church, 1999.

————. *De Hominis Opificio* [On the making of man]. Patrologia Graeca 44:123–256. Critical edition by G. H. Forbes, "De Conditione Hominis," in *Sancti Patris Nostri Gregorii Nysenni Basilli Magni fratris quae supersunt omnia* t.1, fasc. 1–2. Burntisland, 1855, pp. 96–319. English translation in vol. 5 of *The Nicene and Post-Nicene Fathers*, ser. 2, edited by Philip Schaff. Repr., Albany, OR: Ages Electronic Library, 1997.

————. *De Instituto Christiano.* Patrologia Graeca 46:289. *Gregorii Nysseni opera*, edited by Werner Jaeger, with others, 8:1. Leiden: Brill, 1963. English translation by Virginia Callahan in *St. Gregory Ascetical Works*. Fathers of the Church 58. Repr., Washington, DC: Catholic University of America Press, 1999.

————. *De Perfectione* [On perfection]. Patrologia Graeca 46:249. *Gregorii Nysseni opera*, edited by Werner Jaeger, with others, 8:1. Leiden: Brill, 1963. English translation by Virginia Callahan in *St. Gregory Ascetical Works*. Fathers of the Church 58. Repr., Washington, DC: Catholic University of America Press, 1999.

————. *De Professione Christiana.* Patrologia Graeca 46:237. *Gregorii Nysseni opera*, edited by Werner Jaeger, with others, 8:1. Leiden: Brill, 1963. English translation by Virginia Callahan in *St. Gregory Ascetical Works*. Fathers of the Church 58. Repr., Washington, DC: Catholic University of America Press, 1999.

————. *De Virginitate* [On virginity]. Patrologia Graeca 45.317–416. *Grégoire de Nysse, Traité de la virginité*, edited and translated by Michel Aubineau. Sources chrétiennes 119. Paris: Éditions du Cerf, 1966. *Gregorii Nysseni opera*, edited by Werner Jaeger, with others, 8:1. Leiden: Brill, 1963. English translation by Virginia Callahan in *St. Gregory Ascetical Works*. Fathers of the Church 58. Repr., Washington, DC: Catholic University of America Press, 1999.

————. *De Vita Moysis* [The life of Moses]. Patrologia Graeca 44:297. Edited by Herbert Musurillo. *Gregorii Nyssenii, De Vita Moysis*, in *Gregorii Nysseni opera*, edited by Werner Jaeger and Hermannus Langerbeck, vol. 7, pt. 1. Leiden: Brill, 1964. *La vie de Moïse; ou, Traité de la perfection en matière de vertu*, translated by Jean Daniélou. Sources chrétiennes 1bis. Paris: Éditions du Cerf, 1968. English translation by Abraham Malherbe and Everett Ferguson in *The Life of Moses*. New York: Paulist, 1978.

————. *De Vita Sanctae Macrinae* [The life of Saint Macrina]. Patrologia Graeca 46:960–1000. *Grégoire de Nysse, Vie de sainte Macrine*, edited and translated by Pierre Maraval. Sources chrétiennes 178. Paris: Éditions du Cerf, 1971. *Gregorii Nysseni opera*, edited by Werner Jaeger, with others, 8:1. Leiden: Brill, 1963. English translation by Virginia Callahan in *St. Gregory Ascetical Works*. Fathers of the Church 58. Repr., Washington, DC: Catholic University of America Press, 1999. English translation by W. K. L. Clarke in *The Life of Saint Macrina*. London: SPCK, 1916.

————. *Epistle 3, To Ablabius. Grégoire de Nysse: Lettres.* Edited and translated by Pierre Maraval. Sources chrétiennes 363. Paris: Éditions du Cerf, 1990. Also in *Gregorii Nysseni opera*, 2nd ed., edited by Werner Jaeger, vol. 8, pt. 2. Leiden: Brill, 1959. English translation by Anna Silvas in *Gregory of Nyssa: The Letters*. Brill: Leiden, 2007.

————. *Epistle 13, To the Nicomedians. Grégoire de Nysse: Lettres*, edited and translated by Pierre Maraval. Sources chrétiennes 363. Paris: Éditions du Cerf, 1990. Also in *Gregorii Nysseni opera*, 2nd ed., edited by Werner Jaeger, vol. 8, pt. 2. Leiden: Brill,

1959. English translation in vol. 5 of *The Nicene and Post-Nicene Fathers*, ser. 2, edited by Philip Schaff. Repr., Albany, OR: Ages Electronic Library, 1997.

———. *Epistulae*. Edited by G. Pasquali. In *Gregorii Nysseni opera*, 2nd ed., edited by Werner Jaeger, vol. 8, pt. 2. Leiden: Brill, 1959.

———. *A Homily of Consolation concerning Pulcheria*. Patrologia Graeca 46:864–77. English translation in vol. 5 of *The Nicene and Post-Nicene Fathers*, ser. 2, edited by Philip Schaff. Repr., Albany, OR: Ages Electronic Library, 1997.

———. *Homily 6, On the Beatitudes*. Patrologia Graeca 44:1264. *Gregory Nysseni De oratione dominica, De beatitudinibus*, edited by Johannes F. Calahan, in *Gregorii Nysseni opera*, vol. 7, pt. 2, 136–48. Leiden: Brill, 1992. English translation by Anthony Meredith in *Gregory of Nyssa*. London: Routledge, 1999.

———. *In Canticum Canticorum* [Commentary on the Canticle]. Patrologia Graeca 44:756–1120. *Gregorii Nysseni opera*, edited by H. Langerbeck, vol. 6. Leiden: Brill, 1960. English translation by Herbert Musurillo in *From Glory to Glory: Texts from the Gregory of Nyssa's Mystical Writings*. Crestwood, NY: St. Vladimir's Seminary Press, 2001. See also *Homilies on the Song of Songs*, translated by C. McCambley. Brookline, MA: Hellenic College Press, 1987.

———. *Oratio Catechatica* [The great catechism]. Patrologia Graeca 45:10. *Gregorii Nysseni opera*, edited by Ekkehard Mühlenberg, vol. 3, pt. 4. Leiden: Brill, 1996. *Discours catéchétique*, Greek text of Mühlenberg, edited and translated by R. Wingling. Sources chrétiennes 453. Paris: Éditions du Cerf, 2000. English translation by H. Swraley in *The Catechetical Oration of Gregory of Nyssa*. Cambridge: Cambridge University Press, 1903. Also in vol. 5 of *The Nicene and Post-Nicene Fathers*, ser. 2, edited by Philip Schaff. Repr., Albany, OR: Ages Electronic Library, 1997.

———. *Vita Gregorii Thaumaturgii* [The life of Gregory the Wonderworker]. Patrologia Graeca 46:893–957. In *Gregorii Nysseni Sermones, pars II. Gregorii Nysseni opera*, edited by G. Heil, vol. 10, pt. 1. Leiden: Brill, 1990. English translation by M. Slusser in *St. Gregory Thaumaturgus: Life and Works*. Fathers of the Church 98. Washington, DC: Catholic University of America Press, 1998. See also English translation by David A. Solomon, http://web.archive.org/web/20010617133640/www.bhsu.edu/dsalomon/nyssa/thaum.html.

Gregory Thaumaturgus. *Oration and Panegyric Addressed to Origen*. Patrologia Graeca 10:1049. *Grégoire le Thamaturge, Remerciement à Origéne, suivi de la Lettre d'Origéne à Grégoire*, edited and translated by Henri Crouzel. Sources chrétiennes 148. Paris: Éditions du Cerf, 1969. English translation by S. D. F. Salmond, http://www.ewtn.com/library/PATRISTC/ANF6-4.TXT. English translation by W. Metcalf, *Address to Origen*, in vol. 4 of *The Nicene and Post-Nicene Fathers*, ser. 2, edited by Philip Schaff. London: SPCK, 1920.

Irenaeus. *Against Heresies 3, 4, 5*. Patrologia Graeca 7:437–1224. *Irénée de Lyon: Contres les hérésies*, livres 3, 4, 5, edited and translated by A. Rousseau et al. 6 vols. Sources chrétiennes 210, 211, 100.1, 100.2, 152, 153. Paris: Éditions du Cerf, 1974, 1965, 1969. English translation in vol. 1 of *The Ante-Nicene Fathers*, ser. 1, edited by Alexander Roberts and James Donaldson. Repr., Peabody, MA: Hendrickson, 1994.

Jerome. *Epistle 133*. Corpus Scriptorum Ecclesiastical Latinorum 56. Vienna, 1866.

Methodius. *Banquet on the Ten Virgins*. Patrologia Graeca 18. *Methodius*, edited by G. Bonwetsch. Griechischen Christlichen Schriftsteller 27. Berlin: Akademie-

Verlag, 1917. *Le banquet*, edited by H. Musurillo. Sources chretiennes 95. Paris: Éditions du Cerf, 1963. English translation in vol. 6 of *The Ante-Nicene Fathers*, ser. 1, edited by Alexander Roberts and James Donaldson. Repr., Peabody, MA: Hendrickson, 1994.

————. *From the Discourse on the Resurrection.* Patrologia Graeca 18. *Methodius*, edited by G. Bonwetsch. Griechischen Christlichen Schriftsteller 27. Berlin: Akademie-Verlag, 1917. English translation in vol. 6 of *The Ante-Nicene Fathers*, ser. 1, edited by Alexander Roberts and James Donaldson. Repr., Peabody, MA: Hendrickson, 1994.

Origen. *Against Celsus 3.* Patrologia Graeca 11:956. *Contra Celsum*, edited by M. Borret, 5 vols. Sources chrétiennes nos. 132, 136, 147, 150, 227. Paris: Éditions du Cerf, 1967–1976. Some English portions may be found in Jules Gross, *The Divinization of the Christian according to the Greek Fathers*, translated by Onica. Anaheim: A & C, 2002. English translation by Henry Chadwick in *Origen: Contra Celsum*. Cambridge: Cambridge University Press, 1953. English translation in vol. 4 of *The Ante-Nicene Fathers*, ser. 1, edited by Alexander Roberts and James Donaldson. Repr., Peabody, MA: Hendrickson, 1994.

————. *Commentary on John.* Patrologia Graeca 14:39. *Commentarii in evangelium Joannis*, edited and translated by C. Blanc, vols. 1, 2, 4, 5; 6, 10; 13; 19–29; 28, 32. Sources chrétiennes 120, 157, 222, 290, 385. Paris: Éditions du Cerf, 1966, 1970, 1975, 1982, 1992. English translation in vol. 9 of *The Ante-Nicene Fathers*, ser. 1, edited by Alexander Roberts and James Donaldson. Repr., Peabody, MA: Hendrickson, 1994.

————. *Commentary on Matthew.* Patrologia Graeca 14:936. English translation by John Patrick. http://mb-soft.com/believe/txua/origenmt.htm.

————. *Commentary on the Song of Songs.* Patrologia Graeca 13:61–216. English translation in vol. 4 of *The Ante-Nicene Fathers*, ser. 1, edited by Alexander Roberts and James Donaldson. Repr., Peabody, MA: Hendrickson, 1994.

————. *De Principiis.* Patrologia Graeca 11:333. *De principiis*, edited by H. Görgemanns and H. Karpp, *Origenes vier Bücher von den Prinzipien*. Darmstadt: Wissenschaftliche Buchgesellschaft, 1976. English translation in vol. 4 of *The Ante-Nicene Fathers*, ser. 1, edited by Alexander Roberts and James Donaldson. Repr., Peabody, MA: Hendrickson, 1994.

————. *Homily on the Song of Songs.* Patrologia Graeca 13:47. English translation by R. P. Lawson in *Ancient Christian Writers*. Mahwah, NJ: Paulist, 1956. English translation in vol. 4 of *The Ante-Nicene Fathers*, ser. 1, edited by Alexander Roberts and James Donaldson. Repr., Peabody, MA: Hendrickson, 1994.

————. *A Letter from Origen to Gregory.* Patrologia Graeca 11. English translation in vol. 4 of *The Ante-Nicene Fathers*, ser. 1, edited by Alexander Roberts and James Donaldson. Repr., Peabody, MA: Hendrickson, 1994.

————. *Treatise on the Passover.* English translation in *Ancient Christian Writers*, edited by Robert J. Daley. Mahwah, New Jersey: Paulist, 1992.

Plato. *The Dialogues of Plato.* English translation by B. Jowett. 3rd ed. 5 vols. Oxford: Oxford University Press, 1892. http://oll.libertyfund.org/title/766/93700.

————. *Symposium.* Original Greek, http://www.perseus.tufts.edu/cgi-bin/ptext?doc =Perseus%3Atext%3A1999.01.0173;layout=;query=toc;loc=Phaedrus%20279c. English translation by Benjamin Jowett, http://classics.mit.edu/Plato/symposium. html.

————. *Theaetetus.* Original Greek, http://old.perseus.tufts.edu/cgi-bin/ptext?doc=Pe rseus%3Atext%3A1999.01.0171. English translation by Harold N. Fowler in *Plato in Twelve Volumes,* vol. 12. Cambridge: Harvard University Press, 1921.

Plotinus. *Ennaedes.* Original Greek (downloadable), http://hiphi.ubbcluj.ro/fam/texte/ plotin/enneade.htm. English translation by Stephen MacKenna and B. S. Page in *Plotius the Ennaedes.* New York: Larson, 1992.

Pseudo-Dionysius. *Works.* English translation by Colm Luibheid in *Pseudo-Dionysius: The Complete Works.* Mahwah, NJ: Paulist, 1987. English translation by John Parker in *Complete Works,* bk. 2, *Ecclesiastical Hierarchy,* 1.3, http://www.ccel.org/ ccel/dionysius/works.iv.iii.i.html.

Socrates Scholasticus. *Ecclesiastical Letter* 4. Edited by Günther Christian Hansen, *Sokrates Kirchengeschichte.* Griechischen Christlichen Schriftsteller neue Folge 1. Berlin: Akademie-Verlag, 1995. English translation in vol. 2 of *The Nicene and Post-Nicene Fathers,* ser. 2, edited by Philip Schaff.

Tertullian. *On Baptism. Traité du baptême,* edited by R. F. Refoulé and M. Drouzy. Rev. ed. Sources chrétiennes 35. Paris: Éditions du Cerf, 2002. English translation by Ernest Evans in *Tertullian's Homily on Baptism.* London: SPCK, 1964.

————. *On the Apparel of Women. La toilette des femmes (De cultu feminarum),* edited by M. Turcan. Sources chrétiennes 173. Paris: Éditions du Cerf, 1971. English translation in vol. 4 of *The Ante-Nicene Fathers,* ser. 1, edited by Alexander Roberts and James Donaldson. Repr., Peabody, MA: Hendrickson, 1994.

Secondary Sources

Abramowski, Luise. "Des Bekenntnis des Gregory Thaumaturgus bei Gregory von Nyssa und das Problem seiner Echtheit." *Zeitschrift für Kirchengeschichte* 87 (1976) 145–66.

Albrecht, Ruth. *Das Leben der heiligen Makrina auf dem Hintergrund der Thekla-Traditionen: Studien zu dem Ursprüngen des weiblichen Mönchtums im 4. Jahrhundert in Kleinasien.* Göttingen: Vandenhoek & Ruprecht, 1986.

Allen, Pauline. *Severus of Antioch: The Early Church Fathers.* London: Routledge, 2004.

Anatolios, Khalid. "The Soteriological Significance of Christ's Humanity in St. Athanasius." *St. Vladimir's Theological Quarterly* 40:4 (1996) 265–86.

Ayres, Lewis. *Nicaea and Its Legacy: An Approach to Fourth-Century Trinitarian Theology.* Oxford: Oxford University Press, 2004.

Balthasar, Hans Urs von. *Presence and Thought: Essay on the Religious Philosophy of Gregory of Nyssa.* Translated by Mark Sebanc. San Francisco: Ignatius, 1995.

Barrier, Jeremy. *The Acts of Paul and Thecla: A Critical Introduction and Commentary.* Wissenschafliche Untersuchungen zum Neuen Testament 2. Tübingen: Mohr, 2009.

Bartos, Emil. *Deification in Eastern Orthodox Theology.* Eugene, OR: Wipf & Stock, 1999.

Bassett, Paul M. *Holiness Teaching: New Testament Times to Wesley.* 3 vols. Great Holiness Classics. Kansas City: Beacon Hill, 1997.

Beagon, Philip M. "The Cappadocian Fathers, Women and Ecclesiastical Politics." *Vigiliae Christianae* 49 (1995) 165–79.

Beeley, Christopher A. *Gregory of Nazianzus on the Trinity and the Knowledge of God: In Your Light We Shall See Light*. Oxford: Oxford University Press, 2008.

Behr-Sigel, Elisabeth. *The Ministry of Women in the Church*. Crestwood, NY: St. Vladimir's Seminary Press, 1999.

Blevins, Dean G. "'Holy Church, Holy People': A Wesleyan Exploration in Congregational Holiness and Personal Testament." *Wesleyan Theological Journal* 39 (2004) 54–73.

Børtnes, Jostein. "Rhetoric and Mental Images in Gregory." In Børtnes and Hägg, *Gregory of Nazianzus*, 37–57.

Børtnes, Jostein, and Tomas Hägg, eds. *Gregory of Nazianzus: Images and Reflections*. Copenhagen: Museum Tusculanum Press, 2006.

Brown, Peter. *The Body and Society: Men, Women and Sexual Renunciation in Early Christianity*. London: Faber and Faber, 1989.

———. "The Rise and Function of the Holy Man in Late Antiquity." *Journal of Roman Studies* 61 (1971) 80–101.

Burrus, Virginia. *"Begotten, Not Made": Conceiving Manhood in Late Antiquity*. Stanford: Stanford University Press, 2000.

———. "Life after Death: The Martyrdom of Gorgonia and the Birth of Female Hagiography." In Børtnes and Hägg, *Gregory of Nazianzus*, 153–70.

———. "Macrina's Tatoo." *Journal of Medieval and Early Modern Studies* 33:3 (2003) 403–17.

———. "Torture and Travail: Producing the Christian Martyr." In Levine, *Feminist Companion to Patristic Literature*, 56–72.

Bynum, C. Walker. *Holy Feast and Holy Fast: The Religious Significance of Food to Medieval Women*. Berkeley: University of California Press, 1987.

Callahan, Virginia Woods, trans. *St. Gregory Ascetical Works*. Father's of the Church 58. Repr., Washington, DC: Fathers of the Church, 1999.

Cameron, Averil, ed. *History as Text: The Writing of Ancient History*. London: Duckworth, 1989.

———. "Sacred and Profane Love: Thoughts on Byzantine Gender." In James, *Women, Men and Eunuchs: Gender in Byzantium*, 1–23.

———. "Virginity as Metaphor: Women and the Rhetoric of Early Christianity." In Cameron, *History as Text*, 181–205.

Castelli, Elizabeth. "Virginity and Its Meaning in the Early Church." In Levine, *Feminist Companion to Patristic Literature*, 72–101.

———, ed. *Women, Gender, Religion: A Reader*. New York: Palgrave, 2001.

Chadwick, Henry. *Early Christian Thought and the Classical Tradition*. New York: Oxford University Press, 1966.

Chowning, Magaret. *Rebellious Nuns: The Troubled History of a Mexican Convent, 1752–1863*. New York: Oxford University Press, 2006.

Chrestou, Panagiotes. *Partakers of God*. Brookline, MA: Holy Cross Orthodox Press, 1984.

Christensen, Michael J. "Theosis and Sanctification: John Wesley's Reformulation of a Patristic Doctrine." *Wesleyan Theological Journal* 31:2 (1996) 71–94.

Clark, Elizabeth A. *Ascetic Piety and Women's Faith: Essays on Late Ancient Christianity*. Studies in Women and Religion 20. Lewiston: Mellen, 1986.

———. "Authority and Humility: A Conflict of Values in Fourth-Century Female Monasticism." *Byzantinische Forschungen* 9 (1985) 17–33.

————. "Early Christian Women: Sources and Interpretation." In *That Gentle Strength: Historical Perspectives on Women in Christianity*, edited by L. L. Coon et al., 19–35. Charlottesville: University of Virginia Press, 1990.

————. *History, Theory, Text: Historians and the Linguistic Turn*. Harvard: Harvard University Press, 2004.

————. "Holy Women, Holy Words: Early Christian Women, Social History, and the 'Linguistic Turn.'" *Journal of Early Christian Studies* 6:3 (1998) 413–30.

————. "Ideology, History and the Construction of 'Woman' in Late Antique Christianity." *Journal of Early Christian Studies* 2 (1994) 155–84.

————. "The Lady Vanishes: Dilemmas of a Feminist Historian after the 'Linguistic Turn.'" *Church History* 67:1 (1998) 1–31.

————. "Theory and Practice in Late Ancient Asceticism: Jerome, Chrysostom and Augustine." *Journal of Feminist Studies in Religion* 5 (1989) 25–46.

————. "Women, Gender, and the Study of Christian History." *History* 70:3 (2001) 395–426.

————. *Women in the Early Church: Message of the Fathers of the Church*. Wilmington, DE: Glazier, 1983.

Clark, Gillian. *Women in Late Antiquity: Pagan and Christian Lifestyles*. Oxford: Oxford University Press, 1994.

Clarke, Kempe Lowther. *St. Basil the Great: A Study in Monasticism*. Cambridge: Cambridge University Press, 1913.

Cloke, Gillian. *This Female Man of God: Women and Spiritual Power in the Patristic Age*. London: Routledge, 1995.

Coakley, Sarah. "Kenosis: Theological Meanings and Gender Connotations." In Polkinghorne, *Work of Love*, 192–209.

————, ed. *Re-thinking Gregory of Nyssa*. Oxford: Blackwell, 2003.

Coon, Lynda L. *Sacred Fictions: Holy Women and Hagiography in Late Antiquity*. Philadelphia: University of Pennsylvania Press, 1997.

Crouzel, Henri. *Origen*. Translated by A. S. Worrall. Edinburgh: T. & T. Clark, 1989.

Crump, David. "Re-examining the Johannine Trinity: Perichoresis or Deification?" *Scottish Journal of Theology* 59:4 (2006) 395–412.

Cutsinger, James S., ed. *Reclaiming the Great Tradition: Evangelicals, Catholics & Orthodox in Dialogue*. Downers Grove: InterVarsity, 1997.

Daley, Brian E. *Gregory of Nazianzus: The Early Church Fathers*. London: Routledge, 2006.

Damascene, Hieromonk. "The Way of Spiritual Transformation." Talk given at the Parish Life Conference of the Antiochian Orthodox Diocese of Wichita and Mid-America, Sioux City, Iowa, June 9, 2005. http://orthodoxinfo.com/praxis/spiritualtransformation.aspx.

Daniélou, Jean. *From Glory to Glory: Texts from the Gregory of Nyssa's Mystical Writings*. Translated and edited by Herbert Musurillo. Crestwood, NY: St. Vladimir's Press, 2001.

————. "Grégoire de Nysse à travers les lettres de Saint Basile et de Saint Grégoire de Nazianze." *Vigiliae Christianae* 19:1 (1965) 31–41.

————. "Le Mariage de Grégoire de Nysse et la chronologie de sa vie." *Revue des études Augustiniennes* 2 (1956) 71–78.

Davis, Stephen J. *The Cult of Saint Thecla: A Tradition of Women's Piety in Late Antiquity*. New York: Oxford University Press, 2001.

Delcogliano, Mark. "Basil of Caesarea on Proverbs 8:22 and the Sources of Pro-Nicene Theology." *Journal of Theological Studies*, n.s., 59:1 (2008) 183–90.

Dillon John. *The Middle Platonists: 80 B.C. to A.D. 220*. Ithaca: Cornell University Press, 1977.

Doohan, Leonard. "Scripture and Contemporary Spirituality." *Spirituality Today* 42:1 (1990) 62–74.

Dreuille, Mayeul de. *Seeking the Absolute Love: The Founders of Christian Monasticism*. New York: Crossroad, 1999.

Drewery, Benjamin. "Deification." In *Christian Spirituality: Essays in Honor of Gordon Rupp*, edited by Peter Brooks, 35–62. London: SCM, 1975.

Dunbar, Agnes B. C. *A Dictionary of Saintly Women*. Vol. 2. London: Bell, 1905. http://www.archive.org/stream/saintlywomen02dunbuoft/saintlywomen02dunbuoft_djvu.txt.

Elm, Susanna. *"Virgins of God": The Making of Asceticism in Late Antiquity*. Oxford: Clarendon, 1994.

Finlan, Stephen, and Vladimir Kharlamov. *Theosis: Deification in Christian Theology*. Princeton Theological Monograph. Eugene, OR: Pickwick, 2006.

Florovsky, George. "St. Gregory Palamas and the Tradition of the Fathers." In *The Collected Works of Georges Florovksy*, vol. 1, *Bible, Church, Tradition: An Eastern Orthodox View*, 105–20. Vaduz: Buchervertriebsanstaltr, 1987.

Ford, David, and Mary Ford. *Marriage as a Path to Holiness: Lives of Married Saints*. South Canaan, PA: St. Tikhon's Seminary Press, 1999.

Frank, Georgia. "Macrina's Scar: Homeric Allusion and Heroic Identity in Gregory of Nyssa's 'Life of Macrina.'" *Journal of Early Christian Studies* 8:4 (2000) 511–30.

Frantzen, Allen J. "When Women Aren't Enough." *Speculum* 2 (1993) 445–71.

Fry, E. J. B., and A. H. Armstrong, eds. *Rediscovering Eastern Christendom: Essays in Memory of Don Bede Winslow*. London: Darton, Longman & Todd, 1963.

Gambero, Luigi. *Mary and the Fathers of the Church: The Blessed Virgin Mary in Patristic Thought*. San Francisco: Ignatius, 1999.

Goldstein, Valerie Saiving. "The Human Situation: A Feminine View." In *Womenspirit Rising*, edited by Carol Christ and Judith Plaskow, 25–42. San Francisco: Harper & Row, 1979.

Goody, Jack. *The Development of the Family and Marriage in Europe*. Cambridge: Cambridge University Press, 1990.

Greek New Testament (Textus Receptus) with Strong's Numbers. OakTree Software Inc., vers. 1.2, 2003.

Grillmeier, Aloys, et al. *Christ in Christian Tradition: From the Council of Chalcedon*. Vol. 2, pt. 2. London: Mowbray, 1995.

Gross, Jules. *The Divinization of the Christian according to the Greek Fathers*. Translated by P. A. Onica. Anaheim: A&C, 2002.

Hanson, R. P. C. *The Search for the Christian Doctrine of God: The Arian Controversy 318–381*. Edinburgh: T. & T. Clark, 1988.

Hardy, Edward, ed. *Christology of the Later Fathers*. Philadelphia: Westminster, 1954.

Harrison, Verna F. "Allegory and Eroticism in Gregory of Nyssa." *Semeia* 57 (1992) 113–30.

———. "Gender, Generation, and Virginity in Cappadocian Theology." *Journal of Theological Studies*, n.s., 47:1 (1996) 38–67.

————. "Male and Female in Cappadocian Theology." *Journal of Theological Studies*, n.s., 41:2. (1990) 441–70.

Harrison, Nonna Verna. "Women, Human Identity, and the Image of God: Antiochene Interpretations." *Journal of Early Christian Studies* 9:2 (2001) 205–49.

Harvey, Susan Ashbrook. "Sacred Bonding: Mothers and Daughters in Early Syriac Hagiography." *Journal of Early Christian Studies* 4:1 (1996) 27–57.

————. "Women in Early Byzantine Hagiography: Reversing the Story." In *That Gentle Strength: Historical Perspectives on Women in Christianity*, edited by L. L. Coon et al., 36–59. Charlottesville: University Press of Virginia, 1990.

Hastings, James, ed. *Encylopaedia of Religion and Ethics*. Vol. 3. Edinburgh: T. & T. Clark, 1910.

Havel, Václev. "The End of the Modern Era." *New York Times*, March 1, 1992. http://www.gse.buffalo.edu/FAS/Bromley/classes/theory/Havel.htm.

Hawkins, Aly, and Bryan Ashmore. *My Lover Is Mine: Words and Images Inspired by the Ancient Love Poetry of Solomon*. Ventura, CA: Regal, 2006.

Hayne, Léonie. "Thecla and the Church Fathers." *Vigiliae Christianae* 48:3 (1994) 209–18.

Henderson, Katharine Rhodes. *God's Troublemakers: How Women of Faith Are Changing the World*. New York: Continuum, 2006.

Herrin, J. "In Search of Byzantine Women: Three Avenues of Approach." In *Images of Women in Antiquity*, edited by Averil Cameron and Amelie Kuhrt, 167–89. Abingdon: Routledge, 1993.

Hildebrand, Stephen M. *The Trinitarian Theology of Basil of Caesarea*. Washington, DC: Catholic University of America Press, 2007.

Horowitz, Maryann Cline. "The Image of God in Man: Is Woman Included?" *Harvard Theological Review* 7 (1979) 175–206.

Hudson, Nancy J. *Becoming God: The Doctrine of Theosis in Nicholas of Cusa*. Washington, DC: Catholic University of America Press, 2007.

Jaeger, Werner. *Early Christianity and Greek Paideia*. Cambridge: Belknap of Harvard University Press, 1961.

————. *Gregor Von Nyssa's Lehre Vom Heilgen Geist*. Leiden: Brill, 1966.

————. *Two Rediscovered Works of Ancient Christian Literature: Gregory of Nyssa and Macarius*. Leiden: Brill, 1965.

James, Carolyn Custis. *Lost Women of the Bible: The Women We Thought We Knew*. Grand Rapids: Zondervan, 2005.

James, Liz, ed. *Women, Men and Eunuchs: Gender in Byzantium*. London: Routledge, 1997.

Johnson, Scott Fitzgerald. *The Life and Miracles of Thekla: A Literary Study*. Cambridge: Harvard University Press, 2006.

Jones, Serene. "Divining Women: Irigaray and Feminist Theologies." *Yale French Studies* 87 (1995) 42–67.

Kannengiesser, Charles. "Christology." In *The Westminster Handbook to Origen*, edited by John Anthony McGuckin, 73–78. Louisville: Westminster John Knox, 2004.

Kärkkäinen, Veli-Matti. *One with God: Salvation as Deification and Justification*. Collegeville: Liturgical, 2004.

Kassian, Mary. "The History of Feminism and the Church: Part II, An Excerpt and Summary from *The Feminist Gospel*." *Journal for Biblical Manhood and*

Womanhood 4:1 (1999) no pages. www.cbmw.org/Journal/Vol-4-No-1/The-History-of-Feminism-and-the-Church-Part-II.

Keenan, Mary Emily. "De Professione Christiana and De Perfectione: A Study of the Ascetical Doctrine of Saint Gregory of Nyssa." *Dumbarton Oaks Papers* 5 (1950) 169–207.

Keener, Craig. *Paul, Women and Wives: Marriage and Women's Ministry in the Letters of Paul.* Peabody, MA: Hendrickson, 1998.

Kelly, J. N. D. *Golden Mouth: The Story of John Chrysostom.* Grand Rapids: Baker, 1995.

Kirsch, Johann Peter. "Sts. Thecla." In *The Catholic Encyclopedia*, vol. 14. New York: Appleton, 1912. http://www.newadvent.org/cathen/14564a.htm.

Knight, Douglas. *The Theology of John Zizioulas: Personhood and the Church.* Burlington, VT: Ashgate, 2007.

Köstenberger, Margaret Elizabeth. *Jesus and the Feminists: Who Do They Say That He Is?* Wheaton, IL: Crossway, 2008.

Kraemer, Ross Shepard, and Mary Rose D'Angelo, eds. *Women and Christian Origins.* Oxford: Oxford University Press, 1999.

Krawiec, Rebecca. "'From the Womb of the Church': Monastic Families." *Journal of Early Christian Studies* 11:3 (2003) 283–307.

Kruger, Derek. "Writing and the Liturgy of Memory in Gregory of Nyssa's *Life of Macrina.*" *Journal of Early Christian Studies* 8:4 (2000) 483–510.

Ladner, Gerhart B. "The Philosophical Anthropology of Saint Gregory of Nyssa." *Dumbarton Oaks Papers* 12 (1958) 59–94.

Leclerc, Diane. *Discovering Christian Holiness: The Heart of Wesleyan-Holiness Theology.* Kansas City: Beacon Hill, 2010.

———. *Singleness of Heart: Gender, Sin, and Holiness in Historical Perspective.* Lanham, MD: Scarecrow, 2001.

Levin, Amy-Jill, ed. *A Feminist Companion to Patristic Literature.* New York: T. & T. Clark, 2008.

Lienhard, Joseph T. "Ps-Athanasius, Contra Sabellianos, and Basil of Caesarea, Contra Sabellianos et Arium et Anomoeos: Analysis and Comparison." *Vigiliae Christianae* 40:4 (1986) 365–89.

Lilla, R. C. Salvatore. *Neoplatonisches Gedankengut in den "Homilien über die Seligpreisungen" Gregors von Nyssa.* Leiden: Brill, 2004.

Lim, Richard. "The Politics of Interpretation in Basil of Caesarea's 'Hexaemeron.'" *Vigiliae Christianae* 44:4 (1990) 351–70.

Limberis, Vasiliki M. *Architects of Piety: The Cappadocian Fathers and the Cult of the Martyrs.* Oxford: Oxford University Press, 2011. Kindle ed.

Lossky, Vladimir. *In the Image and Likeness of God.* Crestwood, NY: St. Vladimir's Seminary Press, 1985.

———. *The Mystical Theology of the Eastern Church.* Cambridge : Clarke, 1957.

———. *Orthodox Theology: An Introduction.* Crestwood, NY: St. Vladimir's Seminary Press, 1989.

Luck, Georg. "Notes on the *De Vita Macrinae Macrinae* by Gregory of Nyssa. " In *The Biographical Works of Gregory of Nyssa*, edited by Andreas Spira, 21–31. Patristic Monograph 12. Cambridge, MA: Philadelphia Patristic Foundation, 1984.

Luckman, Harriet A. *Basil of Caesarea and Purity of Heart.* In *Purity of Heart in Early Ascetic and Monastic Literature*, edited by Harriet A. Luckman and Linda Kulzer, 89–106. Collegeville: Liturgical, 1999.

Ludlow, Morwenna. *Gregory of Nyssa, Ancient and (Post)modern.* Oxford: Oxford University Press, 2007.

Maddix, Mark A., and Adrienne M. Meier. "Listening to Voice: Revisioning Feminist Pedagogy for Christian Education and Formation." *Didache: Faithful Teaching* 11:1 (2011) no pages. http://didache.nazarene.org.

Madigan, Kevin, and Carolyn Osiek, eds. *Ordained Women in the Early Church: A Documentary History.* Baltimore: Johns Hopkins University Press, 2007.

Mathews-Green, Frederica. *The Illumined Heart.* Brewster, MA: Paraclete, 2007.

McCarty, Mary Stanislaus. *A Saint among Saints: A Sketch of the Life of Saint Emmelia, Mother of St. Basil the Great, by S.m.s.* 1882. Repr., Whitefish, MT: Kessinger, 2009.

McClendon, James William, Jr. *Biography as Theology: How Life Stories Can Remake Today's Theology.* Eugene, OR: Wipf & Stock, 1974.

McCormick, Steve. "Theosis in Chrysostom and Wesley: An Eastern Paradigm on Faith and Love." *Wesleyan Theological Journal* 26:1 (1991) 38–103.

McGuckin, John Anthony. *St. Gregory of Nazianzus: An Intellectual Biography.* Crestwood, NY: St. Vladimir's Seminary Press, 2001.

———. "The Strategic Adaptation of Deification." In *Partakers of the Divine Nature: The History and Development of Deification in the Christian Traditions,* 95–114. Grand Rapids: Baker Academic, 2007.

———, ed. *The Westminster Handbook to Origen.* Louisville: Westminster John Knox, 2004.

McLynn, N. B. "The Other Olympias: Gregory of Nazianzen and the Family of Vitalianus." *Journal of Ancient Christianity* 2 (1998) 227–46.

Meconi, David V. "Deification in the Thought of John Paul II." *Irish Theological Quarterly* 71 (2006) 127–41.

Meredith, Anthony S. J. *Gregory of Nyssa: The Early Church Fathers.* London: Routledge, 1999.

Meyendorff, John. *Christ in Eastern Christian Thought.* Crestwood, NY: St. Vladimir's Seminary Press, 1987.

———. *Marriage: An Orthodox Perspective.* Crestwood, NY: St. Vladimir's Press, 1975.

———. "Theosis in the Eastern Christian Tradition." In *Christian Spirituality: Post-Reformation and Modern,* edited by Louis Dupre and Don E. Saliers, 470–76. New York: Crossroad, 1989.

Miles, Margaret R. "Image." In *Critical Terms for Religious Studies,* edited by Mark Taylor, 160–72. Chicago: University of Chicago Press, 1998.

———. *Practicing Christianity: Critical Perspectives for an Embodied Spirituality.* New York: Crossroad, 1988.

Miller, Nancy K. "The Text's Heroine: A Feminist Critic and Her Fictions." In *Conflicts in Feminism,* edited by Marianne Hirsch and Evelyn Fox Keller, 112–20. London: Routledge, 1990.

Morison, E. F. *St. Basil and His Rule: A Study in Early Monasticism.* Edinburgh: Oxford University Press, 1912.

Nauser, Michael. "Toward Community Beyond Gender Binaries: Gregory of Nyssa's Transgendering as Part of His Transformative Eschatology." *Theology Sexuality* 16 (2002) 55–65.

Nicol, D. M. *The Byzantine Lady.* Cambridge: Cambridge University Press, 1994.

Noble, T. A. "Gregory Nazianzen's Use of Scripture in Defence of the Deity of the Spirit." *Tyndale Bulletin* 39 (1988) 101–23.

Norris, F. W. "Deification: Consensual and Cogent." *Scottish Journal of Theology* 43:4 (1996) 411–28.

———. "Gregory Contemplating the Beautiful: Knowing Human Mystery and Divine Mystery Through and Being Persuaded By Images." In Børtnes and Hägg, *Gregory of Nazianzus*, 19–36.

———. "Gregory Nazianzen's Doctrine of Jesus Christ." PhD diss., Yale, 1970.

O'Donovan, Theresa. "Doing It Differently: Unleashing Student Creativity." *Teaching Theology* and *Religion* 6:3 (2003) 159–63.

Orthodox Eastern Church. *The Lives of the Spiritual Mothers: An Orthodox Materikon of Women Monastics and Ascetics throughout the Year.* Buena Vista, CO: Holy Apostles Convent, 1991.

Osborn, Ronald E. "I'm Looking Over a Four-Leaf Clover That I Overlooked. . . ." *Impact* 8 (1982) 15–30.

Osiek, Carolyn. "The Patronage of Women in Early Christianity." In Levine, *Feminist Companion to Patristic Literature*, 173–93.

Otis, Brooks. "Cappadocian Thought as a Coherent System." *Dumbarton Oaks Papers* 12 (1958) 97–124.

———. "The Throne and the Mountain: An Essay on St. Gregory Nazianzus." *Classical Journal* 56:4 (1961) 146–65.

Palmer, Phoebe. *Promise of the Father.* New York: Palmer, 1872.

Papanikolaou, Aristotle. "Divine Energies or Divine Personhood: Vladimir Lossky and John Zizioulas on Conceiving the Transcendent and Immanent God." *Modern Theology* 19:3 (2003) 357–85.

Parvis, Sara. "The Canons of Ancyra and Caesarea (314) Lebon's Thesis Revisited." *Journal of Theological Studies* 25:2 (2001) 625–36.

Patrologia Graeca. Edited by J. P. Migne. 162 vols. Paris, 1857–1886.

Patrologia Latina. Edited by J. P. Migne. 217 vols. Paris, 1844–1864.

Pederson, Rena. *The Lost Apostle: Searching for the Truth about Junia.* San Francisco: Jossey-Bass, 2006.

Pelikan, Jaroslav. *The Christian Tradition: A History of the Development of Doctrine.* Vol. 1. Chicago: University of Chicago Press, 1971.

———. *Christianity and Classical Culture: The Metamorphosis of Natural Theology in the Christian Encounter with Helenism.* New Haven: Yale University Press, 1993.

Pfister, J. Emile. "A Biographical Note: The Brothers and Sisters of St. Gregory of Nyssa." *Vigiliae Christianae* 18:2 (1964) 108–13.

Polkinghorne, John, ed. *The Work of Love: Creation as Kenosis.* Grand Rapids: Eerdmans, 2001.

Pomazansky, Michael. *Orthodox Dogmatic Theology.* Platina, CA: Saint Herman, 2005.

Pope, Marvin. *Song of Songs.* Anchor Bible Commentary 19. New York: Doubleday, 1977.

Prestige, G. L. *Fathers and Heretics.* London: SPCK, 1940.

Ramelli, Ilaria. *The Christian Doctrine of "Apokatastasis": A Critical Assessment from the New Testament to Eriugena.* Leiden: Brill, 2013.

———. "Theosebia: A Presbyter of the Catholic Church." *Journal of Feminist Studies in Religion* 26:2 (2010) 79–102.

Rapp, Claudia. "Storytelling as Spiritual Communication in Early Greek Hagiography: The Use of Diegesis." *Journal of Early Christian Studies* 6:3 (1998) 431–48.

Reid, Barbara. *Choosing the Better Part? Women in the Gospel of Luke.* Collegeville: Liturgical, 1996.

Rist, John M. "Basil's 'Neoplatonism'": Its Background and Nature." In *Basil of Caesarea, Christian, Humanist, Ascetic,* edited by Paul Jonathan Fedwick, 137–219. Toronto: Pontifical Institute of Mediaeval Studies, 1981.

Roberts, Alexander, and James Donaldson, eds. *The Ante-Nicene Fathers.* 1885–1887. 10 vols. Repr., Peabody, MA: Hendrickson, 1994.

Roberts, Benjamin Titus. *Ordaining Women: Biblical and Historical Insights.* Indianapolis: Light and Life, 1997.

Robinson, Cecilia. *The Ministry of Deaconess.* London: Methuen, 1898.

Roth, Catherine. "Platonic and Pauline Elements in the Ascent of the Soul in Gregory of Nyssa's *Dialogue on the Soul and Resurrection.*" *Vigiliae Christianae* 46 (1992) 20–23.

Rousseau, Philip. *Basil of Caesarea.* Berkeley: University of California Press, 1994.

———. "Orthodoxy and the Coenobite." *Studia Patristica* 30 (1997) 241–48.

———. "The Pious Household and the Virgin Chorus: Reflections on Gregory of Nyssa's *Life of Macrina.*" *Journal of Early Christian Studies* 13:2 (2005) 165–86.

Ruether, Rosemary. "Mothers of the Church: Ascetic Women in the Late Patristic Age." In *Women of Spirit: Female Leadership in the Jewish and Christian Traditions,* edited by Rosemary Ruether and Eleanor McLaughlin, 30–70. New York: Simon & Schuster, 1979.

———. *Women and Redemption: A Theological History.* Minneapolis: Fortress, 1998.

Russell, Norman. *The Doctrine of Deification in the Greek Patristic Tradition.* Oxford: Oxford University Press, 2004.

Salter, Darius. *Spirit and Intellect: Thomas Upham's Holiness Theology.* Lanham, MD: Scarecrow, 1986.

Schaff, Philip. *History of the Christian Church: Nicene and Post-Nicene Christianity from Constantine the Great to Gregory the Great.* Vols. 1–2. Edinburgh: T. & T. Clark, 1981.

Schaff, Philip, and Henry Wace, eds. *Cyril of Jerusalem, Gregory Nazianzen.* Vol. 7 of *A Select Library of Nicene and Post-Nicene Fathers of the Christian Church,* 2nd ser. Grand Rapids: Eerdmans, 1972.

———. *Gregory of Nyssa: Dogmatic Treatises, etc.* Vol. 5 of *A Select Library of Nicene and Post-Nicene Fathers of the Christian Church,* 2nd ser. Grand Rapids: Eerdmans, 1972.

———. *Saint Chrysostom: Homilies on the Epistles of Paul to the Corinthians.* Vol. 12 of *The Nicene and Post-Nicene Fathers.* Edinburgh: T. & T. Clark, 1889.

———. *St. Basil: Letters and Select Works.* Vol. 8 of *The Nicene and Post-Nicene Fathers.* Grand Rapids: Eerdmans, 1968.

Schmemann, Alexander. *Historical Road of Easter Orthodoxy.* Crestwood, NY: St. Vladimir's Seminary Press, 1992.

Schüssler Fiorenza, Elisabeth. *Bread Not Stone: The Challenge of Feminist Biblical Interpretation.* Boston: Beacon, 1995.

———. *In Memory of Her: A Feminist Theological Reconstruction of Christian Origins.* New York: Crossroad, 2000.

———. *Rhetoric and Ethics: The Politics of Biblical Study.* Minneapolis: Augsburg, 1999.

———. *Sharing Her Word: Feminist Biblical Interpretation in Context.* Boston: Beacon, 1998.

Shaw, Teresa M. "The Virgin Charioteer and the Bride of Christ: Gender and the Passions in Late Ancient Ethics and Early Christian Writings on Virginity." In Levine, *Feminist Companion to Patristic Literature*, 193–210.

Sheldrake, Philip. *Spirituality & History: Questions of Interpretation and Method.* Maryknoll: Orbis, 2007.

Silvas, Anna. *Gregory of Nyssa: The Letters.* Leiden: Brill, 2007.

———. *Macrina the Younger, Philosopher of God.* Turnhout: Brepols, 2008.

Smith, Warren J. "A Just and Reasonable Grief: The Death and Function of a Holy Woman in Gregory of Nyssa's *Life of Macrina*." *Journal of Early Christian Studies* 12:1 (2004) 57–84.

Spiegel, Gabrielle. *Practicing History: New Directions in Historical Writing after the Linguistic Turn.* London: Routledge, 2005.

Spira, Andreas, ed. *The Biographical Works of Gregory of Nyssa.* Patristic Monograph 12. Philadelphia: Philadelphia Patristic Foundation, 1984.

Stavropoulos, Christoforos. *Partakers of Divine Nature.* Translated by Stanley Harakas. Minneapolis: Light and Life, 1976.

Stephenson, Christopher A. "The Rule of Spirituality and the Rule of Doctrine: A Necessary Relationship in Theological Method." *Journal of Pentecostal Theology*, 15:1 (2006) 83–105.

Stramara, Daniel F., Jr. "Double Monasticism in the Greek East, Fourth through Eighth Centuries." *Journal of Early Christian Studies* 6:2 (1998) 269–312.

———. "Gregory of Nyssa's Terminology for Trinitarian Perichoresis." *Vigiliae Christianae* 52:3 (1998) 257–63.

———. "'Prosopon': Two Frequently Overlooked Meanings." *Vigiliae Christianae* 51:3 (1997) 316–20.

Святитель Василий Великий. *Творения. Том Первый. Догматико полемические творения экзегетические сочинения беседы.* В *Полное собрание творений святых отцов церкви и церковных писателей в русском переводе.* Сибирская Благозвонница: Москва, 2008.

———. *Творения. Том Второй. Догматико полемические творения экзегетические сочинения беседы.* В *Полное собрание творений святых отцов церкви и церковных писателей в русском переводе.* Сибирская Благозвонница: Москва, 2008.

Святитель Григорий Богослов. *Полное Собрание Творений Святых Отцов Церкви и Церковных Писателей в Русском переводе: Творения: Том второй.* Сибирская Благозвонница, Москва 2006.

Swan, Laura. *The Forgotten Desert Mothers: Sayings, Lives, and Stories of Early Christian Women.* Mahwah, NJ: Paulist, 2001.

Taft, Robert F. "Women at Church in Byzantium: Where, When—And Why?" *Dumbarton Oaks Papers* 52 (1998) 27–87.

Talbot, Mary-Alice. "The Byzantine Family and the Monastery." *Dumbarton Oaks Papers* 44 (1990) 119–29.

———. "Holy Women of Byzantium: Ten Saints' Lives in English Translation." Washington, DC: Dumbarton Oaks Research Library and Collection, 1996.

Tanner, Norman P., ed. *Decrees of the Ecumenical Councils.* Washington, DC: Georgetown University Press, 1990. https://www.ewtn.com/library/councils/chalcedo.htm.

Taylor, Mark C. *Critical Terms for Religious Studies*. Chicago: University of Chicago Press, 1998.

Torjesen, Karen Jo. *When Women Were Priests: Women's Leadership in the Early Church & the Scandal of their Subordination in the Rise of Christianity*. San Francisco: Harper, 1995.

Torrance, T. F. *The Incarnation: Ecumenical Studies in the Nicene-Constantinopolitan Creed A.D. 381*. Eugene, OR: Wipf & Stock, 1998.

———. *The Trinitarian Faith*. London: T. & T. Clark, 1995.

Tredget, Dermot. "Basil of Caesarea and His Influence on Monastic Mission." EBC Theology Commission, Belmont, March 2005. https://www.scribd.com/document/45605259/Basil-of-Cesarea-and-Monasticism.

Trigg, Joseph W. "God's Marvelous Oikonomia: Reflections of Origen's Understanding of Divine and Human Pedagogy in the Address Ascribed to Gregory Thaumaturgus." *Journal of Early Christian Studies* 9:1 (2001) 27–52.

"Troparion to St. Emilia." Tune 8. www.monachos.net/conversation/topic/4414-being-stalked-by-st-emilyemilia.

Van Dam, Raymond. *Family and Friends in Late Roman Cappadocia*. Philadelphia: University of Pennsylvania Press, 2003.

———. "Hagiography and History: The Life of Gregory Thaumaturgus." *Classical Antiquity* 1:2 (1982) 272–308.

———. *Kingdom of Snow: Roman Rule in Greek Culture in Cappadocia*. Philadelphia: University of Pennsylvania Press, 2002.

Volf, Miroslav. *After Our Likeness: The Church as the Image of the Trinity*. Grand Rapids: Eerdmans, 1998.

Wallace, William Ross. "The Hand That Rocks the Cradle Is the Hand That Rules the World." Poem. First published 1865 under the title "What Rules the World." http://en.wikipedia.org/wiki/The_Hand_That_Rocks_the_Cradle_(poem).

Ware, Kallistos. *The Orthodox Way*. Crestwood, NY: St. Vladimir's Seminary Press, 1995.

White, Hayden. "The Question of Narrative in Contemporary Historical Theory." *History and Theory* 23:1 (1984) 1–33.

Wilken, Robert Louis. *The Spirit of Early Christian Thought: Seeking the Face of God*. New Haven: Yale University Press, 2003.

Williams, A. N. *The Ground of Union: Deification in Aquinas and Palamas*. New York: Oxford University Press, 1999.

Winslow, Donald F. "Christology and Exegesis in the Cappadocians." *Church History* 40:4 (1971) 389–96.

———. *The Dynamics of Salvation: A Study in Gregory of Nazianzus*. Cambridge, MA: Philadelphia Patristic Foundation, 1979.

Witherington, Ben, III. *Women and the Genesis of Christianity*. Cambridge: Cambridge University Press, 1990.

Yarbrough, Anne. "Christianization in the Fourth Century: The Example of Roman Women." *Church History* 45:2 (1976) 149–56.

Young, Frances. "Sexuality and Devotion: Mystical Readings of the Song of Songs." *Theology Sexuality* 7 (2001) 80–96.

Index of Names

Index of Subjects

Index of Ancient Documents

Old Testament

New Testament

Cappadocian Fathers

Gregory of Nyssa

Apocrypha and Septuagint

Early Theological and Philosophical Works

An environmentally friendly book printed and bound in England by www.printondemand-worldwide.com

PEFC Certified

This product is
from sustainably
managed forests
and controlled
sources

www.pefc.org

PEFC/16-33-415

This book is made of chain-of-custody materials; FSC materials for the cover and PEFC materials for the text pages.

Reprint of # - C0 - 229/152/13 - PB - Lamination Gloss - Printed on 16-Sep-18 09:13